dictionary of
computer and internet words

[an A to Z guide to hardware,

software, and cyberspace]

Houghton Mifflin Company
Boston   New York

Words are included in this Dictionary on the basis of their usage. No investigation has been made of common-law trademark rights in any word, because such investigation is impracticable. The inclusion of any word in this Dictionary is not, however, an expression of the Publisher's opinion as to whether or not it is subject to any proprietary rights. Indeed, no definition in this Dictionary is to be regarded as affecting the validity of any trademark.

Visit our website: www.houghtonmifflinbooks.com

Library of Congress Cataloging-in-Publication Data

Dictionary of computer and internet words : an A to Z guide to hardware, software, and cyberspace.
    p. cm.
  ISBN 0-618-10137-3
    1. Computers--Dictionaries. 2. Internet--Dictionaries.
QA76.15 .D5255 2001
004'.03--dc21

                                                    2001016890

Manufactured in the United States of America

DOH   10   9   8   7   6   5   4   3   2   1

editorial and production staff

Editor
Steven Kleinedler, Project Director

Managing Editor
Chris Leonesio

Production Supervisor
Chris Granniss

Senior Art & Production Coordinator
Margaret Anne Miles

Contributing Editor
Julie A. Kent

Consulting Editor
Stephen Gilliard, Jr.

Associate Editor
Jacquelyn Pope

Editorial Assistant
Uchenna Ikonné

Design
Melodie Wertelet

preface

As we enter the 21st century, technology involving computer science proliferates in most areas of our lives. How we work, how we study, how we run errands, how we spend our leisure time, and how we communicate all entail the use of computers. The past decade has seen an explosion of new growth on the Internet and the introduction of personal computers into millions of homes. Along with this growth has come the proliferation of specialized terminology—related not just to the Internet, but to software, multimedia systems, information processing, and more. *The Dictionary of Computer and Internet Words* includes the newest terminology and makes it accessible to anyone who works with a computer at home, school, or work. New words defined here, such as *digital signature, MP3, packet sniffer,* and *portal,* will help the reader keep up to date with the latest technologies and products.

Much of this new terminology reflects one of the most prominent areas of interest today: the Internet. The Dictionary defines clearly such Internet-related terms as *banner, cookie, netiquette,* and *newsgroup,* to name a few. To help demystify terms for the reader, dozens of acronyms and abbreviations such as *ANSI, DES, FTP, IMAP, ISP, ODBC, PGP, TCP/IP,* and *VRML* have been defined. Entries that have been culled from earlier editions of Houghton Mifflin's *Dictionary of Computer Words* have been completely reviewed and revised to reflect changing technology.

The proliferation of computer-related terms has been one of the most notable developments in American English over the past 15 years. Many terms, such as *byte* and *hyperlink,* are entirely new. Others, such as *frame* and *thread,* are familiar English words that have taken on new, specialized meanings. To the novice, the language surrounding computers can be intimidatingly complex, and that is where the *Dictionary of Computer and Internet Words* is a lifesaver, explaining special terms with clear, exact, and plain-spoken definitions. It has been designed both to answer specific questions and to encourage browsing. The areas it covers are many: the Internet, multimedia, software, hardware, artificial intelligence, networks, and much more.

Vocabulary defined in the Dictionary was chosen for its high utility: this is the language that is most likely to be encountered by the average computer user and is most in need of elucidation.

Entries in the *Dictionary of Computer and Internet Words* are fully defined in clear, precise language, free of unnecessary technical jargon. Examples of usage enhance the reader's understanding by putting a word in a context in which it is commonly heard or read.

Cross-references are used extensively throughout the *Dictionary of Computer and Internet Words*. A term that is closely related to another entry has a "See also" cross-reference following its definition. Thus, at *freeware*, the reader will find: "*See also* **shareware**." When appropriate, cross-references are also provided to tables and illustrations. For example, at the words *head* and *platter*, cross-references will lead the reader to the illustration at *hard disk*. In addition, when a term often goes by another name or names, the entry will list these names at the end—for example, at *alert box*, the last line of the entry reads, "*Also called* **message box**."

As computer technology evolves, computer language—"computerese"—adjusts and expands to cover it. The *Dictionary of Computer and Internet Words* covers the essential language of this exciting, active field. It will give the new and not-so-new computer user a solid grounding in a way that will be interesting, informative, and even, we hope, fun.

[A]

abort To cancel while in progress. A procedure or program can be aborted on request. When this happens, you usually lose any unsaved work and are returned to the operating system shell. *See also* **crash**.

absolute Defined with respect to some fixed, universally accepted reference point. *See also* **relative**.

absolute address An address that is fixed in memory, referencing that location in memory by its byte number. *Also called* **direct address, machine address, real address**.

absolute cell reference In a spreadsheet, a reference to a cell that remains constant, regardless of moving or copying formulas or modifying the spreadsheet's size or shape. This reference appears as a symbol in front of the column letter and the row number. For example, B4 refers to the cell that is the intersection of the second column and the fourth row; whereas B4, a relative cell reference, may start out referring to that cell but could change if the spreadsheet is modified or if that reference is copied to another cell. *See also* **relative cell reference**.

absolute path A directory path that is fully specified. The names of all the directories that are needed to locate the file are shown.

Accelerated Graphics Port *See* **AGP**.

accelerator board A printed circuit board that can be added to a computer to enhance its performance by substituting a faster microprocessor without replacing the entire motherboard and associated components. Accelerator boards are now largely used in Apple Macintosh computers and specialized IBM-compatible PCs. Most consumer PCs usually have their chips replaced on the motherboard. *Also called* **accelerator card**. *See also* **expansion board, graphics accelerator**.

Acceptable Use Policy *Abbreviated* **AUP** A set of rules that determine what type of transactions are allowed on a given network. For example, at one time commercial activity was not allowed on the Internet. Also, some online service providers do not allow the posting of pornographic material.

access *n.* The ability to locate, gain entry to, and use a directory, file, or device on a computer system or over a network.

v. To locate and be able to use a directory, file, or device on a computer system or over a network.

access code   An alphanumeric sequence that permits access to a computer system, network, or online service.

access control   The means of securing a computer system by forbidding access to unauthorized users, including the use of passwords.

access control list   A list of users authorized to access a computer system, accompanied by any restrictions or permissions governing their access to files and directories on the system.

access number   A telephone number you call to connect to an ISP (Internet Service Provider) or another network provider such as an online service.

access time   The time required for a program or device to locate and retrieve a piece of data, as from a computer's memory or from a storage device. Often it refers to disk drives and is the amount of time needed for a disk drive to respond to a request to read or write data. When such a request is made by the operating system, the disk drive must move the read/write heads over the proper location on the disk, settle the heads into position, and wait for the desired location on the disk to rotate under them. The fastest current hard drives for personal computers have average access times under 6 milliseconds. The quoted access time for hard disks is an average that may be affected by the presence of a cache. Therefore a single instance of accessing may take significantly longer than the average. Table 1 lists typical access times for various devices.

ACM   *Abbreviation of* **Association for Computer Machinery**.

acoustic coupler   A device, usually containing a modem, that attaches to the earpiece and mouthpiece of a telephone so that a com-

TABLE 1 Access Times for Various Storage Mediums

Storage Medium	Access Time
Static RAM	5–50 nanoseconds
Dynamic RAM	50–70 nanoseconds
ROM, EPROM	55–250 nanoseconds
Hard disk	6–12 milliseconds
Erasable optical disk	19–100 milliseconds
CD-ROM	80–800 milliseconds
DAT, QIC	20–40 seconds

puter can make a connection over the telephone. The coupler allows digital signals to be changed to sound and back again. This device is rarely used nowadays, because of the widespread availability of modular phone jacks, allowing modems to connect directly with a telephone using a telephone connector.

ACPI *Abbreviation of* **Advanced Configuration and Power Interface.** A power-saving system that allows control of the amount of electricity each peripheral attached to the computer uses, so that power to items such as a CD-ROM can be shut off when you're not using them. This feature is included in Microsoft Windows 98 and subsequent versions.

Acrobat A suite of programs developed by Adobe Systems that allows you to place documents formatted by a desktop publishing program to be read by anyone using an Apple Macintosh or IBM-compatible PC. This allows printable documents to be placed online without being reformatted in HTML, which would cause them to lose their original format and design. The Acrobat products allow users of different platforms to view a document exactly as the person who wrote it.

active Of or relating to a file, device, or portion of the screen that is currently operational and ready to receive input.

active cell In a spreadsheet, the cell that is currently highlighted or selected and ready to be acted upon, as by entering or editing data. *Also called* **current cell.**

Active Desktop The collective set of desktop features available in Microsoft Windows that are integrated into Microsoft Internet Explorer, giving the desktop the look and feel of a webpage interface.

Active Directory A directory service for Microsoft Windows that allows you to maneuver through the directories in your computer's local area network (LAN).

active file A file that is currently open and is capable of accepting or transmitting data. Although it is possible to have numerous files open at the same time, only one of them is active at any given moment.

active-matrix display A type of liquid-crystal display that uses individual transistors to control the charges on each cell in the liquid-crystal layer, as opposed to passive-matrix displays that use electrodes that extend the full length of the layer. Active-matrix displays produce a brighter display and better color.

active program   A program that is currently running and is capable of processing data.

Active Server Page   A standard for webpages that use either Visual Basic or Jscript code from a remote server. This allows a webpage to be dynamically rewritten every time you view it.

active window   The window that is currently receiving data from input devices (such as a mouse or a keyboard). The onscreen cursor is found in the active window.

ActiveX   An object linking and embedding technology developed by Microsoft for running programs through web browsers. Programmers can write ActiveX components that can be embedded in any webpage. A person reading the webpage can invoke this program by selecting the ActiveX component. This technology has been largely supplanted by Java and JavaScript.

ActiveX control   A program that allows other programs to share data, using ActiveX technologies.

Ada   A high-level programming language, based on Pascal and developed for the US Department of Defense in the late 1970s. Ada was designed to be a standard, general-purpose language that would save the military the expense and trouble of maintaining many incompatible computer systems. It also supports real-time applications necessary for control processes, such as launching a guided missile. Several versions of Ada are available for personal computers.

Ada is named after Augusta Ada Byron (1815–1852), Countess of Lovelace and daughter of Lord Byron. She worked with Charles Babbage in developing programs for the Analytical Engine, the first mechanical computer, and is often called the world's first programmer.

adapter   A printed circuit board or an interface card that can be installed in a personal computer to allow it to use additional peripheral devices or hardware. A network adapter, for example, allows a computer to be connected to a network. *See also* **expansion board, video adapter.**

adaptive differential pulse code modulation   *Abbreviated* **ADPCM** A form of pulse-code modulation (PCM) that produces a lower bit rate than standard PCM. Applications use ADPCM to digitize voice signals to allow them to be sent with data on lines designed for digital signals. When used on CD-ROMs, ADPCM allows for up to 16 hours of audio recording while maintaining or improving sound quality.

ADB   *Abbreviation of* **Apple Desktop Bus**.

add-in   An accessory program designed to be used in conjunction with an existing application program to extend its capabilities or provide additional functions. Sometimes an add-in provides a major improvement, such as new functions or bug fixes. Games usually have improvements included as add-ins, which are also called *scenarios* in this context. *Also called* **add-on**, **plug-in**.

add-on   1. A hardware device that is added to a computer to increase its capabilities. Common add-ons include additional hard drives, tape backup and CD-ROM drives, graphics accelerators, sound cards, and modems. *See also* **expansion board, peripheral**.   2. *See* **add-in**.

address   *n.* The name assigned to a location in memory or a peripheral storage device.
v. To locate data or to find places where data can be written in memory or a peripheral storage device.

One source of failures in personal computer systems is address conflicts, which can occur when a program attempts to address a location that is unavailable or is being used by another program. Input/output ports such as serial ports are also assigned specific addresses so that they can be located and identified by the operating system and BIOS (basic input/output system). Addresses are usually expressed in hexadecimal notation. *See also* **physical address, virtual address**.

address book   A feature in email programs that allows you to store, organize, and access email addresses.

address bus   A bus that carries the addresses of data storage locations back and forth between the CPU (central processing unit) and RAM. The address bus enables the CPU to select a specific location in memory for the transfer of data that the CPU needs in order to execute a specific instruction.

Address Resolution Protocol   *See* **ARP**.

address space   The set of all memory addresses that are available for a microprocessor or an application to store and retrieve data. The size of the address space depends on the number of bits that the address register can effectively access. If an address register can access 8 bits, then there are 256 (or 2^8) possible addresses, and the size of the address space is 256 bytes.

In early microprocessors, the available address space was limited to the system's actual physical memory. More recent microprocessors make use of virtual memory to create address spaces much larger than the available physical memory.

ADPCM   *Abbreviation of* **adaptive differential pulse code modulation**.

ADSL   *Abbreviation of* **assymetric digital subscriber line**.   A digital telephone technology using the traditional copper telephone lines that allows users to receive data at speeds of up to 9 Mbps and to send data at speeds of up to 640 Kbps. You need a special ADSL modem to use this service, which is currently available in the US in most urban areas.

Advanced Research Projects Agency   *See* **ARPA**.

Advanced Research Projects Agency Network   *See* **ARPANET**.

agent   A program that performs a task such as data transfer on behalf of a particular machine or human.

AGP   *Abbreviation of* **Accelerated Graphics Port**.   A port specification developed by Intel Corporation that enables the graphics controller to access the main memory directly. It provides enough speed for the use of high-resolution and 3-D graphics.

AI   *Abbreviation of* **artificial intelligence**.

AIFF   *Abbreviation of* **Audio Interchange File Format**.   The standard audio format for storing and transmitting sound on Apple computers. This format is also often utilized on the Internet and on Silicon Graphics machines. It does not compress the data, so the AIFF files are comparatively large.

AIX   *Abbreviation of* **Advanced Interactive eXecutive**.   A version of Unix developed by IBM.

alert box   In a graphical user interface, a window or box that appears on the screen to alert the user to an event requiring attention. An alert box may warn you, for example, that the directory you want to place a file in cannot be located. An alert box does not request user input, unlike a dialog box, although you may need to click on it to close it. *Also called* **message box**.

algorithm   A finite set of unambiguous instructions performed in a prescribed sequence to achieve a goal. Algorithms are the basis for most computer programming. The use of algorithms extends beyond computations to everyday tasks. Examples of common algorithms are recipes for cooking and the procedure for placing a telephone call. An advantage of this method of problem solving is that it is not necessary to understand how the steps rely upon each other to produce the result, as long as each individual step is understood; if the instructions are followed in the prescribed sequence and valid input is provided, the result can be achieved.

alias **1.** An alternate name given to an object, such as a computer, computer user, or variable. Aliases are useful, for example, in assigning simple names to email addresses that are hard to remember—when sending that person an email, you can simply address it to the alias instead of the full address. **2.** A false signal in telecommunication links from beats between signal frequency and sampling frequency.

aliasing In computer graphics, the appearance of jagged distortions, called *jaggies,* in curves and diagonal lines. Aliasing occurs because of limited display screen resolution. Pixels are arranged in rows and columns. If the pixel grid is too coarse, the pixels cannot be turned on in a pattern that will be perceived as a smooth curve or diagonal. *See also* **antialiasing.**

alignment **1.** The placement of objects in fixed rows or columns, such as icons in a folder or on the desktop. **2.** The placement of the read/write heads of disk drives over the tracks that they read and write. **3.** *See* **justification.**

Alpha Chip A 64-bit RISC CPU (central processing unit) developed by Digital Equipment Corporation. The Alpha Chip is used in many high-end workstations and is capable of running either Unix or Microsoft Windows NT operating systems.

alphanumeric Consisting of any combination of alphabetic characters and the decimal numerals 0 through 9. In some contexts certain punctuation characters and other symbols are also included.

alpha testing The initial stage in the testing of a new software or hardware product conducted by testers within the company that developed the product, before it is released to independent testers outside the company.

alpha version The first version of a software or hardware product, used during alpha testing.

AltaVista A proprietary Internet search engine and portal.

Alt key On keyboards for IBM PC and compatible computers, a key that is pressed in combination with another key to execute an alternate function. In Microsoft Windows applications, for example, Alt-F4 exits and closes a running program. *See also* **Control key, Shift key.**

ALU   *Abbreviation of* **arithmetic logic unit.**

American National Standards Institute   *See* ANSI.

American Standard Code for Information Interchange   *See* ASCII.

America Online or **AOL**   A commercial online service that provides access to services such as chatrooms, instant messaging, as well as the World Wide Web and other Internet-based services.

Amiga   A model of computer made by Commodore that favored by many designers, artists, and musicians because of its powerful microprocessors that allowed for advanced graphics and sound capabilities. Ownership of Amiga has changed hands several times since Commodore sold it.

analog   **1.** Measuring or representing data by means of one or more physical properties that can express any value along a continuous scale. Analog modes are contrasted with digital modes, in which a variable must assume one of a number of discrete values and can only approximate values that lie between these points. A mercury thermometer and a clock with hands, for example, are analog devices. Most computers are strictly digital devices; they can accept input and produce output in analog form, but only with the help of digital-to-analog and analog-to-digital converters. Analog computers, which operate on continuously varying input data, are primarily used in specialized industrial and scientific contexts.   **2.** Designating a type of display, as on a watch or radio, that makes use of a pointer or other indicator moving against a fixed scale rather than a series of changing numerical digits.

analog monitor   A monitor that can accept continuously varying or analog signals from the computer's video adapter. This allows the monitor to display a continuous range of colors rather than a limited number of color values. VGA and Super VGA monitors are analog. VGA monitors combined with advanced graphics adapters can now display as many colors on screen as the human eye can distinguish. *See also* **digital monitor, fixed-frequency monitor, multifrequency monitor, multiscanning monitor.**

analog-to-digital converter   A device that converts an analog signal, such as sound waves, into digital form that can be stored or manipulated by a computer. Voice-recognition products use analog-to-digital converters to allow computers to accept spoken input.

anchor **1.** A formatting code that is used to fix an object, such as a graphical item, to a place that is permanent or relative to another object, so that it remains in that position when the document is repaginated. For example, in dictionary publishing, marginal artwork may be anchored to the entry words with which it corresponds, so that if text shifts cause an entry associated with a piece of art to flow to the following page, the art will follow along with it. **2.** An HTML tag that sets off an item of text or graphics as a hyperlink to another item in the same or another HTML document.

AND A Boolean operator that returns the value TRUE if both of its operands are TRUE. If either operand is false, AND returns the value FALSE. Table 2 shows the results of the AND operator.

TABLE 2 Results of AND Operator

a	b	a AND b
FALSE	FALSE	FALSE
FALSE	TRUE	FALSE
TRUE	FALSE	FALSE
TRUE	TRUE	TRUE

animated GIF A series of GIF files saved as one large file. When you view an animated GIF through a browser or graphics program, it gives the appearance of being animated. This technology has largely been replaced by dedicated animation programs.

animation The creation of the illusion of motion through the display of a series of static pictures that change slightly from one to the next. Computer software can facilitate the production of cartoons or animated multimedia presentations by eliminating the need for a human to redraw each image; instead, the computer can modify each step.

anonymous ftp A function that allows a user to transfer files or other data from a publicly accessible FTP server. To log on to an anonymous ftp server, use *anonymous* as your login name and your email address as your password. *See also* **file transfer protocol.**

ANSI *Abbreviation of* **American National Standards Institute.** A US government organization responsible for approving US standards in many areas, including computers and communications. ANSI is a member of the ISO.

answer mode   An operating condition in which a modem is ready to answer an incoming call and establish a connection with the calling modem.

antialiasing   In computer graphics, a software process for removing or reducing jaggies, the jagged distortions created by a graphic display with limited resolution. Antialiasing diminishes the conspicuousness of jaggies by surrounding them with shades of gray (for gray scale images) or color (for color images). This makes the jaggies less prominent but makes the character's edges fuzzier. Another method for reducing jaggies is called smoothing. *See illustration. See also* **aliasing**.

bit map (with jaggies)   antialiasing   smoothing

ANTIALIASING

antistatic mat   A mat that absorbs static electricity. By standing on such a mat, you can minimize damage from electrical shock to a computer that you're using, especially when you have the cabinet open for tasks such as adding expansion cards.

antivirus program   A utility that checks memory and disks for computer viruses and removes those that it finds. Since new viruses can erupt, you should periodically update the antivirus program on your computer; however, many antivirus products now do this automatically over the Internet as updates become available. It is a good idea to scan disks that have been in other machines or software that has been downloaded from the Internet before use on your own computer unless you're certain the disks or software come from a virus-free computer.

any key   Any of the keys on a keyboard. Some programs or manuals may prompt you to "press any key," which means that you can press any key on the keyboard to continue. Keyboards do not include a key labeled "Any Key."

AOL *Abbreviation of* **America Online**.

Apache server Free, open-source software for running web servers, based on code originally developed by the NCSA and supplemented by a number of patches (hence, *a patchy server*). The software is regarded as highly reliable and is widely used. Originally written for Unix machines, versions now exist for other platforms, including Microsoft Windows.

API *Abbreviation of* **application program interface**. The interface through which one program can communicate with another. Different database or systems programs may be interchangeable on your computer if they share the same API, for example.

app An application.

append *v.* To add data or another file to the end of a file or string.
n. A DOS command that instructs the operating system where to search for data files, analogous to the PATH command for executable files. *See also* **path**.

Apple Desktop Bus *Abbreviated* **ADB** An interface developed by Apple Computer that is built into Macintosh computers. The Apple Desktop Bus allows up to sixteen serial input devices (mouse, keyboard, trackball, etc.) to be connected to the computer through two 4-pin ports on the back. When more than two devices are connected, they are linked together in a configuration called a daisy chain. To avoid conflicts, each device on the bus listens to be sure the line is clear before attempting to access the computer.

Apple Key A key found on Apple Macintosh keyboards, labeled with the Apple logo. On most Macintosh computers, it functions as the command key. *See also* **command key**.

applet A small program that has limited features, requires limited memory resources, and is designed to be downloaded from the Internet to run on a webpage that the user is accessing. Such a program is considered more secure than other, similar components because it cannot read or write data on the user's machine.

AppleTalk A local area network (LAN) standard developed by Apple Computer that is built into Macintosh computers. AppleTalk uses a bus topology to link other Macintosh computers and LaserWriter printers. Although considerably slower than other LAN systems, it has the advantage of being easy to set up and connect with standard telephone cables. It is also possible to connect IBM PC and compatible computers to AppleTalk if they are provided with suitable hardware; also, AppleTalk can be linked to other networks through gateways.

application   A program or set of programs that enables people to use the computer as a tool to accomplish some task. A huge variety of applications software has been developed, including word processors and text editors, spreadsheet and accounting packages, database management programs, communications software, and programs for entertainment and education. In addition to specialized applications written for specific jobs, there are also integrated applications packages that provide relatively less comprehensive tools for a wider variety of tasks. Many programs fall between these extremes; for example, Microsoft Word includes some graphics and desktop publishing capabilities, and some database programs include basic word processing facilities. *See also* **software, systems software, utility.**

application program interface   *See* **API.**

applications software   *See* **software.**

application window   The main window of an application. This window consists of a title bar, which lists the name of the application; the menu bar, which hierarchically lists the names of the available commands or options; and a work area, which itself may consist of multiple windows. In the Microsoft Windows and Apple Macintosh operating systems, you can adjust the size of windows, have multiple windows open on your desktop, and move or copy items from one window to another.

archie   A searchable database of anonymous ftp sites and their contents. Archie is used on the Internet to find, organize, and access files through an FTP server. *See also* **file transfer protocol.**

architecture   The overall design or structure of a computer system. In general, architecture applies to the entire system including all the hardware components and systems software needed to make it run. More specifically, it refers to the internal structure of a microprocessor, either in terms of its data-handling capacity (8 bits, 16 bits, 32 bits, or 64 bits) or the type of instruction set it uses. The instruction set consists of all instructions or commands in the computer's machine language that the microprocessor can recognize and execute.

archival backup   1. *See* **full backup.**   2. *See* **incremental backup.**

archive   1. A long-term storage area, often on magnetic tape, for backup copies of files or files that are no longer in active use. 2. A file containing one or more files in compressed format for more efficient storage and transfer, which must be decompressed by a file compression program in order to be used. *See also* **data compression, packed file.**   3. An attribute in DOS and Microsoft Windows that indicates files that have been changed since the last backup.

ARCnet   *Abbreviation of* **Attached Resource Computer network.**   A popular, inexpensive local access network (LAN) first produced in 1968 by Datapoint Corporation. Simple to install and use, ARCnet employs a star topology and a token-ring architecture and allows a mixture of different kinds of cables on the same network. ARCnet is capable of transmitting data at rates of up to 2.5 megabytes per second.

areal density   The amount of data that can be fit on a storage medium, expressed in megabits or gigabits per square inch.

arg   *Abbreviation of* **argument.**

argument   *Abbreviated* **arg**   In spreadsheet programs and in programming languages, a value that is passed to a function so it can be operated on to produce a result. For example, if a function called LOG computes the common logarithm of a number, then the statement LOG(100), where the argument is 100, would return the value   2. The term is often used as a synonym for both option and parameter, as in *command line argument,* which refers to an option to a command.

arithmetic expression   An expression that can be calculated to yield a numerical value. Arithmetic expressions can contain constants and variables. Examples are 6 * (5 + 4) and PRICE * QUANTITY * 0.05.

arithmetic-logic unit   *Abbreviated* **ALU**   The component of the CPU (central processing unit) that performs all of the arithmetic computations, logical operations, and comparative functions.

arithmetic operator   A symbol that stands for a numerical operation, such as addition or multiplication. Table 3 on page 14 lists arithmetic operators and their results. *See also* **Boolean operator, relational operator.**

TABLE 3 **Arithmetic Operators and Their Results**

Operator	Operation	Example	Result
+	Addition	D2+D3	Finds the sum of the values in cells D2 and D3.
-	Subtraction	D2-10	Subtracts 10 from the value in cell D2.
*	Multiplication	D2*D3	Multiplies the value in cell D2 by the value in cell D3.
/	Division	D2/100	Divides the value in cell D2 by 100.
^	Exponentiation	D2^3	Raises the value in cell D2 to the third power.

ARP *Abbreviation of* **Address Resolution Protocol**. A protocol often used in conjunction with TCP/IP to determine the MAC address of a given IP address. The requester broadcasts a message giving the IP address and requesting the MAC address. The machine with that IP address responds with its own MAC address. *See also* **MAC address**.

ARPA *Abbreviation of* **Advanced Research Projects Agency**. The former name of a research agency at the US Department of Defense that funded and researched undertakings in computer technology. This agency is now called DARPA (Defense Advance Research Projects Agency).

ARPANET *Abbreviation of* **Advanced Research Projects Agency**. A network developed by ARPA in the 1960s and 1970s as a means of communication between research laboratories and universities. Used by researchers for testing networking technologies, it is the predecessor of the Internet.

array **1.** A group of many single elements, all of the same kind, arranged in a regular pattern and connected together to perform a single task. **2.** In mathematics and computer programming, a structure consisting of a collection of single elements or pieces of data, all having the same data type, any of which can be located and retrieved by specifying the name of the array and the element's location within the array. A one-dimensional data structure, with values arranged in a single row or column, is known as a vector. A two-dimensional array, with values in both rows and columns, is a matrix.

arrow keys A set of four or more keys labeled with arrows pointing left, right, up, and down, that control the movement of the cursor or insertion point on the display screen. Depending on which program is running, the arrow keys may have additional functions when combined with the Shift, Control, or Alt keys (on IBM PC computers) or the Shift, Option, or Command keys (on Apple Macintosh computers). For example, Shift-Up arrow may send the cursor to the beginning of a document. *Also called* **cursor control keys**.

artificial intelligence *Abbreviated* **AI** A branch of computer science whose goal is to develop electronic devices that can operate with some of the characteristics of human intelligence. Among these properties are logical deduction and inference, creativity, the ability to make decisions based on past experience or insufficient or conflicting information, and the ability to understand natural language.

One of the earliest goals of AI research was machine translation of natural languages. Although this effort has attracted a great deal of attention, it has never progressed beyond a rudimentary and mostly unreliable stage, because few researchers have been prepared to recognize the enormous complexity and subtlety of human language. More recent work in the modeling and emulation of neural networks and in speech recognition has shown more promise.

Although many of the early hopes of AI have yet to be fulfilled, this fact in itself has helped to reveal how much still remains to be understood about the processes of human thought and intelligence.

ascender The part of a lowercase letter that rises above the main body of the letter, as in a *b,* a *d,* or an *h. See illustration at* **baseline**.

ascending sort A sort in which the items are listed from first to last or smallest to largest, as from A to Z or from 0 to 9. *See also* **descending sort**.

ASCII [AS-kee] *Abbreviation of* **American Standard Code for Information Interchange**. A code that assigns the numbers 0 through 127 to letters, the digits 0 to 9, punctuation marks, and certain other characters. For example, uppercase D is coded as decimal 68 (binary 1000100); an exclamation point is coded as decimal 33 (binary 0100001). By standardizing the values used to represent text, ASCII enables computers to exchange information.

Basic, or standard, ASCII uses 7 bits for each character code, giving it 2^7, or 128, unique symbols. Various larger character sets, called extended ASCII, use 8 bits for each character, yielding 128 additional codes numbered 128 through 255. EBCDIC is another set of codes that is used on IBM mainframes and minicomputers. Due to the proprietary nature of the IBM extended ASCII Character Set, not all platforms share the same characters. To prevent incompatibility problems, web browsers and some operating systems use the ISO Latin-1 coding scheme.

Tables 4a–4c list the standard ASCII and IBM extended ASCII character sets. *See also* **ISO Latin-1**.

TABLE 4A **Standard ASCII Character Set—Control Codes and Space Characters**

Decimal Value	Hexadecimal Value	Character	Decimal Value	Hexadecimal Value	Character
0	00	NUL Null	17	11	DC1 Device control 1
1	01	SOH Start of heading	18	12	DC2 Device control 2
2	02	STX Start of text	19	13	DC3 Device control 3
3	03	ETX End of text	20	14	DC4 Device control 4
4	04	EOT End of transmission	21	15	NAK Negative acknowledge
5	05	ENQ Enquiry	22	16	SYN Synchronous idle
6	06	ACK Acknowledge	23	17	ETB End transmission block
7	07	BEL Audible bell	24	18	CAN Cancel
8	08	BS Backspace	25	19	EM End of medium
9	09	HT Horizontal tab	26	1A	SUB Substitute
10	0A	LF Line feed	27	1B	ESC Escape
11	0B	VT Vertical tab	28	1C	FS File separator
12	0C	FF Form feed	29	1D	GS Group separator
13	0D	CR Carriage return	30	1E	RS Record separator
14	0E	SO Shift out	31	1F	US Unit separator
15	0F	SI Shift in	32	20	SP Blank space character
16	10	DLE Data link escape			

TABLE 4B **Standard ASCII Character Set — Alphanumeric Characters**

Decimal Value	Hexadecimal Value	Character	Decimal Value	Hexadecimal Value	Character
33	21	!	45	2D	–
34	22	"	46	2E	.
35	23	#	47	2F	/
36	24	$	48	30	0
37	25	%	49	31	1
38	26	&	50	32	2
39	27	'	51	33	3
40	28	(	52	34	4
41	29	)	53	35	5
42	2A	*	54	36	6
43	2B	+	55	37	7
44	2C	,	56	38	8

TABLE 4B Standard ASCII Character Set — Alphanumeric Characters (continued)

Decimal Value	Hexadecimal Value	Character	Decimal Value	Hexadecimal Value	Character
57	39	9	93	5D	]
58	3A	:	94	5E	^
59	3B	;	95	5F	_
60	3C	<	96	60	`
61	3D	=	97	61	a
62	3E	>	98	62	b
63	3F	?	99	63	c
64	40	@	100	64	d
65	41	A	101	65	e
66	42	B	102	66	f
67	43	C	103	67	g
68	44	D	104	68	h
69	45	E	105	69	i
70	46	F	106	6A	j
71	47	G	107	6B	k
72	48	H	108	6C	l
73	49	I	109	6D	m
74	4A	J	110	6E	n
75	4B	K	111	6F	o
76	4C	L	112	70	p
77	4D	M	113	71	q
78	4E	N	114	72	r
79	4F	O	115	73	s
80	50	P	116	74	t
81	51	Q	117	75	u
82	52	R	118	76	v
83	53	S	119	77	w
84	54	T	120	78	x
85	55	U	121	79	y
86	56	V	122	7A	z
87	57	W	123	7B	{
88	58	X	124	7C		
89	59	Y	125	7D	}
90	5A	Z	126	7E	~
91	5B	[	127	7F	DEL
92	5C	\			

ASCII

TABLE 4C IBM Extended ASCII Character Set

Decimal Value	Hexadecimal Value	Character	Decimal Value	Hexadecimal Value	Character
128	80	Ç	181	B5	╡
129	81	ü	182	B6	╢
130	82	é	183	B7	╖
131	83	â	184	B8	╕
132	84	ä	185	B9	╣
133	85	à	186	BA	║
134	86	å	187	BB	╗
135	87	ç	188	BC	╝
136	88	ê	189	BD	╜
137	89	ë	190	BE	╛
138	8A	è	191	BF	┐
139	8B	ï	192	C0	└
140	8C	î	193	C1	┴
141	8D	ì	194	C2	┬
142	8E	Ä	195	C3	├
143	8F	Å	196	C4	─
144	90	É	197	C5	┼
145	91	æ	198	C6	╞
146	92	Æ	199	C7	╟
147	93	ô	200	C8	╚
148	94	ö	201	C9	╔
149	95	ò	202	CA	╩
150	96	û	203	CB	╦
151	97	ù	204	CC	╠
152	98	ÿ	205	CD	═
153	99	Ö	206	CE	╬
154	9A	Ü	207	CF	╧
155	9B	¢	208	D0	╨
156	9C	£	209	D1	╤
157	9D	¥	210	D2	╥
158	9E	P$_t$	211	D3	╙
159	9F	ƒ	212	D4	╘
160	A0	á	213	D5	╒
161	A1	í	214	D6	╓
162	A2	ó	215	D7	╫
163	A3	ú	216	D8	╪
164	A4	ñ	217	D9	┘
165	A5	Ñ	218	DA	┌
166	A6	ª	219	DB	█
167	A7	º	220	DC	▄
168	A8	¿	221	DD	▌
169	A9	⌐	222	DE	▐
170	AA	¬	223	DF	▀
171	AB	½	224	E0	α
172	AC	¼	225	E1	β
173	AD	¡	226	E2	Γ
174	AE	«	227	E3	π
175	AF	»	228	E4	Σ
176	B0	▒	229	E5	σ
177	B1	▓	230	E6	µ
178	B2	▓	231	E7	τ
179	B3	│	232	E8	Φ
180	B4	┤	233	E9	θ

TABLE 4C IBM Extended ASCII Character Set (continued)

Decimal Value	Hexadecimal Value	Character	Decimal Value	Hexadecimal Value	Character
234	EA	Ω	245	F5	∫
235	EB	δ	246	F6	÷
236	EC	∞	247	F7	≈
237	ED	φ	248	F8	°
238	EE	ε	249	F9	•
239	EF	∩	250	FA	·
240	F0	≡	251	FB	√
241	F1	±	252	FC	η
242	F2	≥	253	FD	2
243	F3	≤	254	FE	▪
244	F4	⌠	255	FF	

ASCII file   A text file that contains only characters in the standard ASCII character set, without extended characters or formatting codes.

ASCII sort   A sort in which items are listed in order according to their numerical position in the ASCII character set. Numbers precede uppercase letters, which precede lowercase letters. *See also* **dictionary sort**.

ASP   A scripting language used to write web applications. ASP has a structure similar to the BASIC programming language.

aspect ratio   The ratio of width to height of an image on a given output device. Images may become distorted if forced into a different aspect ratio during enlargement, reduction, or transfer.

assembler   A program that converts a set of instructions written in assembly language into machine language.

assembly language   A programming language that is only one step removed from machine language. Assembly languages have the same structure as machine language, the major difference being that commands and functions are expressed in words rather than in numbers. Programs are converted into machine language by an assembler. Assembly language has certain advantages over high-level languages, including high speed, relatively low memory demands, and the ability to act directly on the system's hardware. For this reason many operating systems and utility programs are written in it. For everyday programming, however, assembly language code is difficult and tedious to write. All procedures must be spelled out in minute detail, and repeating an operation requires writing its entire block of code again. Assembly programs also must be rewritten if they are transferred from one type of microprocessor to another.

Association for Computer Machinery *Abbreviated* **ACM** The first professional society for computer technology experts, founded in 1947. The ACM fosters advances in computer and information technologies, sponsors an annual conference, publishes journals and books, promotes computing standards, and has formulated a code of ethics and professional conduct.

asterisk **1.** A character (*) used to indicate multiplication, as in 4 * 2 = 8. **2.** In file names, a character (*) used as a wild card that can stand for any number of unspecified characters. For example, *.EXE specifies all files with the extension .EXE.

Asymmetric Digital Subscriber Line *See* **ADSL.**

asynchronous Of, related to, or being a telecommunications mode that does not rely on an independent timing signal to identify the beginning and end of each byte of data that is transmitted. In asynchronous mode, the communicating devices are free to send data in a continuous stream whenever both devices are ready. The beginning of each byte is identified by a start bit, and the end by a stop bit. Most communication between personal computers is asynchronous, because the relatively lower transmission speeds permit the use of standard telephone lines. *See also* **modem, parity, synchronous.**

asynchronous transfer mode *See* **ATM.**

AT *Abbreviation of* **Advanced Technology,** used in conjunction with the IBM AT computer, which was introduced in 1984. The IBM AT computer had an Intel 286 processor and a 1.2MB floppy disk drive.

AT Attachment Packet Interface *Abbreviated* **ATAPI.** A standard which allows a CD-ROM drive to be connected to an IDE host adapter.

AT bus A 16-bit expansion bus used in the IBM AT computer, now obsolete.

AT Command Set A standardized set of instructions used to control modems. This standard was developed by Hayes Microcomputer Products. Practically all modern modems made today are compatible with the standard established by Hayes.

AT keyboard An 84-key keyboard that was used with the IBM AT computer. This type of keyboard has largely been replaced by the enhanced keyboard, which has 101 keys, or the Microsoft Windows keyboard, which has 104 keys.

ATM   *Abbreviation of* **asynchronous transfer mode.**   A high-speed communications standard for voice, data, and video traffic. The standard achieves its speed because it does not require the clock signals of the communicating devices to be coordinated. Instead, each device sends signals to the other indicating whether it is ready to receive or send. ATM combines the efficiency of packet switching with the path and bandwidth reliability of circuit switching.

at sign   The symbol @, used in email addresses to separate the name of a mailbox and the computer name at which it resides, as in *trade@hmco.com.*

Attached Resource Computer Network   *See* **ARCNet.**

attachment   A file that is attached to an email. The contents of an attachment usually do not appear within the body of the email, and it is encoded by one of various standards such as MIME, BinHex, or UUENCODE. Many email programs automatically encode documents that are sent as attachments and automatically decode received attachments if the program is capable of doing so.

attribute   **1.** In applications, a characteristic of a block of text or of a database field. Style and size are text attributes; a database field's attribute might specify that the field contains only numerical data in the form of percentages.   **2.** In file management, a property that can be assigned to a file to indicate whether it is a read-only file, a system file, or a hidden file; or whether it has been changed since the last backup.

audio card   *See* **sound card.**

Audio Interchange File Format   *See* **AIFF.**

audit trail   **1.** In accounting and database management software, a complete record of all transactions and changes made to a document. This allows the document's history to be reconstructed in case of data loss or error.   **2.** In systems management, a record of all activity on a network, used primarily for security purposes.

Audio Video Interleave   *See* **AVI.**

AUP   *Abbreviation of* **Acceptable Use Policy.**

authentication   The process of verifying a user's identity. The use of a username and password is the most common method of authentication on a network. On advanced systems, thumbprints, retinal scans, or other biometrics are also used for authentication.

authoring language   A computer language or application designed to help create graphics and multimedia presentations, hypertext documents, and CAI (computer-aided instruction) programs. Authoring languages provide tools for linking together text, graphic, and sound objects to create new application programs. A well-known authoring language for webpage design is HTML.

AUTOEXEC.BAT   A file that DOS automatically executes when you start or restart the computer. The name stands for the words automatic execute batch. *See also* **batch file.**

auto-redial   A feature that allows a modem to dial a number repeatedly when it receives a busy signal.

autorepeat   A feature that allows a key on a keyboard to repeat its assigned keystroke continuously until the key is released.

autosave   A feature in applications that minimizes loss of data in the event of system failure by automatically saving an open file to disk at periodic intervals. *Also called* **timed backup.** *See also* **save.**

AUX   The logical device name in MS DOS systems for the standard auxiliary port, usually the first serial port. It is also referred to as COM-1.

A/UX   The Apple Computer version of the Unix operating system.

avatar   1. A graphical representation of a person in an IRC chat room, interactive game, or other area of cyberspace. An avatar can be a cartoon drawing, picture, or other item that the user chooses to represent his or her virtual identity.   2. *See* **superuser.**

AVI   *Abbreviation of* **Audio Video Interleave.**   A file format for the Microsoft Windows environment for storing, transmitting, and playing audio and video data. AVI files are named with an .AVI extension.

awk   An interpretive programming language designed for processing string data. Awk has a C-like syntax and is available on almost all versions of the Unix operating system.

[B]

backbone   The top level of a hierarchical network. Other networks and subnetworks usually connect to the backbone.

back end   The part of a program in a application that is stored and runs on the file server. This allows processing tasks to be done on a powerful server instead of a user's machine. *See also* **front end.**

background   1. One or more operations that a computer is carrying out in addition to the one that is the main focus of the user's attention. The operation that once most commonly occurred in the background was printing, as most operating systems and word processors enabled the user to direct one document to a printer while returning to work on another document without having to wait for the printer to release control of the computer.

   With the more widespread use of multitasking operating systems, however, the concept of background processing became more general. In a multitasking environment it is possible to have multiple programs running simultaneously and sharing CPU time. This allows you to continue working while the CPU completes time-consuming operations such as large spreadsheet recalculations or modem-to-modem file transfers. It also makes it possible to leave facilities such as email and fax modems active and waiting to notify you when a message is received. *See also* **foreground, spooling**. 2. The area of a display screen over which characters and graphics appear. On many monitors, the user can set the color, shading, or pattern of the background.

backlighting   A technique used in laptops, notebooks, and personal digital assistants to increase the legibility of a liquid crystal display screen by illuminating it from behind. This heightens the contrast between the text and the background, but at the cost of more quickly running down the computer's batteries.

back slash   also **backslash**   A character (\) used to indicate the root directory and to separate subdirectories in DOS, several versions of Microsoft Windows, and OS/2 file names.

Backspace key   A key that moves the cursor one space to the left and deletes whatever character is there. *See also* **Delete key**.

backup   1. The process or an instance of backing up.   2. A disk or tape that contains files copied in a backup. *See also* **data compression, DMA**.

back up   To copy files from one storage area, especially a hard disk, to another to prevent their loss in case of disk failure. For today's personal computers, where a typical hard disk can easily contain up to 16 gigabytes of data, regular backups are crucial. You should consider making at least two backups and keep the extra backup in another location in case of fire or theft. Since modern hard drives are so large, complete backups might be impractical or impossible;

however, backing up key files is critical. Files can be backed up by using operating system commands or a backup utility program. Backup utilities are faster and usually compress the data so that fewer disks or tapes are required.

backward compatible Of or relating to a computer system or software program that does not make earlier versions obsolete. For example, IBM PC-compatibles based on the Pentium microprocessor can run all software that will run on the earlier 486. Similarly, later versions of most application programs can read files generated with earlier versions.

Manufacturers strive to maintain downward compatibility when they develop new hardware and software, because it avoids the need for users to start from scratch every time they upgrade to a new version. Occasionally, however, the capabilities of newer products become so far advanced that a certain amount of compatibility has to be given up. *Also called* **downward compatible**. *See also* **compatible, upward compatible**.

bad break In word processing and desktop publishing, a place where a word, line, or page is improperly divided. Examples include setting the second part of a hyphenated word at the beginning of a left-hand page, hyphenating *minute* at the end of a line as *min-ute* when the word in a document is actually *mi-nute,* and leaving a section title stranded at the very bottom of a page.

bad sector A sector of a hard disk or floppy disk that cannot be used for reading and writing information because of a manufacturing defect or a flaw in the surface. It is normal for a new hard disk to have a small number of bad sectors; the operating system or a disk utility program can locate and mark these areas so they will not be used. As a hard disk gets older, more sectors may occasionally fail, but if this happens frequently it is a sign of a malfunctioning disk drive or impending disk failure. If bad sectors appear on a floppy disk, some data will usually be lost and the entire disk may become unusable; the safest policy generally is to copy the remaining files to a fresh disk, if possible, and discard the one that has failed. *See also* **disk, format, head crash, sector**.

.BAK A file extension in MS-DOS appended to a file of backup data. For many programs, when you save a document such as foo.doc, many programs create a document called foo.bak that is a copy of the previous version of foo.doc.

bandwidth   A measure of the amount of data that can be passed by a communications channel in a given amount of time. For analog devices, bandwidth is the range of frequencies that can be transmitted and is expressed in hertz (cycles per second). A standard telephone line, for example, has a usable bandwidth of about 3,000 Hz. For digital devices, bandwidth is often measured in bps (bits per second). In general, the bandwidth of a channel directly affects the speed of data transfer — the wider the bandwidth, the faster data can be sent. *Also called* **pipe**.

banner   A rectangular box for advertisements on webpages. Banners are usually 50 points high (one point equals 1/72 of an inch) and 400 points across, and are generally placed near the top or bottom of a webpage. Clicking on a banner links you to the advertiser's website and often supplies the advertiser with data about you or your computer that is used to track the effectiveness of the advertisement and to generate leads.

bar graph   A graph consisting of parallel, usually vertical bars or rectangles with lengths proportional to the frequency with which specified quantities occur in a set of data. *Also called* **bar chart**.

barrel distortion   The distortion on a monitor in which the horizontal and vertical lines curve outward away from the center of the screen. Most monitors have controls that allow you to correct distortion. *See also* **pincushion distortion**.

baseband transmission   A digital signal transmission technique that allows only a single signal to be sent across a connection at a time. Baseband transmission is typically used for radio, infrared, and other mediums, as well as for wired networking such as modems.

base font   In word processing, the default font that is used in a document wherever a different font is not specifically selected.

baseline   The horizontal line on which the base of letters are aligned, excluding descenders. *See illustration.*

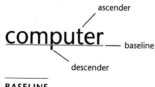

BASELINE

base memory   *See* **conventional memory.**

BASIC   *Abbreviation of* **Beginners' All-purpose Symbolic Instruction Code.**   A simple, widely used high-level programming language. It was first developed in the mid-1960s by John Kemeny and Thomas Kurtz of Dartmouth College, and many other versions with proprietary extensions have also been developed over the years. Despite being criticized by professional programmers for its unwieldiness, BASIC is still widely taught to students as a first programming language. Visual Basic is based on BASIC.

basic input/output system   *See* **BIOS.**

batch file   A text file that consists of a number of commands to be executed one after the other. Batch files offer a convenient way to carry out a frequently executed sequence of commands by simply typing the name of the batch file. They are easy to create and can include a small number of programming functions, such as IF . . . THEN, GOTO, and FOR . . . IN . . . DO constructs, which make the command line interface much faster and more powerful. It is also possible to call one batch file from within another, executing the second file and then returning control to the first. All batch files in DOS have the extension .BAT; hence they are often called BAT files.

   As the last step in the boot-up sequence, most DOS-based computers automatically run the file AUTOEXEC.BAT, which can be used to set a number of system parameters and install device drivers and terminate and stay resident programs without the user's having to enter the commands one by one. *See table at* **file.**

batch processing   A mode of computer operation in which a complete program or set of instructions is carried out from start to finish without any intervention from a user. Batch processing is a highly efficient way of using computer resources, but it does not allow for any input while the batch is running, or any corrections in the event of a flaw in the program or a system failure. For these reasons it is primarily used for CPU-intensive tasks that are well established and can run reliably without supervision, often at night or on weekends when other demands on the system are low. *See also* **transaction processing.**

battery pack   A rechargeable battery for portable computers.

BAT file   *See* **batch file.**

baud   A unit of speed in data transmission usually equal to one bit per second (bps). *See also* **baud rate.**

baud rate   In telecommunications, the number of changes in state that can occur in a given communications circuit in one second. For a modem, this is the number of times per second that it can change the frequency of its analog signal. At speeds under 1,200 baud, the data transmission rate, measured in bits per second, is generally equivalent to the baud rate: at 1,200 baud, 1,200 bits per second are transmitted. At higher rates, more bits per second can be transmitted than the equivalent baud rate. For example, 9,600 bps can be transmitted at a baud rate of 4,800 by sending 2 bits of data with each frequency change. As typical modem speeds increase, the term *baud* is becoming outdated. Transmission speed is now generally measured in bits (or kilobits or megabits) per second.

bay   A space in the cabinet of a personal computer where a storage device such as a disk drive, CD-ROM drive, or removable storage drive can be installed. A bay is *internal* or *hidden* when it cannot be used for removable media, such as floppy disk drives; otherwise it is called *exposed* or *accessible*. *Also called* **drive bay**.

BBS   *Abbreviation of* **bulletin board system**.

bells and whistles   The features or enhancements of a product that are that are intended especially to add commercial appeal. Usually bells and whistles are viewed as unnecessary, attention-grabbing annoyances with functions that aren't really important but are added to differentiate the product from previous versions.

benchmark   A standard by which the performance of hardware or software is measured. Benchmark tests typically measure efficiency and the speed at which a program or computer component performs a certain task, but these measurements are not reliable in gauging the actual performance of the whole computer system. For example, the output from a microprocessor that performs well in a benchmark test could be held up by slow disk drives. Throughput, a measurement of a computer's ability to send data through all of its components, is often a better overall indication of a computer's speed than individual benchmark measurements. *See also* **throughput**.

Bernoulli Box   [ber-NOO-lee]   A mass storage device developed by Iomega Corporation that uses removable cartridges similar to floppy disks. As the flexible disk spins, the decreased air pressure along its surface causes it to be pulled nearly into contact with the read/write head. However, a thin cushion of air remains to isolate the head from the disk's surface, making the drive unlikely to suffer a head crash. Its high rotation speed made the Bernoulli Box significantly faster than previous kinds of floppy drives. It is now obsolescent, largely replaced by optical storage disks, CD-RW disks, and other technologies. *Also called* **Bernoulli disk drive**.

beta testing   The final stage in the testing of new software or hardware, conducted by independent testers outside the company that developed it, before it is released commercially.

beta version   The version of a software or hardware product used during beta testing, usually the second major revision of the product. Beta versions are often released to the public for use.

Bézier curve   [BEZ-ee-ay]   A smooth free-form curve used in nearly all draw programs. The shape of the curve is determined mathematically by the location of two midpoints called control handles, or simply handles. Usually the handles appear on the screen as two small boxes. By clicking on the handles and dragging them with the mouse, you can change the shape of the curve. *See illustration.*

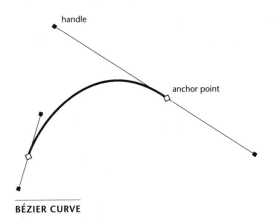

BÉZIER CURVE

Big Blue   A nickname for the International Business Machines (IBM) Corporation, stemming from the blue in IBM's corporate logo.

binary   Of or relating to a number system with a base of two. Each place in a binary number represents a power of two, in contrast with the decimal (base ten) system most of us use every day, in which each place in a number represents a successive power of ten. Thus the decimal number 165, which really stands for

$$(1 \times 10^2) + (6 \times 10^1) + (5 \times 10^0)$$

is written in binary notation as 10100101, which stands for

$$(1 \times 2^7) \times (0 \times 2^6) + (1 \times 2^5) + (0 \times 2^4) +$$
$$(0 \times 2^3) + (1 \times 2^2) + (0 \times 2^1) + (1 \times 2^0).$$

This kind of notation is unnatural and difficult for humans to read, but it is ideal for computers, because an electronic circuit that only has to differentiate between two states — on or off, open or closed, 0 or 1 — is easier to build and can operate faster than one that must detect and work with ten possible states. Table 5 lists decimal, binary, octal, and hexadecimal equivalents. *See also* **hexadecimal, octal**.

TABLE 5 Binary, Octal, and Hexadecimal Values

Decimal	Binary	Octal	Hexadecimal	Decimal	Binary	Octal	Hexadecimal
0	0	0	0	9	1001	11	9
1	1	1	1	10	1010	12	A
2	10	2	2	11	1011	13	B
3	11	3	3	12	1100	14	C
4	100	4	4	13	1101	15	D
5	101	5	5	14	1110	16	E
6	110	6	6	15	1111	17	F
7	111	7	7	16	10000	20	10
8	1000	10	8				

binary coded decimal A coding scheme in which each decimal digit 0-9 is represented by a string of four binary digits, as a means of preventing calculation errors due to rounding and conversion. For example, since the binary equivalent of 3 is 0011 and the binary equivalent of 6 is 0110, 36 is represented as 0011 0110.

binary digit *See* **bit**.

binary file A file containing numeric data or program instructions in a computer-readable form. *See also* **ASCII file, text file**. *See table at* **file**.

BinHex A scheme for encoding the data in binary text files as ASCII characters for Internet transmission. In order to read email or files sent in this manner, your computer must have software for decoding BinHex files. BinHex is especially common among Apple Macintosh users.

BIOS *Abbreviation of* **basic input/output system**. A set of instructions and routines that enable the computer to communicate with the various devices in the system, such as memory, disk drives, keyboard, monitor, printer, and communications ports. Just as the operating system lets applications programs interact with the computer without having to tell it exactly how to carry out every operation, the BIOS mediates between the operating system and the hardware, taking care of the intricate details of getting the various devices to work smoothly together. The BIOS in IBM PC and compatible computers may be contained in the system's read-only memory, making it available when the system boots up and keeping it safe in case of system failure.

B-ISDN *Abbreviation of* **Broadband ISDN**.

bit The smallest unit of memory and therefore information within a computer. A bit can hold only one of two values, 0 or 1. In the binary number system, the digits 0 and 1 are also called bits. The term comes from the phrase **binary digit**. *See also* **byte**.

bit map also **bitmap** A set of bits that represents a graphic image. Each bit corresponds to a dot in a pattern. For a monochromatic image, the bit map consists of rows and columns of 0s and 1s. Each value determines whether its dot is to be filled in (1) or not (0). For a color image or one with shades of gray, each dot requires more than one bit of data. To print the image on a printer, the computer translates the bit map into ink dots. To display the image on a screen, the computer translates the bit map into pixels. Optical scanners and fax machines convert text or pictures into bit maps. *See illustrations at* **antialiasing, outline font**. *See also* **resolution**.

bit-mapped font A font in which each character is represented by a pattern of dots. To display or print a bit-mapped font, the computer or printer must have a bit map of each character in memory. This means bit-mapped fonts require huge amounts of memory and disk space. Furthermore, bit-mapped fonts cannot be scaled up or down, as from Times Roman 12 point to Times Roman 16 point, without developing jaggies. *See also* **antialiasing, scalable font**. *See illustration at* **outline font**.

bit-mapped graphics Graphic images that are stored in memory as arrays of bits that specify the appearance of each individual pixel on the screen. Bit-mapped graphics are commonly produced by paint programs. Because they are not mapped in memory as sets of objects but only as undifferentiated sequences of dots, it is difficult to pick out one element of a bit-mapped drawing for editing. The resolution of bit-mapped images is limited to that of the display screen, scaling them up or down to different sizes does not work very well, and they require large amounts of memory and storage space. *See also* **bit map, object-oriented graphics, raster graphics**. *See illustration at* **pixel**.

BITNET *Abbreviation of* **Because It's Time Network**. A wide area network (WAN) founded in 1981 and run by the Corporation for Research and Educational Networking in Washington, DC. BITNET links North American, European, and Japanese universities and research institutions. Unlike the Internet, it does not use the TCP/IP protocol for its email and ftp services. Instead, it uses IBM's Network Job Entry protocol; nonetheless, it is capable of sending email over the Internet.

bits per second *See* **bps**.

blank character A character that produces no visible representation other than a space on the screen, usually generated by pressing the space bar.

bleed Text or graphics that extend to the edge of the page or that are printed so as to go off the edge after trimming. A bleed may be used as part of a design element; they are also used in bookmaking to mark off a block of pages as a tab index when the pages of book are viewed from the side.

bloatware Software with large, often unused additional features, especially as compared with previous versions. Generally bloatware results when software developers add more complex features to new versions to appeal to commercial consumers.

block **1.** In word processing, a section of text that is selected so that some operation can be performed on it as a unit. The ability to manipulate marked blocks of text is perhaps the most important feature that distinguishes word processing from manuscript preparation with a typewriter. Marking is usually done by highlighting the desired text with the arrow keys or by using the mouse to drag the cursor over it. Once a block is selected, it can be deleted, copied, moved to another document or another location in the same document, saved as a named file, or printed with a few keystrokes or mouse clicks. Another powerful kind of operation that can be performed on a block of text is reformatting, in which the margins, spacing, and size and appearance of the type can be changed quickly for any portion of a document. **2.** In telecommunications, an amount of data transferred from one system to another as a unit. When a block is created, additional information is usually included that can be used to check if the block was garbled during transmission. In general, the larger the block size, the faster the data transfer rate, but if noisy telephone lines or other disruptions cause errors that make it necessary to repeat blocks, smaller block sizes are more efficient. The most common transfer protocols use block sizes from 128 bytes to 1,024 bytes.

block graphics   Onscreen graphic images that are made of characters in the ASCII extended character set having the decimal values 176 through 223. These characters consist of rectangles and horizontal and vertical lines of various thicknesses, sizes, and shadings. Being elements in the character set, they are processed in the same way that other characters, such as the letters and numbers, are. As a result, block graphics are processed and displayed more rapidly than bit-mapped graphics. However, images created with block graphics are more limited and are low-resolution. *See the IBM Extended ASCII Character Set table at* **ASCII**.

block protection   In word processing, a feature that allows a block of text to be kept together as a unit when moved to a location where it would otherwise be interrupted by page breaks.

.BMP   A file extension in MS-DOS for files with bit-mapped graphics.

BNC connector   A connector used to connect coaxial cables. By placing a cable having this connector into the end of another, you can lock them together by turning a ring that surrounds the end of the connector. *See illustration.*

BNC CONNECTOR   A male BNC connector

board   *See* **printed circuit board**.

boilerplate   Text or graphical elements that need to be used frequently in numerous documents, such as standard language required in mortgage documents, or a company logo and letterhead. By saving boilerplate to a memory device, you can copy it into any documents or programs that require its use.

boldface   A typeface in which the letters are heavier and darker than normal. The entry words in this dictionary are printed in boldface. *See illustration at* **font family**.

bomb *n.* An abrupt and complete failure, especially of a running program.

v. To fail suddenly and completely. *See also* **crash**.

bookmark A marker used in a program such as a web browser or a help utility that allows you to go directly to a specific webpage.

Boolean expression An expression that yields a value of TRUE or FALSE. Boolean expressions can contain relational operators such as = for *is equal to*, < for *is less than*, and > for *is greater than*. For example, the statement 26 > 30 returns the value FALSE. The other main type of operator in Boolean expressions is a Boolean (sometimes called logical) operator, such as AND, OR, NOT, NOR, or XOR. For example, if A is the statement *Ice is cold* (and we assume that the statement is true), the result of the expression NOT A is FALSE.

Boolean logic A form of algebra that employs only two values, TRUE and FALSE. Boolean logic, developed by the 19th-century English mathematician George Boole, is particularly well suited for use with computers because it works so well with the binary number system. A bit with value 1 corresponds to TRUE; a bit with value 0 corresponds to FALSE. *See also* **fuzzy logic**.

Boolean operator An operator whose result can only be one of two values, TRUE or FALSE. Boolean operators are widely used in programming, spreadsheets, and databases. Common Boolean operators are AND, OR, XOR, and NOT. For example, the database query

find all where last_name = "Jones" AND balance_owed > 100

would yield the records of everyone named Jones who owed more than $100. The query

find all where last_name = "Jones" OR balance_owed > 100

would yield the records of everyone named Jones regardless of the balance owed and the records of everyone who owed more than $100 regardless of last name. *Also called* **logical operator**.

boot *v.* To load the software, usually the operating system, that starts the computer.

n. The process of loading the software that starts the computer. *See also* **cold boot**, **warm boot**.

boot disk *See* **startup disk**.

boot sector A track on a disk containing the instructions that automatically run to begin the operation of the computer when the computer is turned on. Usually the boot sector is located on a hard drive's first track in the first partition.

bot   A software program that imitates the behavior of a human, as by querying search engines or participating in chatroom or IRC discussions.

bounced mail   An email message that never arrives at its destination and is returned to its sender.

box   **1.** An enclosed area in a graphical user interface. Boxes are similar to a windows in appearance, but they generally cannot be resized. Alert boxes and dialog boxes are two kinds of boxes. **2.** *Slang.* A particular kind of computer: *a Unix box*.

bps   *Abbreviation of* **bits per second.**   A measure of data transmission rate. For example, a common rate for a modem to transmit and receive data is 33,600 bps, and many modems can reach a rate of 56,000 bps.

branch   In a tree structure, a line of the tree that ends in a leaf. In MS-DOS, a branch corresponds to a subdirectory.

Break key   A key that causes a computer to pause in the middle of an operation, such as sorting a file, or to break a modem connection. Not all keyboards have a Break key, nor do all programs recognize it. In many cases a break is executed by pressing a combination of two keys. *See also* **Ctrl-Break**.

bridge   A device that connects two local area networks and allows them to exchange data, even though they may have different topologies or communications protocols. *See also* **router**.

Broadband ISDN   *Abbreviated* **B-ISDN**   A standard for data transmission over fiber optic cable at rates of up to 1.5 megabits per second.

broadband transmission   A digital signal transmission technique whereby multiple signals are sent over a single wire. Broadband transmission typically is done over coaxial cable and allows the simultaneous transmission of voice, data, fax, and video. B-ISDN and cable modems are examples of technologies using broadband transmission.

broadcast   To simultaneously send one message to a number of receivers, as in an email system or over a network.

brouter   A device that combines the functions of bridges and routers.

brownout   A reduction in electric power, usually as a result of a shortage, a mechanical failure, or overuse by consumers. A computer subject to these power interruptions can lose data or even crash. *See also* **surge protector**, **UPS**.

browse   *v.* **1.** To view information without manipulating it. Browsing enables the user to move through a large number of files or database records quickly, but usually does not allow the user to change data. *See also* **surf.**   **2.** To use a browser to access the Internet.

n. In a database, a mode in which the user may view data without manipulating it.

browser   A program, such as Netscape Navigator or Microsoft Internet Explorer, that allows you to find and access documents from anywhere on the Internet.

bubble-jet printer   A printer consisting of a grid of ink-containing nozzles that forms an image when the ink is heated and expanded, forcing it out onto the page. *See table at* **printer.**

bubble memory   A memory that stores data in the form of bubbles, or circular areas, on a thin film of magnetic silicate. It is similar to RAM but does not lose the stored information when the computer is turned off. The use of bubble memory has become almost obsolete since the introduction of flash memory.

buffer   A temporary storage area for data, usually located in the computer's RAM. The CPU (central processing unit) of a computer can process data much faster than a printer can, for example. When the user enters a print command, the operating system copies the data to a print buffer, from which the printer pulls characters at its own pace. A print buffer is often called a *spooler.*

Since writing to disk is another relatively slow task, many text editors and word processors save changes to text in a buffer. Then, either at set intervals or at the end of an editing session, they transfer the updated text from the buffer to the document's disk file. Saving the file during the editing session forces the editor or word processor to write the changes to disk.

Many operating systems employ a disk buffer to temporarily store data they have read from disk. DOS allows the user to specify the memory allocated to disk buffers by placing a BUFFER command in the CONFIG.SYS file. Each DOS buffer uses 528 bytes, so the command BUFFERS=10 reserves about 5 kilobytes of RAM for buffers. In Apple Macintosh computers, the disk buffer is called a *cache,* and its memory allocation is set via the Control Panel.

buffer overflow   *See* **overflow error.**

bug   A defect in software or hardware that causes it to perform inconsistently, crash, or otherwise malfunction. The word was allegedly coined when a moth caused a short circuit in one of the earliest computers.

built-in font   *See* **resident font.**

bullet   A graphical element used to highlight a particular passage, as an item in a list or outline. Bullets are typically heavy, filled-in dots (•), but can also have other shapes (■, ♦, ○) serving a similar function.

bulletin board system   *Abbreviated* **BBS**   An electronic communication system that allows users to leave messages, review messages, play games, and upload and download software, including shareware. Computers are connected to a BBS by modem. Thousands of BBSs are active in the United States, although due to the proliferation of the Internet, much of the information and camaraderie they provide is duplicated by newsgroups and websites.

bundled software   **1.** Programs that are included as part of the package when you buy a computer.   **2.** Several programs packaged and sold together. *See also* **suite.**

burn-in   *v.* To run a new computer continuously for an extended period, usually 24 to 48 hours, in order to test for defective memory chips, microprocessors, and other components.
n. See **ghosting.**

bus   **1.** A circuit that connects the components of a computer, allowing the transfer of electric signals from one connected component to any other. The electric signals encode data, and the bus is the pathway on which data travels throughout the computer. The size of a bus, called its width, determines how much data it can carry at once. More technically, the width of the bus is the number of signal lines used to transmit data in parallel, each line carrying one data bit. A 16-bit bus transmits 16 bits of data at one time, just like 16 trucks traveling side by side on a 16-lane highway. Another characteristic of buses is that their clock speed is measured in megahertz (MHz). Most new personal computers now have two or more buses. Table 6 shows a comparison of some popular buses. **2.** One of the three principal topologies for a local area network (LAN) in which all computers and devices, known as nodes, are connected to a central cable along which data is passed. *See also* **ring, star.** *See illustration at* **network.**   **3.** The central cable used in a bus topology.

TABLE 6 **Expansion Bus Varieties and Connection Types***

Expansion Bus Name	Clock Speed
ISA	8.33 megahertz
EISA	8.33 megahertz
Micro Channel Architecture	10 megahertz
NuBus	10 or 20 megahertz
PCI local bus	33 megahertz
VESA local bus	40 or 66 megahertz (max.)
Connection Type	**Transfer Rate**
serial	115 kilobits/second
parallel	115 kilobits/second
SCSI-2	10 megabits/second
USB	12 or 1.5 megabits/second
Ultra 2 SCSI	40 megabits/second
Ultra 3 SCSI	80 megabits/second
USB 2.0	480 megabits/second
FC-AL Fiber Channel	100–400 megabits/second

*An expansion bus is commonly used to connect hardware that is internal to the CPU box. A connection is used to connect hardware that is external to the CPU box.

bus mouse   A mouse connected to the computer through an expansion board or through the motherboard, as opposed to a serial mouse, which is connected through a serial port. One advantage of using a bus mouse is that it does not tie up one of the computer's serial ports.

button   1. In graphical user interface systems, a small outlined area within a dialog box that is clicked to select a command. *Also called* **pushbutton**.   2. In a hypertext database, an icon that when selected allows a user to view a particular associated object. Text, pictures, recorded music, and other forms of information are called objects; associated objects are linked together. *See illustration at* **desktop**.

byte   A unit of data equal to eight bits. Each bit has a value of either 0 or 1, and the various eight-bit combinations represent all of the data in a computer. Amounts of computer memory are often expressed in terms of megabytes (1,048,576 bytes). *See also* **megabyte**.

bytecode   The compiled format for programs written in Java, usually having the extension *.class*.

[C]

C A high-level language widely used in writing professional software. Known as an efficient and flexible programming language, C was developed at AT&T Bell Laboratories in the 1970s. C is a highly portable language because it is so compact that a compiler for it can easily be built on almost any platform.

C++ A programming language originally based on C that uses object-oriented programming. C++ was developed in the early 1980s at AT&T Bell Laboratories. C++ has become one of the most commonly used languages for the development of new products.

cable modem A communications device that allows computers to transmit data over cable TV lines. Because of the high bandwidth of the cable TV lines, cable modems are much faster than modems that use telephone lines.

cache **1.** An area of storage devoted to the high-speed retrieval of frequently used or requested data. Data can be retrieved much more quickly from a cache than it can from another storage area, such as a disk or RAM. A cache typically mimics a larger, slower area of storage. **2.** A part of RAM set aside to facilitate access to the data that is needed most often. The cache uses faster, more expensive static RAM chips. Every time a request for data is sent to RAM, the cache intercepts the request. If the data is already in the cache, it can be sent immediately. Otherwise, the cache accesses the data from the slower chips in RAM and sends it to the microprocessor, but also keeps a copy in case it is needed again soon. When no requests are made, the cache copies and stores data from RAM addresses near the data most recently needed on the theory that they may be needed next. When the cache is full, it erases the data that has waited the longest without being needed. *Also called* **RAM cache**.

CAD *Abbreviation of* **computer-aided design**. The use of computer programs and systems to design detailed two- or three-dimensional models of physical objects, such as mechanical parts, buildings, and molecules. Many CAD systems allow the user to view models from any angle, to move about inside of the model, and to change its scale. When the designer or engineer changes one part of a model, the CAD system is able to reconfigure the rest of the model around this new specification. CAD systems require fast microprocessors and high-resolution video displays. Until the last few years, all CAD systems were dedicated minicomputers. CAD software that runs on general-purpose workstations and personal computers is now available.

CADD   *Abbreviation of* **computer-aided design and drafting**.   A CAD system that incorporates extra features specific to drafting, especially the capability to annotate architectural or engineering designs with size specifications and notes.

CAD/CAM   *Abbreviation of* **computer-aided design/computer-aided manufacturing**.   A computer system that designs and manufactures products. An object is designed with the CAD component of the system, and the design is then translated into manufacturing or assembly instructions for specialized machinery.

CAI   *Abbreviation of* **computer-aided instruction**.   The use of computer programs as teaching tools. CAI software usually offers tutorials, drills, and tests and allows the student to proceed at his or her own pace.

calculated field   In a database or spreadsheet, a field that contains results of calculations performed on other fields. In a database showing each country's area and population, for example, the calculated field could give population density figures.

calculator   A program or a part of an operating system that enables the user to perform arithmetic calculations, usually on an onscreen representation of a hand-held calculator. The calculator is operated with the keyboard or with a mouse.

calendar   An application that works as an electronic datebook. Besides allowing you to set appointments, many calendar programs can automatically set entries for weekly or monthly events. Some calendar programs can issue a signal to remind you of an important engagement or a significant day.

call   *v.* In programming, to invoke and transfer control to a routine, subroutine, or function. When the called procedure is completed, program execution resumes at the next instruction after the calling point.
   n. An invocation of a routine, subroutine, or function.

CAM   *Abbreviation of* **computer-aided manufacturing**.   The process of using specialized computers to control, monitor, and adjust tools and machinery in manufacturing.

camera-ready copy   The final stage in the preparation of a document prior to printing. Originally, items at this stage were photographed as part of the offset printing process. Now, in instances where offset printing plates are made electronically, skipping the photograph step, or where the document is printed by a high-resolution printer, *camera-ready* is still used to indicate that something is ready to be printed.

Caps Lock key   A toggle key on a computer keyboard that when activated locks the keyboard so that you can enter uppercase letters without pressing the Shift key. The key has no effect on number and punctuation keys, unlike a Caps Lock key on a typewriter. Most keyboards have a light that illuminates when the Caps Lock key is pressed.

capture   To save data, especially that which is visible on a screen, to a file for storage or later analysis.

card   **1.** A printed circuit board, especially one designed to fit an expansion slot in a personal computer; an adapter.   **2.** In HyperCard and similar programs, an onscreen representation of an index card on which information can be written and "filed."

cardinal number   A number, such as 3 or 11 or 412, used in counting to indicate quantity but not order.

caret   A symbol (^) usually found above the 6 on the keyboard. This symbol sometimes indicates the control key, especially in manuals or documentation; that is, ^A would indicate to press the control key and the A together. It is also used to indicate that the number following it is an exponent; that is, 2^4 is the same as 2^4.

carpal tunnel syndrome   A condition characterized by pain and numbing or tingling sensations in the hand and caused by compression of a nerve in the carpal tunnel, a passageway in the wrist through which nerves and the flexor muscles of the hands and fingers pass.

carriage   The mechanism that feeds paper through a printer. On inkjet printers, the assembly that moves the print head across the page is called the print head carriage assembly.

carriage return   *Abbreviated* **CR**   On personal computers, a code that brings the cursor back to the beginning of the same line. (In the ASCII character set, a carriage return is coded as the decimal value 13.) To move the cursor to the beginning of a new line you press the Enter key or the Return key. Most word processing and desktop publishing programs feature word wrap, which automatically starts a new line once the current line is filled. *See also* **hard return, line feed**.

carrier **1.** A telecommunications company. **2.** *See* **carrier signal**.

Carrier Sense Multiple Access with Collision Detection *See* CSMA/CD.

carrier signal A steady signal or tone of a specified frequency that is sent along a communications line. The carrier can be modulated, or changed, as in frequency or amplitude, by a device such as a modem in order to transmit information from one computer to another.

Cartesian coordinate system A system of representing points in a space by coordinates, in which a point's coordinates are its distances from a set of perpendicular lines that intersect at an origin, such as two lines in a plane or three in space. *See illustration.*

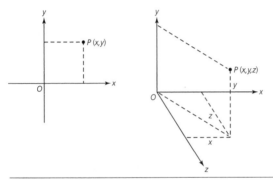

CARTESIAN COORDINATE SYSTEM Two-dimensional coordinate system (left) and three-dimensional coordinate system

cartridge **1.** A removable unit that contains a data storage medium such as tape, disks, or memory chips. The term removable cartridge generally refers to a type of portable hard disk. **2.** A removable unit used to load fonts into some printers, giving you the option to print in other fonts besides the base font. *See also* **font cartridge**.

cartridge font *See* **font cartridge**.

cascading menu A submenu that appears on the screen when a choice from another menu is selected. *See illustration at* **menu**.

cascading style sheet *See* **CSS**.

cascading windows *See* **overlaid windows**.

CASE *Abbreviation of* **computer-aided software engineering**. The use of computer software and systems as an aid in complex programming. CASE software may now be run on personal computers.

case-sensitive Able to distinguish between uppercase (capital) and lowercase (small) letters. Programs that are case-sensitive and have a search feature will distinguish between *APPLE, apple,* and *Apple,* for example. Case-sensitive programs will respond differently to commands issued in uppercase versus lowercase letters. Most passwords are case-sensitive.

cathode-ray tube *Abbreviated* **CRT** The basic element in standard computer monitors and television sets. In a monochrome monitor, the video adapter sends signals to an electron gun at the back of the CRT. In response, the electron gun shoots out a stream of electrons. Another mechanism, also controlled by signals from the adapter, focuses and aims the electron beams so that they strike the phosphors coating the inside of the display screen. Phosphors are materials that glow when they are struck by electrons. The electron beams sweep across the screen about 60 to 120 times a second, continually re-illuminating, or refreshing, the appropriate phosphors. Color monitors work on the same principle, but use 3 electron guns (one each for red, blue, and green) and 3 different phosphor materials.

CAV *Abbreviation of* **constant angular velocity**.

CBT *Abbreviation of* **computer based training**.

CCD *Abbreviation of* **charge-coupled device**.

CCITT *Abbreviation of* **Comité Consultatif International Télégraphique et Téléphonique.** A former organization based in Geneva, Switzerland, that developed and recommended transmission standards for modems, computer networks, serial ports, and fax machines. Its duties were subsumed in 1993 by its parent, the International Telecommunications Union (ITU).

CCITT protocol Any of a set of standards for data transmission developed by the CCITT.

CD *Abbreviation of* **compact disk**.

CD burner A device used to write data onto compact disks. Recently, drives have become available for PCs which allow CDs to be both read and written in the same drive. These devices write at a speed of 1x (150 kilobytes per second) to 8x (1.2 megabytes per second). Larger CD burners may be used to make scores or hundreds of identical CDs at the same time.

cdev [SEE-dev] *Abbreviation of* **control panel device.** Any of various utility programs for the Apple Macintosh computer that appear as options in the Control Panel and work from the system folder.

CD-I *Abbreviation of* **compact disk-interactive**. A format for combining and storing audio, video, and text on high-capacity compact disks. The technology is designed for interactive viewing of video images on a computer screen, using a CD-I drive.

CD-R *Abbreviation of* **compact disk-recordable**. A compact disk that can have data written onto it once, which can then be read on a CD-ROM drive. These are typically less expensive than CD-RW disks and are commonly used for distributing software.

CD-ROM *Abbreviation of* **compact disk read-only memory**. A compact disk that functions as ROM (read-only memory). CD-ROMs can store over 600 megabytes (MB) of data. The data must be input with special equipment, and it can be used only on a CD-ROM drive. Additional data or files appended to a CD-ROM can only be read with a multisession drive. *See also* **DVD, erasable optical disk, optical disk**. *See table at* **access time**.

CD-ROM drive A disk drive that reads data stored on CD-ROMs. Originally single-speed and having a data transfer rate of 150 kilobytes per second, CD-ROMS now available are 40-speed (40x), with a transfer rate of 6 megabytes per second. *Also called* **CD-ROM player**.

CD-ROM player *See* **CD-ROM drive**.

CD-ROM/XA *Abbreviation of* **CD-ROM extended architecture**. A specification standard developed by several companies that allows the interleaving of audio and data sectors on CD-ROM tracks.

CD-RW *Abbreviation of* **CD-rewritable**. A compact disk that allows data to be written onto it more than once.

Celeron A microprocessor designed by Intel as in inexpensive alternative to the Pentium II microprocessor. *See table at* **Intel microprocessor**.

cell **1.** One box or unit for entering information within a spreadsheet. The information can be in the form of text, numbers, formulas, or functions. The spreadsheet is formed by intersecting rows and columns of cells. **2.** An elemental storage unit for data or electrical power. A binary cell is an example of a storage unit for data that can hold one bit of information.

cell block *See* **range**.

central processing unit *See* **CPU**.

Centronics interface **1.** An older standard for connecting the parallel port of an IBM PC or compatible computer with a parallel device, usually a printer. The standard provides for 8 bits of data to be sent simultaneously over 8 parallel lines. The cable connecting the computer's parallel port with the device uses a 25-pin connector. Eight of the pins are for the data lines; the rest are either lines for sending control character codes or simply ground lines. *See also* **parallel interface.** *See illustration at* **connector.**

CERN *Abbreviation of* **Conseil Européen pour la Recherche Nucléaire** (European Laboratory for Particle Physics).   A laboratory in Geneva, Switzerland for research in physics. The World Wide Web was developed here in the late 1980s as a means of facilitating the transmission of information among scientists.

CGA *Abbreviation of* **Color Graphics Adapter.**   The first color video adapter and video standard used with IBM PC and compatible computers, introduced in 1981. The CGA system has been superseded by VGA and Super VGA systems.

CGI *Abbreviation of* **Common Gateway Interface.**   A standard that specifies how programs run from a web server. The CGI specification defines how arguments are passed and how programs are executed. A typical CGI program returns an HTML page formatted in a manner completely dependent on the user's request. A CGI program, for example, can access information from an airline schedule database and format the results to show up as a table on the browser. *See also* **ISAPI, NSAPI.**

CGM *Abbreviation of* **Computer Graphics Metafile.**

channel 1. A specified frequency band for the transmission and reception of electromagnetic signals, as for television signals. 2. A site on a network, as on IRC, where online conversations are held in real time by a number of computer users. *Also called* **chat room.** 3. In streaming media such as Real Audio, a link to a specific content provider or a specific set of content.

character A symbol, such as a letter, number, punctuation mark, or graphics symbol, that occupies one byte of memory. Each symbol represented by an ASCII or extended ASCII code is a character. *See also* **control character.**

character-based Of or relating to programs that can display only ASCII and extended ASCII characters. Character-based programs for IBM PC and compatible computers treat display screens as an array of boxes, each of which can hold one character. Because the extended ASCII character set includes shapes for drawing pictures, character-based programs can simulate graphics objects that consist mostly of straight lines, such as menus, windows, and bar charts.

Many old DOS applications were written as character-based programs so that they could be run on any IBM PC or compatible computer, even one with limited memory and graphics capabilities. Nowadays, software manufacturers usually develop graphics-based applications that use operating environments such as Microsoft Windows. Graphics-based programs treat the display screen as a grid of millions of pixels. The Apple Macintosh computer is graphics-based. *See also* **graphical user interface**.

character mode   A mode of resolution supported by a video adapter that allows the screen to display characters only, with no complex graphical images. In the character mode the screen is split into boxes. Each box can hold one ASCII character, and these characters do not necessarily look exactly as they will in print. The other display mode, graphics mode, splits the screen into millions of pixels rather than boxes, and is able to display text as it will appear in print, as well as complex graphics. *See also* **text mode**.

character recognition   *See* **optical character recognition**.

character set   A set of alphabetic, numeric, and often graphic characters that constitute the keyboard coding scheme of a particular computer system.

characters per inch   *Abbreviated* **cpi**   The number of characters that fit into a one-inch long line of type of a particular font. In monospace fonts, all characters have a constant width. But in proportional fonts characters have varying widths, so measurements of the number of characters must be averaged to compute characters per inch.

characters per second   *Abbreviated* **cps**   **1.** A measure of the speed of dot-matrix printers.   **2.** A measure of data transmission rate.

character string   *See* **string**.

charge-coupled device   *Abbreviated* **CCD**   A device that converts light into electrical signals that a computer can read. Its semiconductors are connected in such a way that the electrical output of one provides the input to the next one. Scanners and digital cameras are common products that make use of this technology.

chart   A diagram that illustrates quantitative relationships in pictoral form instead of numeric or textual form. *See also* **bar graph, pie chart**.

chat   To communicate in real-time on a computer network using typed messages. A person chatting with another person or group of people on the network types in a message and waits for the other party to type in a response. As one person types in a message, the other participants can usually see the characters appear on their screen when the person typing hits the return key.

chat room *See* **channel** (sense 2).

check box In a dialog box, a square box that allows you to turn a function or feature on and off by clicking on it. When the box is clicked on, an X or a checkmark appears in it. If a list of items with check boxes appear, more than one may be clicked on simultaneously.

checksum A technique for detecting errors in the transmission of digital data. The computer transmitting information calculates a number based on the pattern of bits in the data and includes this number in its transmission. The receiving computer performs the same calculation and compares the two numbers. If the two numbers match, the data is presumed to have been transmitted without error. *See also* **communications protocol**.

child directory A subdirectory in a parent dictionary. *See also* **parent directory**.

child process A process that initiated by another process. *See also* **parent process**.

chip A minute slice of semiconductor material, usually silicon, arranged into circuits that are built up from layers of metal and semiconductor deposited on the silicon substrate. These circuits are called integrated circuits because they are located on a single slice of a semiconductor. A chip smaller than a fingernail can hold millions of circuits. Computers consist of chips soldered onto printed circuit boards or inserted into appropriate sockets. Chips called microprocessors house an entire CPU. Memory chips contain blank memory.

See **DIMM**, **DIP switch**, **PGA**, **SIMM**, **SIP**. *See illustration.*

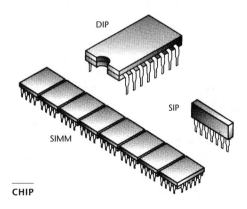

DIP

SIP

SIMM

CHIP

chip set   The set of chips that function as a unit to perform a task and are mounted together on one circuit board.

choose   To select a command or option in a graphical user interface, as by clicking a dialog box button or selecting an item from a pull-down menu.

Chooser   A desk accessory for the Apple Macintosh computer that enables the user to select a printer. The Chooser displays the icons of all printer drivers (programs that control a computer's communication with a printer) currently installed in the operating system. Since a Chooser printer driver is at the operating system level, it works for any application on a Macintosh computer.

ciphertext   The result of encrypting a piece of text for transmission. *See also* **encryption, plaintext**.

circuit board   *See* **printed circuit board**.

circuit switching   A technology for establishing a continuous circuit connection including a reserved bandwidth for communication between two remote sites over a network. Once a connection is achieved, and until it is broken, all of the data is transmitted over this circuit — including all of the gaps in data transmission. This technology is used, for example, in maintaining telephone communication and computer networks. *See also* **packet switching**.

CISC   [sisk] *Abbreviation of* **complex instruction set computer**.   A CPU (central processing unit) that recognizes and carries out a relatively large set of instructions. Most personal computers have CPUs with CISC architecture. RISC (reduced instruction set computer) architecture supports a smaller number of simpler instructions and is found mostly in workstations and newer Apple Macintosh computers.

Class A   A standard, set by the FCC (Federal Communications Commission), for how much radiation a personal computer can emit. Computers with Class A certification are suitable for office and industrial use.

Class A address   An IP address that allocates the first 8 bits to the network portion of the address and the remaining 24 bits to the host portion. Class A addresses have a first octet between 1 and 126.

Class B   A standard, set by the FCC (Federal Communications Commission), for how much radiation a personal computer can emit. Class B is a tougher emissions standard than Class A. Computers with Class B certification are unlikely to interfere with radio and television reception in residential areas and are suitable for use in the home.

Class B address An IP address that allocates the first 16 bits to the network portion of the address and the remaining 16 bits to the host portion. Class B addresses have a first octet between 128 and 191.

Class C address An IP address that allocates the first 24 bits to the network portion of the address, leaving 8 bits for the host portion. Class C addresses have a first octet between 192 and 223.

Class D address An IP address whose first octet is between 224 and 239. These addresses are reserved for multicast group usage and cannot be assigned to individual hosts.

Class E address An experimental Internet address whose first octet is between 240 and 255. These addresses are not available to the public.

clean boot A computer start-up using the fewest number of files possible, loading only the files necessary to run the operating system. Running a clean boot allows you to troubleshoot the computer to figure out which elements of the regular booting process are creating problems, such as system crashes.

clear To erase data from a display screen or document. The clear command in Microsoft Windows and Apple Macintosh environments deletes the selected data. The cut command copies the selected data to the clipboard. *See also* **undo**.

click To press down and immediately release a button on a mouse. In graphical user interfaces, clicking the mouse when its pointer is touching an object on the screen will select that object. This operation is also called *clicking on. See also* **double-click, drag, shift clicking**.

client 1. In a local access network or over the Internet, a program running on a personal computer or workstation that requests information from a server. 2. A program, task, or other process that requests a service from another program.

client/server A systems configuration in which a client requests services from another program, running on the server. In a client/server configuration, the server controls a central repository of data that is manipulated in some way by the client.

client/server network The most common model for a network of personal computers. One centralized, high-powered computer, called the server, is the network's hub. It is connected to many less powerful personal computers or workstations, called clients, throughout an organization. The clients run programs that are stored on the server. They also access data stored there, such as a common schedule of meetings or a database of customers. The server typically acts as an electronic mail post office. *See also* **peer-to-peer network**.

clip art   In word processing and desktop publishing, illustrations that are stored on disk and can be inserted into a document. Many collections of professional-quality clip art are available.

clipboard   A file or an area in memory where cut or copied text and graphics can be temporarily stored before being moved to another location within the same document or into a new document. The information on the clipboard is lost if another unit of information is moved to the clipboard.

Clipper Chip   An encryption chip using an algorithm developed by the National Security Agency. Allowing computer users to encrypt messages, it also allows for the government to decrypt them. Although the government would need a warrant to do so, just as it does to wiretap a phone line, foes of the Clipper Chip fear governmental abuse of power. The efforts by the United States government to make its use mandatory have been unsuccessful.

clock   1. *See* **real-time clock**.   2. *See* **system clock**.

clock-doubled   Running at twice the clock speed of the bus or motherboard to which it is attached. Used of a CPU.

clock speed   The speed of a computer's internal system clock, which determines the shortest amount of time it takes the CPU (central processing unit) to carry out each instruction. The clock in a computer is a circuit that generates a stream of evenly paced pulses. Clock speed is expressed in megahertz (MHz), and standard personal computer clock speeds range from about 500 MHz to about 800 MHz. Some computers have an adjustable clock speed, a useful feature if one is using software that runs poorly at a particular speed.

Clock speed alone does not determine the performance of a computer. An expansion bus has its own clock speed, which is often slower than the CPU clock speed. Also, the CPU must often wait for data it needs from slower memory chips or disk drives. These differences cause the faster components to lie idle while the slower components catch up. These idle periods are called *wait states*.

clock-tripled   Running at three times the clock speed of the bus or motherboard to which it is attached. Used of a CPU.

clone   A computer, program, or component that resembles an original model in appearance and function. Personal computer clones often have the same components, run the same software, and use the same peripherals as the well-known IBM PC computers that they imitate.

   The IBM PC was cloned almost immediately after its development because both its operating system and many of its components came from outside companies. Cloners were able to purchase these components from the same places and build near-perfect replicas of the IBM PC. In some cases, cloners have improved upon the product that they are imitating.

close   **1.** To exit a data file and save it.   **2.** In graphical user interfaces, to exit a file and remove its window from the screen.

closed architecture   **1.** A computer system design whose specifications are proprietary; that is, not available to outside software developers and peripheral manufacturers. This prevents outside companies from developing products for such a computer.   **2.** A computer design that does not include expansion slots to accommodate additional printed circuit boards. *See also* **open architecture**.

cluster   **1.** A unit of storage on a disk. When a disk is formatted, it is divided into tracks, concentric circles around the disk, and sectors, sections of each concentric track. A cluster, typically consisting of two to eight sectors in a single track, is the smallest unit used by DOS to store data. Data from one file may be fragmented and stored in many clusters throughout a disk; the disk's file allocation table (FAT) keeps track of the location of these clusters. *See also* **fragmentation, sector, track**.   **2.** A group of computers that run the same programs on copies of the same data at the same time. When a computer in a cluster is shut down another one takes over so that processing is not interrupted.

CLV   *Abbreviation of* **constant linear velocity**.

CMOS   [SEE-moss] *Abbreviation of* **complementary metal oxide semiconductor**.   A chip that draws very little power and is therefore used in battery-powered devices, such as laptop computers. Most computers use a CMOS to keep the time, date, and system setup data, since a CMOS retains its data when the computer's power is turned off, so long as it receives a trickle of energy from a battery.

CMY *Abbreviation of* **cyan-magenta-yellow**. A color model from which all colors can be made using subtractive primary colors that absorb light instead of additive primary colors that emit light. When the spectrum contains the full amount of cyan, magenta, and yellow, the result is white. When these three colors are removed from the spectrum completely, the result is black. By varying the amount of each pigment that is removed, all the colors of the spectrum can be achieved.

CMYK *Abbreviation of* **cyan-magenta-yellow-black**. A color model that also has a black component so that black does not have to be composed by removing cyan, magenta, and yellow from the spectrum. This allows for a deeper, richer black.

coaxial cable A cable consisting of a conducting outer metal tube enclosing and insulated from a central conducting core, used for high-frequency transmission. It is commonly used in the communications industry for cable television and computer networks.

COBOL *Abbreviation of* **common business-oriented language**. A high-level language developed in the late 1950s and early 1960s. It is still widely used, especially in commercial data processing and business applications. COBOL is closer to English than many other high-level languages, making it easier to learn.

code *n.* **1.** A set of symbols for representing characters in binary form for storage in a computer. For example, most computers recognize characters in ASCII code. **2.** The instructions in a computer program. The instructions written by a programmer in programming language are often called source code. Instructions that have been converted into machine language that the computer understands are called machine code or executable code.
v. To write instructions in a programming language.

codec *Abbreviation of* **compression/decompression**. Any of various technologies that compress and decompress data. You can compress information, such as video or audio, to make it easier to store or transmit, and then it can be decompressed when you want to play it back. Examples of codec technologies include MPEGs and GIFs.

cold boot A computer start-up that begins when the power is turned on. The computer then automatically loads its operating system.

collapse To hide sublevels or subdirectories when displaying a hierarchical tree, so that the only items that appear are the ones at the same level or higher as the item you've selected.

color depth   The number of discrete colors that an item of software or hardware (such as a monitor or a scanner) is capable of displaying.

Color Graphics Adapter   *See* **CGA**.

color monitor   A display monitor that is capable of producing text or graphics in color instead of black and white or just one color on a black background.

column   A vertical arrangement of data. On a display screen in character mode, a column is a vertical line that is one character wide and extends from the top of the screen to the bottom. In a spreadsheet, a column is a set of vertically aligned cells.

column graph   A graph in which data is represented by the relative height of vertical columns.

.com   In Internet addresses, a top level domain that signifies an address of a commercial organization.

COM   **1.** *See* **COM port**. **2.** *Abbreviation of* **Component Object Model**.

COM file   In DOS, a file with the extension .COM, indicating that it is an executable command file. COM files are set up for programs and routines that are 64KB or smaller. To execute a COM file, you type the file name and press Enter. *See table at* **file**.

Comité Consultatif International Télégraphique et Téléphonique.   *See* **CCITT**.

comma-delimited file   A file that is formatted in such a way that the segments of data are separated by a comma, to allow for ease in transferring the file.

command   A signal, given to a computer by a user, that tells the computer to do a specific task. In command-driven programs, commands are issued by typing a key or combination of keys. In menu-driven programs, commands are issued by selecting choices from an onscreen menu.

command buffer   An area in memory where commands are kept. With a command buffer, you can repeat a command without having to retype it. In MS-DOS, the command buffer is also called a **template**.

command button   A button in a dialog box that you click on to activate a command.

COMMAND.COM   The DOS file that interprets and performs the commands keyed in by the user and displays prompts and messages. This file must be present on the hard disk or on a floppy disk to run DOS.

command-driven   Of or relating to a program that recognizes and accepts keyed-in command statements. Command-driven software requires that you learn the commands and remember the correct syntax. *See also* **menu-driven**.

Command key   A key on Apple Macintosh computer keyboards that is marked with a four-leaf clover and/or the Apple logo and functions in combination with other keys as a shortcut through menu choices. Table 7 lists some Command key combinations used as shortcuts on the Macintosh computer.

TABLE 7 Command Key Shortcuts for the Apple Macintosh

Key Combinations	Equivalent Menu Items	Key Combinations	Equivalent Menu Items
⌘-A	Select All	⌘-Q	Quit
⌘-C	Copy	⌘-S	Save
⌘-F	Find	⌘-V	Paste
⌘-G	Find Again	⌘-W	Close
⌘-N	New	⌘-X	Cut
⌘-O	Open	⌘-Z	Undo
⌘-P	Print		

command language   A programming language that consists of the commands that you can execute in an operating system. For example, the MS-DOS command language includes the command DIR, which lists the names of the files in the current directory.

command line   1. The line on the screen that has the prompt; the line where the next command that is typed in will appear.   2. A string of characters comprising a command and its arguments.

command processor   The part of the operating system that accepts inputted commands and then interprets and executes them.

comment   A remark within a program that functions as documentation and is not translated into code and therefore is not read by the compiler or assembler. Programmers provide comments for others using the program to impart information about the program. A comment is usually set off from the program using a particular symbol, such as #, so that the compiler knows to ignore what follows.

Common Gateway Interface   *See* **CGI**.

communications protocol A standard that defines the way in which data is passed between two or more pieces of computer equipment over a telephone line or other communications link. Two pieces of equipment must be using the same protocol in order to communicate, and even then may have to negotiate agreement over variable parts of the standard. The process of choosing a common protocol is called handshaking.

There are several different families of communications protocols, each governing a different aspect of the communications process. For example, modem protocols govern the way in which modems convert digital signals into analog signals for transmission over telephone lines, while other protocols govern the way in which computers attached to those modems convert data into a series of bits for transmission. Still more protocols control data compression, encryption, and error detection, for example.

Table 8 lists widely used modem protocols.

TABLE 8 Common Full-Duplex Mode Communications Protocols

Protocol Name	Maximum Transmission Rate (bits per second)	Creator*
Bell 103	300	AT&T
Bell 212	1,200	AT&T
V.21	300	ITU-TSS
V.22	1,200	ITU-TSS
V.22bis	2,400	ITU-TSS
V.27	4,800	ITU-TSS
V.29	9,600	ITU-TSS
V.32	9,600	ITU-TSS
V.32bis	14,400	ITU-TSS
V.32turbo	19,200	AT&T
V.33	14,400	ITU-TSS
V.34	33,800	multiple contributors
V.FC	28,000	Rockwell International
K56 Flex**	56,000	Lucent Technologies/Rockwell Int'l
V.90 (V.PCM)**	56,000	multiple contributors approved by ITU
USR x2**	56,000	3Com Corporation/US Robotics

*ITU-TSS is an abbreviation of International Telecommunications Union-Telecommunications Standards Section, formerly known as CCITT.

** Due to FCC limitations, 53,000 bps is the maximum permissible transmit power during download transmissions.

communications software Software that enables a computer to communicate through a modem over telephone lines. Communications software can have a wide variety of features to speed the exchange of data, such as auto-redial and macros that automatically execute the log on sequence.

compact disk *also* **compact disc** *Abbreviated* **CD** A small plastic disk on which data such as text or music is digitally encoded. CDs are read using laser optics, while conventional disks are read by magnetic means. Until recently, CDs have been encoded with information that cannot be erased or changed, and have been called CD-ROMs in computer applications. However, CD burners are now available for those who want to make their own CDs, as are erasable CDs, making the name CD-ROM somewhat enigmatic. *See also* **disk**.

compact disk-interactive *See* **CD-I**.

compact disk-recordable *See* **CD-R**.

compatibility The ability of one computer, peripheral, program, or file to work with the same commands and formats as another.

One must be careful to distinguish exactly what is meant by compatibility in a given case. Two printers may be compatible in that they can both be attached to the same computer, but that does not mean they will accept the same font cartridges. An IBM PC-compatible is a computer that can run the same software as an IBM PC. Programs are compatible if they can use files in the same data formats. *See also* **compatible, emulate, plug-compatible**.

compatible *n.* A computer, peripheral, file, or program that can be used with or substituted for another. Although the term was once primarily used as shorthand for IBM PC-compatible computers, it now is often used to distinguish the operating system or hardware that a product is able to run with. For example, hardware that is Intel-compatible will run with Intel processors. *See also* **clone, compatibility, plug-compatible**.
adj. Capable of being used with or substituted for another computer, peripheral, file, or program.

compile To translate a program written in a high-level language into object code. The object code may be machine language that can be directly executed by the computer, or it may be an intermediate assembly language. If the latter, the object code must then be transformed into machine language using assemblers, linkers, or loaders.

compiler A program that translates another program written in a high-level language into object code. Compilers translate the entire program into executable code before it is run; interpreters translate and run a program line by line. Since object code is unique to each type of computer, there are many compilers available for each high-level language.

complementary metal oxide semiconductor *See* CMOS.

complex instruction set computer *See* CISC.

component **1.** A self-contained piece of software that can usually be integrated with other applications in order to add predefined functionality. For example, you can add a map that zooms in and out to your web application by adding a mapping ActiveX component. **2.** A completely functional piece of hardware that is part of a larger system. For example, an audio card is a component of a multimedia workstation.

Component Object Model *Abbreviated* **COM** A specification designed by Microsoft Corporation for building software that can be incorporated into larger programs by allowing objects to exchange data, even if the objects were created on different platforms. *See also* **OLE**.

COM port *Abbreviation of* **communications port**. A connection point on a computer for plugging in a serial device, such as a modem or a mouse. There can be up to four COM ports in DOS. The DOS operating system designates them COM1, COM2, COM3, and COM4.

compound document A file that contains two or more applications, such as a document that includes text from a word processing program and a spreadsheet from a spreadsheet program. Within the file, you can edit each element using the program that you used to make it.

compress To encode data so as to minimize the space it requires for storage or transmittal, for example. *See also* **data compression, lossless compression, lossy compression**.

compression *See* **data compression**.

computer A programmable machine that performs high-speed processing of numbers, as well as of text, graphics, symbols, and sound. Modern computers are digital. The computer's physical components are called hardware; its programs and data are called software. All computers include these components:

- a CPU (central processing unit) that interprets and executes instructions

- input devices, such as a keyboard or a mouse, through which data and commands enter the computer
- memory that enables a computer to store programs and data
- mass storage devices, such as disk drives, that store large amounts of data and
- output devices, such as printers and display screens, that show the results after the computer has processed data.

See also **mainframe, minicomputer, supercomputer, workstation.**

computer-aided design   *See* CAD.

computer aided design and drafting   *See* CADD.

computer-aided instruction   *See* CAI.

computer-aided manufacturing   *See* CAM.

computer-aided software engineering   *See* CASE.

computer-based training   *Abbreviated* **CBT**   The use of CAI teaching tools to provide workers with the necessary computer skills to do their jobs.

Computer Graphics Metafile   *Abbreviated* **CGM**   A object-oriented graphics file format for software used by devices such as printers and plotters. This international standard allows computers using different programs or platforms to transmit and use CGM files among themselves.

computer literacy   The ability to operate a computer and to understand the language used in working with a specific system or systems.

computer science   The scientific study of computer software, hardware, and technology.

computer system   A computer along with the software and all of the peripheral devices used in its operation.

computer virus   *See* **virus.**

concatenate   To join together. For example, you can concatenate two files into a single file. You can also concatenate two or more database fields into one field. Or you can concatenate two or more character strings, such as *super* and *computer,* into one string, *supercomputer,* and then search for that concatenated string within your document or program.

condensed type   A type style that narrows characters and places them closer together than in ordinary type. Condensed type increases the number of characters that can fit into a single line.

conditional   Of or relating to an action that is undertaken only if a particular condition is met or is true. The statement *If the output is greater than 10,000, then divide it in half* is conditional; that is, the action of dividing the output in half is dependent on whether it is greater than 10,000 or not. Programming frequently contains conditional statements by which commands are executed conditionally; that is, only if certain other items are met or are true.

CONFIG.SYS   A file that tells the computer what configuration to use for DOS or OS/2 systems. For example, CONFIG.SYS may have a DEVICE statement to let the computer know that you're going to be using a mouse so that it can install the proper device driver. CONFIG.SYS tells the computer how many files can be open at the same time and how much memory to reserve for its buffers.

CONFIG.SYS is one of the first files the computer checks when it boots up. If it finds this file, it immediately sets everything up according to the commands there. If there is no CONFIG.SYS file in the root directory, the computer follows the default configuration settings instead.

configuration   The way in which a computer is set up in terms of both hardware and software. For example, an IBM PC-compatible computer's configuration may consist of 256MB of RAM, a 4GB hard drive, a 3.5-inch floppy drive, a 40x CD-drive, a mouse, a monitor, and the Microsoft Windows 2000 operating system. When you configure your computer, you attach all the physical components with the necessary cables and connectors, set various switches and jumpers, and select the software parameters that tell the computer what the configuration looks like and how its various components should interact with each other. For example, the operating system needs to know what type of monitor and printer the computer is hooked up to.

On DOS-based computers, the system is configured by placing commands in the file CONFIG.SYS. In Windows 98 and Windows NT computers, the system is configured by modifying the registry. In OS/2 systems, many settings are saved in binary INI files. On Apple Macintosh computers, the system's parameters are set with the Control Panel, a Macintosh desk accessory.

configuration file   A file that tells a computer what configuration to use for a specified program. The configuration file for DOS is called

CONFIG.SYS. Whenever you ask your computer to run a program, it checks the configuration file to find the current parameters for that program. In a word processing program, for example, the parameters would include the current settings for line spacing, margin width, and font specifications.

connectivity The ability to make and maintain a connection between two or more points in a telecommunications system.

connector A coupler used to join two cables or to plug a cable into a port or interface. Types of connectors include the DIN connector and the DB connector. *See illustration. See also illustration at* **printed circuit board**.

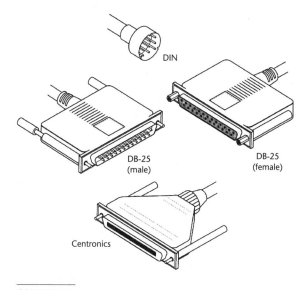

DIN

DB-25
(male)

DB-25
(female)

Centronics

CONNECTOR

connect time The elapsed time during which a user is connected to a remote terminal, especially that of an Internet service provider.

console The portion of a computer that allows you to communicate with the CPU (central processing unit). In a personal computer, the console is made up of the keyboard, the mouse, and the monitor. In a network, the console is the terminal that controls the mainframe or server.

constant A value, such as a number or a string, that does not change. Programs generally use both constants and variables.

constant angular velocity *Abbreviated* **CAV**   A method for playing compact disks by which the disk rotates at a constant speed. The data is retrieved more slowly at the edges of the disk as compared to the center of the disk, but the motor speed stays constant.

constant linear velocity *Abbreviated* **CLV**   The conflict caused by simultaneous message transmission by two or more nodes over a single channel on a local area network.

context-sensitive help   A mode of help in which the primary information available to the user varies according to the operation the user is performing.

context switching   *See* **task switching**.

continuous paper   Computer paper that is produced in a single, long strip, having sheets that are separated by perforations, and often having holes down the margins to allow for use in the tractor feed mechanism of impact printers.

continuous tone   A method of creating an image out of smoothly gradated colors or shades of gray, as in photography. Color printers and some color graphics programs use continuous tone, but some black-and-white printers and most black-and-white graphics software use patterns of black dots of variable size and density to simulate continuous tone. *See also* **halftone**.

control character   A keyboard character that serves, usually in combination with the Control key, to give the computer a command when both keys are pressed together. For example, in some word processing programs the control character *x* means *delete* and the control character *c* means *copy*. The first 32 characters of the ASCII character set are defined as control characters, but a particular application may define its own control characters differently.

Control key   *Abbreviated* **Ctrl**   A key on IBM PC and compatible keyboards that is pressed in combination with another key to produce a control character. For example, when you type *x* in a word processing program the letter *x* appears as part of your text, but when you press the Control key while typing *x*, the computer will interpret *x* as a control character. *See also* **Alt key**, **Shift key**.

controller   A unit that controls the flow of data along the expansion bus between a computer's CPU (central processing unit) and devices such as a display screen, a disk drive, or a printer. Each component or device attached to the expansion bus has its own controller. Personal computers come equipped with controllers for standard components, but if additional devices are added, more controllers, which come installed on expansion boards, can be inserted. *See also* **bus, expansion bus.**

control menu A pulldown menu in Microsoft Windows that allows you to resize, close, or move a window, activated by clicking on its icon in the window's title bar.

Control Panel In Apple Macintosh computers and Microsoft Windows, a utility program used to set such system parameters as screen colors, speaker volume, the date and time in the computer's clock, the double click speed for a mouse, or the keyboard repeat rate.

control panel device *See* **cdev.**

control program 1. *See* **operating environment.** 2. *See* **operating system.**

conventional memory The amount of RAM available to programs running in DOS in real mode. Usually this amounts to 640 kilobytes and is adequate if you want to run only one program at a time. If you want to run more than one program at a time, however, you will need more than conventional memory. *Also called* **base memory.** *See also* **expanded memory, extended memory, protected mode, real mode.**

convergence The relative sharpness of each pixel on the display screen of a color monitor. On a color screen, each pixel is made up of red, blue, and green dots, and the sharpness of an individual pixel depends on how well these colored dots converge.

conversion A change, as from one format or program to another. For example, there are programs that let you change, or convert, a file from the format used by one word processing program to another.

cookie An item, such as a file, that is used to relate one computer transaction with a later one. For example, certain webpages download small cookie files that hold information that can be retrieved by other webpages on the site. Cookies can contain any arbitrary information the server chooses and are typically used to authenticate or identify registered users of a website without requiring them to sign in again every time they access that site. Cookies are also used to customize a website for individual users and to keep track of a user's access to a site. Some cookies are programmed with an expiration date so that they are automatically deleted after a period of time.

cooperative multitasking A kind of multitasking in which a program running in the background can be processed only if the foreground program allows it to run, as opposed to *pre-emptive multitasking*. The Apple Macintosh operating system and Microsoft Windows operating systems prior to Windows 95 use cooperative multitasking.

coprocessor A microprocessor distinct from the CPU (central processing unit). A coprocessor will perform specified functions that the CPU either cannot perform or cannot perform as well and as quickly. For example, while CPUs can do mathematical calculations, certain math coprocessors have been designed to perform these calculations faster. Graphics coprocessors can speed the manipulation of graphics images.

copy To duplicate data. In word processing, for example, you can copy text from the document you're working on into a buffer (often known as the clipboard) in order to paste it into another document. You can also copy a file from one directory or disk to another.

copyleft A form of software licensing introduced by Gnu. In contrast to a copyright, which restricts users and developers of software from unauthorized distribution of applications and source code, a copyleft license encourages the free distribution of such items.

copy protection Any of various methods of preventing software from being copied and used by unauthorized users. This is done by ensuring that copies made of software will be unusable. However, copy protection may prevent the user from making backups of software, so that if a copy-protected program becomes corrupted, the user has to contact the manufacturer to ask for a second copy. For this reason, and because it has been proven to be easily defeated, most companies and software developers have stopped using copy protection. *See also* **dongle, piracy, shareware**.

CORBA *Abbreviation of* **Common Object Request Broker Architecture**. A standard developed by the Object Management Group (OMG) consortium that defines a standard interface for object-oriented applications to utilize each other's functionality.

corrupt To accidentally change or destroy the data in a file. This can happen because of a problem with the software, damage to the disk or disk drive, or because of a power fluctuation. Utility programs, such as PC Tools and Norton Utilities, can sometimes recover data from a corrupted file.

courseware Software that is created for educational or training purposes including CAI (computer-aided instruction) and CBT (computer-based training).

cpi *Abbreviation of* **characters per inch.**

cps *Abbreviation of* **characters per second.**

CPU *Abbreviation of* **central processing unit.**   The part of a computer that interprets and executes instructions. A mainframe or a mini-computer has a CPU consisting of one or more printed circuit boards, but the CPU of a personal computer or small workstation consists of a single chip called a microprocessor.

The CPU fetches, decodes, and executes instructions, and transfers information to and from other components, such as disk drives, expansion boards, or the keyboard, over the computer's bus, its main data highway. The part of the CPU known as the Arithmetic Logic Unit (ALU) performs all arithmetic and logic operations on data. The CPU's Control Unit coordinates the steps necessary to execute each instruction. It tells the other parts of the CPU what to do and when. The data registers of the CPU function as a scratch pad for the ALU and as working memory for the CPU. In some instances, CPU is used more broadly to include main memory, or RAM.

CR *Abbreviation of* **carriage return.**

cracker *See* **hacker** (sense 2).

crash *n.* A failure of a program, operating system, or disk drive, which may cause the loss of data. If an application crashes, the operating system may crash, too, or may ignore it. In many cases the user must reboot after a crash before resuming work.

v. To suddenly stop functioning and become unusable, as an application or operating system.

CRC *Abbreviation of* **cyclical redundancy check.**   A technique for detecting errors in the transmission of digital data using a particular type of checksum. CRC is used in many communications and file transfer protocols. *See also* **checksum.**

crop In a graphics or desktop publishing program, to cut away unwanted parts of an image. For example, you may want to crop a picture before inserting it into a document or layout.

cross-hatching   In a graphics program, a pattern created by intersecting lines and used to fill in an area. For example, you might select several different cross-hatching patterns to distinguish different parts of a pie graph.

cross-platform   Of or relating to the capability of hardware or software to function in the same way on different platforms. Cross-platform applications generally can be run on Apple Macintosh, Unix, or Microsoft Windows operating systems, for example.

cross-posting   The act of posting a single message simultaneously to multiple newsgroups or discussion groups. Cross-posting messages to unrelated newsgroups is considered bad netiquette.

CRT   *Abbreviation of* **cathode-ray tube**.

cryptography   The process or skill of communicating in or deciphering coded information. The security of transmissions across the Internet is dependent upon the ability for messages to be encrypted before they are sent and to be decrypted after they are received.

CSMA/CD   *Abbreviation of* **Carrier Sense Multiple Access with Collision Detection.**   A protocol that determines the procedures for controlling access to data channels when multiple devices try to use the same channel at the same time. In instances where data sent by different nodes collides in a channel, each node stops the transmission and each begins retransmitting after a brief time, the exact duration of which is determined randomly by the protocol.

Ctrl   *Abbreviation of* **Control key**.

Ctrl-Alt-Del   Under DOS and OS/2, a command that causes a warm boot, issued by pressing the Delete key while holding down the Control and Alt keys. If your program crashes, you can sometimes press Ctrl-Alt-Del and do a warm boot instead of turning the computer off and doing a cold boot. This technique may not work, however, if your operating system has crashed as well and does not recognize the command. In Microsoft Windows and Windows NT, Ctrl-Alt-Del gives the user several options, including closing a program that has crashed without rebooting.

Ctrl-Break   A DOS command issued by pressing the Break key while holding down the Control key. Ctrl-Break can cancel the previous command issued in DOS if the program recognizes it.

current cell   *See* **active cell**.

current directory   *See* **default directory**.

current drive   *See* **default drive**.

cursor   The bright, usually blinking indicator on a display screen, marking the position at which a character can be entered, changed, or deleted. A cursor may be a small rectangle, underline, or vertical bar, and it can be moved about the screen with the arrow keys. In applications that use a mouse, the cursor appears as an arrow. In modern graphical user interfaces, the cursor may be customized by the user or the application. Sometimes a change in the cursor is used to indicate that different functions are available to the user.

cursor control keys   *See* **arrow keys**.

cursor movement keys   *See* **arrow keys**.

cut   To remove part of a document or a graphics file and store it in a buffer (often called a clipboard).

cut and paste   To cut part of a document or a graphics file and then insert or paste it into another place in the document or into another document or file.

cut-sheet feeder   *See* **sheet feeder**.

cyber-   A prefix used to refer to computers or computer networks. A large amount of new words have been coined by adding this prefix to already existing words to relate those words to computers or the Internet. For example, *cyberculture* refers to the culture arising from the use of computer networks. *Cyberpunk* is a subgenre of science fiction often involving futuristic computer-based societies. The prefix was taken from the word *cybernetics*.

cybernetics   The theoretical study of communication and control processes in biological, mechanical, and electronic systems, especially the comparison of these processes in biological and artificial systems.

cyberspace   The electronic medium of computer networks, in which online communication takes place.

cyclical redundancy check   *See* **CRC**.

cylinder   The set of all tracks (concentric circles) located in the same corresponding position on each recording surface of a disk or on each side of a platter in a hard disk drive. On a double-sided disk, a cylinder consists of 2 tracks, 1 from each side. On a hard disk, a cylinder consists of 2 tracks (1 from each side) from each platter. If a hard disk has 600 tracks on each of 4 platters, then it will have 600 cylinders, each consisting of a vertical set of 8 tracks.

[D]

DA *Abbreviation of* **desk accessory**.

DAC *Abbreviation of* **digital-to-analog converter**.

daemon A program or process that sits idle in the background until it is invoked to perform its task. For example, a printer spooling program on Unix is a daemon that waits for a request to print a file.

daisy chain A set of hardware devices that are linked in a series.

daisywheel printer An impact printer that produces characters that look typewritten. Instead of a row of typewriter bars that strike the paper, the bars are arranged as spokes around a hub, called a daisywheel. During the printing process, the daisywheel spins around to the proper character and strikes it against a ribbon, imprinting the character on the paper. *See table at* **printer**.

DARPA *Abbreviation of* **Defense Advance Research Projects Agency**. *See* **ARPA**.

DASD [dee-ay-ess-DEE or DAZZ-dee] *Abbreviation of* **direct access storage device**. A storage device, such as a CD-ROM, that is capable of accessing information directly instead of having to read through all of the data on the device sequentially, as is the case with storage on magnetic tape.

DAT *Abbreviation of* **digital audio tape**. A storage medium that uses magnetic tape to store data digitally. A DAT cartridge is smaller than a 3.5-inch floppy disk and can hold from 700 megabytes to 2.3 gigabytes. Because DATs allow only sequential access, they are often used for backups. *See table following* **access time**.

data Facts, as in the form of figures, characters, or words, especially when given to the computer as input to be stored in machine-readable form. When you type words or numbers into a database, for example, the computer stores this as data in binary form. The word *data* is actually the plural form of *datum,* which means *a single fact,* but *data* has taken on a life of its own. This means that you can treat it as a plural out of respect to its origins or as a singular in deference to its independence.

database An organized collection of information that can be searched, retrieved, changed, and sorted using a collection of programs known as a database management system. Many databases are organized into records consisting of data that have been input into fields. For example, an address database may have one record for every person whose address is included. Each record might have one field for names, another field for street addresses, another for Zip codes, and still another for phone numbers. *See also* **flat-file database, hypertext, relational database**.

database administrator   *Abbreviated* **DBA**   A person with a high degree of technical expertise who is responsible for the design and management of an organization's database. A database administrator is usually responsible for evaluating, selecting, implementing, and maintaining the database management system. These functions sometimes include designing and maintaining the structure and content of tables and the relationships between tables, reports, and queries within a database.

database management system   *Abbreviated* **DBMS**   The program or programs that control a database so that the information it contains can be stored, retrieved, updated, and sorted. The scale and capabilities of DBMSs vary widely. There are database management systems that run on personal computers, such as dBASE and MS Access. There are also huge, specialized applications that operate on mainframes and over large networks such as airline flight reservation systems.

Most database management systems let you request a report giving information from the database organized in a way that meets your specific needs. For example, to do a mailing to customers, you may need their names and addresses printed out on mailing labels and sorted by Zip code. Often requests for information must be structured in the form of a query that specifies the criteria for the selection of information. Queries can be structured by simply choosing options from a menu or by query by example, in which the DBMS presents a blank record and you specify the fields and values you want. Sophisticated DBMSs that provide a great deal of power in structuring needed information may require you to use a special query language such as SQL.

database server   A computer system on a network that stores a shared database and enables network users to retrieve the data they request. *See also* **client/server network, server**.

data compression   The transformation of data into a form that minimizes the space required, as to store or transmit it, for example. One system of data compression, for example, assigns special binary codes to frequently used words so that they take up fewer bits than they would if each letter were coded separately. Data compression can speed up transmission of data by fax machine or modem because it enables these devices to transmit the same amount of data using fewer bits. Data compression is also used in backup utilities, in storing bit-mapped graphics files, and in storing video images. A type of expansion board called a compression board will automatically compress data as it is written to disk, then decompress it when it is read. The data compression is not noticeable to the user but can effectively double or triple the capacity of a disk drive.

data dictionary In database management systems, a file that contains the file specifications needed to operate the database.

data-encoding scheme The technique by which a disk controller records data onto a disk. *See also* **MFM, RLL.**

Data Encryption Standard *See* **DES.**

data entry The process of putting data into a computer, especially the typing of text and figures into a database or spreadsheet from the keyboard.

data entry form In database applications, a single record appearing onscreen in a form that is easy for the user to fill in or update. Most database applications let the user create a custom data entry form, in addition to displaying a default form.

data field In database management systems, a place in a data record for a specific kind of information, such as a date of birth or a telephone number.

data file A file containing data created by an application, such as a document, a graphics design, or database records. *See also* **program file.** *See table at* **file.**

datagram *See* **packet.**

data integrity The accuracy of data stored in a database, especially the reliability and consistency of a database system in which data is not accidentally lost or altered when the database is edited or transmitted.

data mining The process of extracting useful information from large databases. Data mining is usually performed using automated processes that search for meaningful patterns in the data without much prior knowledge of the data content or relationships.

data processing *Abbreviated* **DP** The storing or processing of data by a computer, especially the storing or processing of numerical data by a mainframe or minicomputer.

data transfer rate The rate at which data is transmitted between devices or the rate at which a communications channel is capable of transmitting data, usually measured in bits, kilobits, or megabits per second.

data type **1.** In programming, a declaration of the kind of data (floating-point or integer, for example) that is being used in a particular place within a program. The data type determines which operations can be performed on each data object. **2.** In database management systems and spreadsheet programs, a definition for the type of data (name, date, or dollar amount, for example) found in a specific data field.

data warehouse A database system containing large amounts of data that uses sophisticated software optimized for fast searches and data retrieval.

daughter board A printed circuit board that attaches either to a computer's main circuit board (the motherboard) or to an expansion board. Daughter boards are added to improve a computer's performance or enhance its capabilities and are often used with audio or video boards. *See also* **expansion board**.

DBA *Abbreviation of* **Database Administrator**.

DB connector A connector used in serial or parallel transmission of data, as between a computer and a printer. *See illustration at* **connector**.

DBMS *Abbreviation of* **database management system**.

D connector *See* **DB connector**.

DDE *Abbreviation of* **Dynamic Data Exchange**.

debug **1.** To search for and eliminate errors in a program. **2.** To search for and correct malfunctions in hardware.

debugger A program that checks the structure and logic of other programs and determines where errors exist.

decimal Of or relating to a number system with a base of 10. The number system we normally use is a decimal system, unlike the binary system that computers use. The decimal system uses the 10 different symbols 0–9 for numbers. Each place in a decimal number represents a successive power of 10. The values of decimal numbers without decimal points are integer values. Decimal numbers with decimal points can be written in either fixed-point or floating-point notation. *See also* **hexadecimal, octal.** *See table following* **binary.**

decompress *See* **uncompress.**

decompression The act or process of uncompressing.

decrement *n.* The amount by which a variable is decreased; a negative increment.

v. To subtract one value from another; to decrease in value.

decryption The process of unscrambling data using a password or key, so that it is intelligible. Decryption, of course, is necessary only when a file has undergone encryption. *See also* **ciphertext, plaintext, public key cryptography.**

dedicated Designating a computer, device, or program reserved for one use. For example, a dedicated server may be a computer used only as a server for a particular network. If you have separate phone lines for your modem and your telephone, then your modem line is dedicated.

dedicated link A communcations link established for one specific use. It is usually a phone line that is used only for a connection between two computers or networks. A dedicated link is always available to its application. *See also* **leased line.**

default A setting used by your computer unless and until you choose another one. For example, your word processor uses a default font and default margins whenever you begin working on a new document unless you choose different ones.

default directory The directory that an operating system retrieves files from and saves files to by default. The IBM PC and its compatibles have default directories that they will call up unless you select a different directory. You can change the defaults on your computer if they don't suit your needs. *Also called* **current directory.**

default drive The drive that an operating system uses when it is first booted. *Also called* **current drive.**

defragmentation The reorganization of a file on a disk or in memory to eliminate fragmentation. When a file becomes fragmented, the read/write head has to wander all over the disk in order to read that one file. This means that it takes longer to access the data than it would if the file were defragmented. Utility programs called disk optimizers will defragment files without copying files to a new disk.

degausser   A demagnetizing device. Degaussers can erase data from magnetic storage devices. They also balance a monitor's internal magnetic field. Sometimes the color in your monitor appears distorted. This can be caused by power surges, moving your monitor, or disturbances from nearby magnets. A degausser can restore the proper magnetic balance, restoring a normal appearance to screen images.

Del   *Abbreviation of* **Delete key**.

delete   To erase. For example, you can delete a character, block, or file. You can delete using the Delete key, the Backspace key, or a command.

Delete key   *Abbreviated* **Del**   On IBM PC and compatible keyboards, a key that is pressed to erase the character indicated by the cursor. *See also* **Backspace key**.

delimiter   A character marking the start or end of a unit of data or of one of a series of commands. For example, the backslash (\) is used as a delimiter in DOS, OS/2, Windows 95, and Windows NT pathnames, such as C:\WP\MEMOS\CURPROJ.ABC.

Delphi   An object-oriented programming language based on Pascal, developed by Borland International.

demand paging   A type of virtual memory in which programs and data are divided into fixed units of memory of equal size, called pages. The pages are not copied from the computer's hard disk into RAM until they are actually needed. The operating system may move pages about in RAM or copy them out to a special area of the hard disk in order to make room for other pages.

demodulation   The conversion of a modulated carrier wave into a current equivalent to the original signal. One example of a modulated carrier wave is a sound wave. Sound waves must be converted into digital codes in order to be processed by a computer.

denial-of-service attack   *Abbreviated* **DoS attack**   A malicious attack on a computer in a network or an entire network by bombarding (or "flooding") it with large amounts of meaningless or trivial data requests. As a result, the computer or network is unable to provide regular services to people legitimately trying to access it.

density   A measure of how tightly bits of data can be packed together on a tape or disk. The bits are closer together on higher-density disks, making more memory available than in a low-density disk of the same size. High density 3.5-inch diskettes for IBM PCs have a capacity of up to 1.44MB, and 1.2MB for Apple Macintosh computers. High density disks are now standard for floppies.

DES   Acronym for **Data Encryption Standard**.   A popular standard encryption algorithm defined by the US government. It encrypts data by breaking it into 64-bit blocks of data and using a 56 bit key. DES is identical to the ANSI standard Data Encryption Algorithm defined in ANSI X3.92-1981.

descender   The part of a lowercase letter that falls below the baseline, as in a *j, g,* or *y. See illustration at* **baseline**.

descending sort   A sort in which the items are listed from last to first or largest to smallest, as from Z to A or from 9 to 0.

desk accessory   *Abbreviated* **DA**   On Apple Macintosh computers, a program, usually a utility, that can be accessed at any time from any application. For example, the calculator, clock, and Control Panel are desk accessories. In the Microsoft Windows environment, desk accessories are called memory resident programs, terminate and stay resident programs (TSRs), or pop-up utilities.

desktop   **1.** In a graphical user interface, an onscreen metaphor of your work, just as if you were looking at a real desktop cluttered with folders full of work to do. The desktop consists of icons that

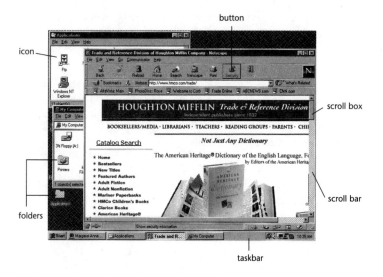

DESKTOP   A desktop showing overlaid windows

show files, folders, and various documents. Common desktop programs come with a set of desk accessories, including such things as a calendar, calculator, and notepad. You can rearrange the icons on the desktop just as you can rearrange objects on a real desktop. On some platforms, you can add or remove features as you desire.
2. The background of the screen, on which windows, icons, and dialog boxes appear. *See illustration.*

desktop computer   A personal computer that is designed to provide a stationary work environment.

desktop configuration   A case for a personal computer system in which components such as the CPU, the power supply, the motherboard, and mass storage devices are housed in one compact box. *See also* **tower configuration.**

desktop publishing   The design and production of publications, such as newsletters, trade journals, books, or brochures, using computers with graphics capability. Usually you work with three separate programs to do desktop publishing: the word processing program; the graphics program; and the page layout program, which lets you insert graphics into the text, organize the layout, make last-minute changes to the text or illustrations, and view the page as it will look when done. Many page layout programs let you create the text and graphics in the same program, which simplifies the procedure.

destination   The location to which you copy or move a file.

device   A hardware component or machine that attaches to your computer. Printers, modems, CD-ROM drives, keyboards, and mice are all devices. *See also* **peripheral.**

device-dependent   Of or relating to software that can be used only with a particular model of computer or kind of hardware. Device-dependent software often makes optimal use of the special features of a specific computer or piece of hardware.

device driver   A piece of software that enables the computer to communicate with a device such as a printer, mouse, CD-ROM drive, or RAM disk. Device drivers convert generic commands from an operating system or applications program into the specific commands needed to perform a requested action on a particular piece of hardware.

Device drivers may be provided along with the operating environment, an applications program, or the piece of hardware. It is always necessary to install the device driver in order to make it available to the programs that use it. This frequently involves adding information to system configuration files such as CONFIG.SYS, and may also involve setting variables in other files.

Microsoft Windows and the Apple MacOS include many such device drivers in the environment itself, for all applications to share. These make it much easier to install a new printer or disk drive. Loading an incorrect device driver is a common cause of problems with peripherals. *Also called* **driver**.

DHTML *Abbreviation of* **dynamic HTML**.

dialog box In a graphical user interface, an onscreen message box that presents information or requests input. A dialog box allows you to carry on a conversation with the program by selecting or deselecting option buttons, typing in text, or selecting from a list of files. Typically, dialog boxes disappear once you have entered the requested information.

In the Apple Macintosh and Microsoft Windows interfaces, any menu option followed by an ellipsis (...) will bring up a dialog box if selected. *See illustration. See also* **alert box**.

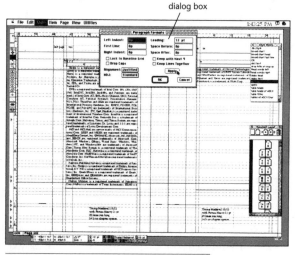

DIALOG BOX   On an Apple Macintosh computer

dictionary sort A lexicographic sort that disregards capitalization and usually punctuation such as hyphens and apostrophes. *See also* **ASCII sort**.

differential backup A procedure for backing up only files that have been changed or added since the last full backup. Earlier versions of these files will be replaced in a differential backup. *See also* **full backup, incremental backup.**

digital Measuring or representing data by means of discrete digits. Digital modes are contrasted with analog modes, in which data is measured or represented by continuously varying physical quantities, such as voltage. A clock with hands is an analog device, because the hands moving continuously around the face can indicate every time of day. A digital clock uses a series of changing digits to represent time at discrete intervals; for example, every second. All modern computers are digital because they use the digits 0 and 1 to represent all data. Computers can accept input and produce output in analog form, but only by simulating analog events.

digital audio tape *See* **DAT.**

digital camera A camera that uses a charge-coupled device to take photographs, storing the images in digital form rather than on film. Pictures taken with digital cameras can can be downloaded to a computer for storage, display, or manipulation.

digital monitor A monitor that takes digital signals from the video adapter and converts them to analog signals. The analog signals then control what is displayed on the screen. Unlike analog monitors, digital monitors display only a limited number of color values; they cannot display a continuous range of colors. Since the analog VGA standard has replaced the older digital standards, digital monitors have largely been superseded by analog monitors.

digital satellite system *Abbreviated* **DSS** A system in which a satellite dish receives a digital signal, decodes the signal, and passes it to a television, radio receiver, or computer. Such a system transmits many of the same programs that cable television operators provide and has become an alternative means of receiving such programming.

digital signal processing *See* **DSP.**

digital signature An encrypted authentication that is unique to an individual or individual computer used for "signing" electronic documents. Attaching a digital signature to an email message allows the recipient to verify that the sender is who he or she claims to be.

Digital Simultaneous Voice and Data *See* **DSVD.**

digital-to-analog converter A device that converts digital data into an analog signal, for example, when modems convert digital data into a signal that can be sent over telephone wires, or a compact disk players covert digital data into audio signals.

Digital Versatile Disk *See* **DVD**.

Digital Video Disk An alternate name for **Digital Versatile Disk**. *See* **DVD**.

Digital Video Interactive *See* **DVI**.

digitize To convert analog data or signals to digital form. For example, optical scanners digitize continuous tone images into bit-mapped graphics. Sound can also be digitized, as for storage on a compact disk, by sampling pitch and volume many times per second and then recording these measurements digitally.

digitizer **1.** A device that digitizes data. Optical scanners are digitizers. **2.** See digitizing tablet.

digitizing tablet A input device consisting of an electronically sensitive tablet and a light pen or puck used to input drawings directly into the computer. A puck, also called a cursor, is a mouselike device with an attached plastic window with cross hairs to aid in precise placement and movement. The tablet records the movement of the puck or light pen and digitizes each point through which the puck or light pen passes. These points are then transferred to the display screen to be viewed or stored on disk. *Also called* **digitizer, graphics tablet**.

DIMM *Abbreviation of* **Dual Inline Memory Module**. A standard form of packaging memory chips on a circuit board with connection pins on both sides of the board. A DIMM package provides space for more pins than a SIMM package. *See illustration. See also* **chip, SIMM**.

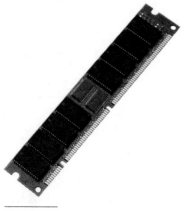

DIMM CHIP

DIN connector   A connector that meets the standards of Deutsche In-
dustrienorm, the organization that sets the standards for German
hardware. DIN connectors are used to connect the keyboard to most
IBM PC and compatible computers and as serial port connectors on
many Apple Macintosh computers. *See illustration at* **connector**.

dingbat   A typographical ornament or symbol, such as a bullet (•),
check mark (✓), or arrow (➡), that can be inserted into a document. Many clip art packages contain dingbats. One of the most
popular sets of dingbats is the Zapf dingbats, available as a Post-
Script font.

DIP   *Abbreviation of* **dual in-line package**.   An electrical component
housing whose connecting pins stick out downward from the two
long sides in two parallel rows. *See illustration at* **chip**.

DIP switch   A series of tiny rocker or slider switches contained in the
housing of a DIP. The housing has downward-facing pins so that it
can be inserted into a socket on a printed circuit board or soldered
directly to the board.

   DIP switches enable you to configure a circuit board for a particular type of computer, printer, or application. Installation instructions should tell you how to set the switches. *See illustration.*

rocker DIP switch

slide DIP switch

DIP SWITCH   Two types of DIP switch

direct access   *See* **random access**.

Direct Access Storage Device   *See* **DASD**.

direct address   *See* **absolute address**.

direct memory access   *See* **DMA**.

directory   A way to organize files into a hierarchical structure. IBM
PC and compatible computers have a top directory called a root
directory (or simply *root*) that is usually labeled "C:\" on the hard
disk. All directories below the root directory are its subdirectories.
The last directory in a chain or path of directories leading from the

root contains files. In the Apple Macintosh environment, directories are called folders.

directory tree　A diagrammatic representation of the branching structure hard disk's directories and subdirectories. The subdirectories are represented as branches stemming from the main directory.

DirectX　An API developed by Microsoft Corporation that allows programmers to create instructions for hardware devices without regard to the specific kind of hardware that will run the program used by the machine. DirectX is used in gaming software and other graphics-intensive programs.

discussion group　A public forum on a network where multiple users can share and discuss ideas about a topic.

disk *also* **disc**　The most common medium for permanent data storage. The two types of disks are magnetic disks and optical disks. A magnetic disk is a round plate, as of plastic or metal, covered with a magnetic coating. Data is encoded on the disk by magnetizing microscopically small iron particles that are scattered throughout the coating. Magnetic disks include floppy disks, hard disks, and removable cartridges.

Optical disks are composed of a layer of reflective material encased in a protective plastic coating. Data is encoded by a pattern of tiny pits or of aligned metal alloy crystals on the reflective layer. The data is read by means of a laser. The laser light is scattered by the pits or crystals, but when it strikes the flat reflective surfaces between them, it is reflected directly into a detector. The three kinds of optical disks are CD-ROMs, WORMs (write once read many), and erasable optical disks.

As for the spelling of *disk* versus *disc*, when new words come into the language, they often have different forms for a period until one form wins out over the others. Sometimes competing forms remain in use for a long time. *Disk* came into English in the mid-17th century and was originally spelled with a *k* on the model of older words such as *whisk*. The *c*-spelling arose a half century later as a learned spelling derived from the word's Latin source *discus*. Both spellings were used interchangeably into the 20th century, with people in Britain tending to use *disc* more often, and Americans preferring *disk*. The spellings also began to be sorted out by function. Late in the 19th century, for reasons that are not clear, people used *disc* to refer to the new method of making phonograph recordings on a flat plate (as opposed to Edison's cylindrical drum). In any case, the *c*-spelling became conventional for this sense. In the 1940s, however, when American computer scientists needed a term to refer to their flat storage devices, they chose the spelling *disk*, and this became conventionalized in such compounds as *hard disk*. When the storage technology of the compact disk arose in the 1970s, both *c*- and *k*-spellings competed for an initial period. Computer specialists preferred the familiar *k*-spelling, while people in the music industry, who saw the shiny circular plates as another form of phonograph record, referred to them as *compact discs*. These tendencies soon became established practice in the different industries. This is why we buy compact disks in computer stores but get the same storage devices with different data as compact discs in music stores.

See illustrations at **floppy disk**, **hard disk**.

disk cache A part of RAM set aside to speed access to a disk. The cache retains a copy of the data most recently read from or written to the disk, under the assumption that the CPU will want it again in the near future. When the CPU requests data that is in the cache, it can be sent back immediately, without waiting through the disk's long access time. If the data must be read from disk, the cache keeps a copy of the entire sector containing it, guessing that the CPU may want some of that sector again soon. Data in the cache that has not been used for a while is thrown out to make room. A well-designed cache may handle 80–90 percent of disk requests without actual disk access (that is, have a hit ratio of 80–90 percent), resulting in a huge improvement in speed. Obtaining higher hit-ratios requires larger cache memory but provides better performance.

Some caches intercept all data to be written to disk and hold it until the CPU is free before actually saving it on disk. While this can make the computer seem much faster, it increases the chance that data may be lost in the event of a crash or power failure.

disk crash *See* **head crash**.

disk drive A hardware device that reads data stored on a disk and writes data to the disk for storage. A hard drive reads hard disks, a floppy drive reads floppy disks, and an optical drive reads optical disks.

Disk drives are distinguished by their data storage capacity and access times, or the amount of time it takes the drive to access a single piece of data. Optical drives can store much more data than floppy or hard drives, but are relatively slow. Hard drives are faster and have larger storage capacities than floppy drives. In practice, techniques such as disk caching and interleaving can significantly improve the performance of disk drives. *See also* **cache.**

diskette   *See* **floppy disk.**

diskless workstation   A workstation or personal computer on a local area network (LAN) that has a CPU and RAM, but does not have its own disk drive. Its program and data files are stored on the network file server.

disk operating system   *See* **DOS.**

disk optimizer   A defragmentation program that reorganizes the data on a disk to eliminate empty spaces that arise when items are deleted, resulting in greater efficiency of storage and retrieval.

disk pack   A removable storage device consisting of a stack of several magnetic disks encased as a unit. Disk packs are used chiefly with minicomputers and mainframes. *See also* **RAID.**

display   *v.* To show information or graphics on a monitor.
n. A display screen.

display adapter   *See* **video adapter.**

display screen   The part of a monitor that gives information in visual form. Commonly, a computer's display screen uses a cathode-ray tube to show images, just as a television does. Laptop and notebook computers, however, use flat-panel displays, typically liquid-crystal or gas plasma displays.

distance learning   Education in which students take academic courses by accessing information and communicating with the instructor asynchronously over a computer network.

distributed processing system   A networked system, such as a local access network, that allows different computers on the network to run the same program at the same time. It also refers to the capability of such a system to use more than one computer in the network to run an application, as by detecting when a particular computer is idle and transmitting out processing tasks to it.

dithering   In computer graphics, a technique for alternating the values of adjacent dots or pixels to create the illusion of intermediate values. In printing color or displaying color on a computer screen, making adjacent dots or pixels different colors gives the effect of a third color. For example, a printed field of alternating cyan blue and yellow dots appears green. On a monochrome display or printer, altering the ratio of black to white dots can create the illusion of a particular shade of gray. Thus dithering can give the effect of more colors or shades of grey on a display or printer. *See also* **halftone**.

DLL *Abbreviation of* **dynamic link library**. A file containing executable code that is called by another program when that program is run. A DLL typically consists of code describing functions that can be used by several different applications. The extension for the files containing this code is .DLL.

DMA *Abbreviation of* **direct memory access**. A feature allowing the transfer of data between memory and a peripheral device, such as a disk drive, without involving the CPU. Computers with DMA can transfer data to and from peripheral devices faster than computers without DMA. DMA is handy for real-time applications and quick backups.

DNS *Abbreviation of* **Domain Name System**. A database system that translates textual network domain names into numeric IP addresses.

docking station A small cabinet to which a laptop or notebook computer is connected for use as a desktop computer. Docking stations usually have a connector for externally connected devices, such as hard drives or scanners, and ports that can be linked to components such as a keyboard, monitor, and printer.

document A piece of work created with an application, especially a word processor, and, if saved on disk, given its own file name.

documentation The instructions, tutorials, and reference materials that come with a program or a piece of hardware. Documentation is usually in the form of printed manuals, but most software includes online documentation that can be displayed on a screen or printed out with a printer. Often software also has an online help system that can be summoned from the application with a help command or by pressing a designated help key.

document type definition *See* **DTD**.

domain 1. A group of networked computers that share a common communications address, such as an Internet address, email address, or Telnet address. 2. *See* **domain name**.

domain name   **1.** An alphanumeric string contained in a communications address, such as an Internet address, email address, or Telnet address, that identifies a host within a group of networked computers. On the Internet, there are usually several domain names in an address. In the United States and on the Internet, the domain names are usually partitioned by periods, follow a string "username@", and conclude with one of the following three-letter suffixes: .com, .edu, .gov, .mil, .net, or .org. Such suffixes are likely to proliferate. Internationally, each country has been assigned a domain name consisting of two letters—for example, Canada is .ca, Italy is .it, and South Africa is .za.   **2.** On the Internet, the final alphanumeric string, usually two or three letters, preceded by a period at the end of a communications address.

Domain Name System   *See* **DNS.**

dongle   A hardware device that serves as copy protection for certain software. A dongle plugs into a printer port and must be present for the software to run.

DOS   *Abbreviation of* **disk operating system.**   An operating system for IBM PC and compatible computers. DOS was published separately by Microsoft, Novell, and IBM. DOS has been replaced by Microsoft Windows operating systems, the most recent of which are Windows 2000 and Windows ME.

   DOS is a command-driven operating system that requires the user to type commands at the keyboard. DOS does not support multitasking or multiple users. It is also limited to using 1 megabyte of memory — an amount seemingly prodigious when the system was first designed, but one which quickly became inadequate despite special memory systems, known as expanded or extended memory, that were developed to surmount this limitation. *See table at* **operating system.**

DoS attack   *See* **denial of service attack.**

dot   **1.** The basic unit of composition for an image produced by a device that prints text or graphics on paper. *See* **dots per inch.**   **2.** A period, as used as in URLs and email addresses, to separate strings of words, as in *www.hmco.com.*

dot-com   *adj.*   **1.** Of or relating to business conducted on the Internet, as in *dot-com advertising.*   **2.** Of or relating to a company whose products or services deal with or are sold on the Internet, as in *a dot-com brokerage firm.*

n. A company whose products and services are a part of the Internet industry.

dot-matrix printer   An impact printer that prints text and graphic images by hammering the ends of pins against an ink ribbon. This produces characters made up of a matrix, or pattern, of dots. Dot-matrix printers are relatively cheap, relatively fast, and able to print graphics. They are also a necessity for printing on multi-layer forms, which a nonimpact laser printer can't do.

On the other hand, dot-matrix printers can be noisy and their print quality is generally poor compared with the typeset look produced by laser printers. Print quality is determined by the number of pins used to print the dots — the more pins, the better the quality. Print heads in dot-matrix printers typically have 9, 18, or 24 pins. Each pin is matched to an electromagnet. When the printer sends a current to the electromagnet, it creates an electromagnetic field that repels the magnet on the pin and sends the pin against an inked ribbon to print a dot on the paper.

Some dot-matrix printers can interpret commands from PostScript or some other page description language, but most are designed to work with bit-mapped fonts controlled by ASCII codes sent to the printer from a personal computer. *See table at* **printer**.

dot pitch   A measure of the distance between each pixel on a display screen, given in millimeters — the lower the dot pitch, the higher the resolution of the display screen. The best high-resolution color monitors have dot pitches of 0.28 mm or less.

dots per inch   *Abbreviated* **dpi**   A measure of the resolution of a printer; the more dots per inch, the higher the resolution. A laser printer with a resolution of 600 dpi can print 600 dots per linear inch, or 360,000 (600 × 600) per square inch. *See illustration at* **resolution**.

double-click   To click a mouse button twice in quick succession without moving the mouse. Double-clicking is a way of rapidly selecting an item and initiating an action, such as selecting and opening a file. Both Microsoft Windows and the Apple Macintosh computer interface let you set the double-click speed, which indicates the longest interval between clicks that the computer will interpret as double-clicking rather than as two separate clicks.

double-density disk   A floppy disk that can hold twice the data of the now obsolete single-density disk. Double-density 3.5-inch disks hold 720,000 bytes of data; double-density 5.25-inch disks hold 360,000 bytes of data. Double-density disks have less data storage capacity than high-density disks.

double-sided disk   A floppy disk that can hold data on both its top and bottom surfaces. You need to use a double-sided disk drive to read from or write onto a double-sided disk.

down   Malfunctioning or not operating, especially temporarily, as a computer, for example.

download   To transfer a copy of a file from a central source to a peripheral device or computer. You can download a file from a network file server to another computer on the network, or from a bulletin board system to a personal computer. You can also download a font from disk to a laser printer. Such a font is called a soft font, as opposed to a hard font that is built into the printer by the manufacturer.

downloadable font   *See* **soft font**.

downward compatible   *See* **backward compatible**.

DP   *Abbreviation of* **data processing**.

dpi   *Abbreviation of* **dots per inch**.

draft-quality   Of or producing a low-quality printed output suitable for drafts of documents. Dot-matrix printers generally support both a draft-quality mode that sacrifices print quality for speed of output and a relatively slow near-letter quality mode. *See illustration at* **letter-quality**.

drag   To hold down the mouse button while moving the mouse. In many word processing programs, for instance, dragging the mouse selects a block of text. In a graphical user interface, an icon or graphics object can be moved by dragging it across the screen.

drag-and-drop   Of or relating to an operation that is executed by dragging an item (such as an icon representing a document) and placing it elsewhere on the desktop (such as the Recycle Bin in Microsoft Windows or the Trash Can in the Apple Macintosh operating system).

DRAM   [DEE-ram] *Abbreviation of* dynamic RAM.   A type of memory chip that stores information as electrical charges in capacitors. Because a capacitor can hold a charge for only a limited time, the RAM chips must be periodically refreshed. If the CPU tries to access the memory during this process, one or more wait states may have to be introduced until the memory can catch up, causing the system to slow down. The fastest current personal computers use DRAM access times on the order of 60–70 nanoseconds to avoid excessive wait states. Although it is slower than static RAM, dynamic RAM is generally used in personal computers because it is simpler and less expensive. *See table at* **access time**.

draw program   A graphics program that allows the user to create line art using objects such as lines, circles, squares, and Bézier curves. Draw programs use object-oriented graphics; that is, they represent each graphic object with a mathematical formula. Objects created in draw programs can be sized and scaled without distortions and moved without affecting surrounding objects. This is in contrast to images created with paint programs, which treat images as bit maps.

drive   *See* **disk drive**.

drive bay   *See* **bay**.

driver   *See* **device driver**.

drop cap   An enlarged capital letter, usually the first letter of the first word of an article, chapter, or other text block. The top of the letter is generally at the same height as the rest of the characters on the first line and descends to the baseline of the second or later line of text.

drop-down menu   *See* **pull-down menu**.

dropout   **1.** A segment of magnetic tape on which expected information is absent.   **2.** The loss of data due an interruption in the data signal.   **3.** A character that is lost during transmission when contact with the data signal is lost.

DSP   *Abbreviation of* **digital signal processing**.   The processing of digital signals, typically audio or images, after converting them from analog signals.

DSS   *Abbreviation of* **Digital Satellite System**.

DSVD   *Abbreviation of* **Digital Simultaneous Voice and Data**.   A protocol that allows the transmission of computer data and digitized audio signals over telephone lines at the same time. If you and another computer user both have DSVD modems, you can talk to each other over the telephone line while you message each other online. This technology is useful to players of real-time computer games as well as technical support people in troubleshooting customer concerns.

DTD   *Abbreviation of* **document type definition**.   A file that specifies formatting and typesetting commands for the data in each of the fields of an SGML document.

DTP   *Abbreviation of* **desktop publishing**.

Dual In-Line Memory Module   *See* **DIMM**.

dual in-line package   *See* **DIP**.

dual-scan display   A passive-matrix display that refreshes at twice the rate of a regular passive-matrix display by dividing the screen into two sections that refresh at the same time. Better than regular passive-matrix displays, they are still lower in quality as compared active-matrix displays, although they do use less power, and are therefore often used in portable computers.

dumb terminal   A terminal that has no internal microprocessor and thus no processing power independent of its host computer.

dummy   A character or other piece of information entered into a computer as a placeholder to meet prescribed conditions, such as word length, and having no effect on operations.

dump   To send a copy of the data in a portion of the computer's RAM, its main memory, to the screen or to a printer. Memory contents are often dumped to the screen while debugging a program to enable the programmer to examine exactly what is happening in memory at a particular stage in the program's execution. *See also* **screen dump**.

duplex   *See* **full duplex**.

DVD   *Abbreviation of* **Digital Versatile Disk** *or* **Digital Video Disk**. An optical disk that can store 7 times as much data as a compact disk. Using the MPEG-2 compression format, a DVD is capable of storing a full-length movie up to 133 minutes long in high-quality video and audio. DVD drives are downward compatible and can read conventional CD-ROMs and music CDs. DVDs have a capacity of 4.7GB, 8.5GB, or 17GB. Write-once DVD-R (recordable) drives will record a 3.9GB DVD-R disc that can be read on any DVD drive. *See also* **compact disk, data compression**.

DVD-ROM   A read-only optical disk with a storage capacity of 4.7 to 17GB of data. DVD-ROM drives are backward compatible so that they can play CD-ROMs as well.

DVI   *Abbreviation of* **Digital Video Interactive**.   A proprietary system developed by RCA, General Electric, and Intel that makes use of data compression to enable computers to store and display moving video. Because of the size of video images, which can easily take up more than 1MB per frame, storing enough of them to make a reasonably long motion video on the hard disk of a typical personal computer would be impractical without some kind of data compression. *See also* **CD-I**.

Dvorak keyboard   An alternative keyboard designed for faster typing. Unlike the QWERTY keyboard, the Dvorak keyboard is designed so that most English words fall in the middle row of keys. Common letter positions are placed together for quicker typing.

Some computers let you choose between QWERTY and Dvorak keyboards. You can redefine QWERTY keys with macros to turn them into Dvorak keys.

The Dvorak keyboard was designed in the 1930s by August Dvorak and his brother-in-law William Dealy. *See illustration.*

DVORAK KEYBOARD

dynamic   Occurring immediately as needed, as opposed to fixed and provided for in advance. For example, in dynamic memory allocation, a program is allowed to call for memory space on demand, rather than being assigned a fixed block of memory when it starts. The program can then yield the memory space if it is later needed by another program. Although this process is somewhat slower than an arrangement using fixed blocks of memory, it provides more flexibility when running multiple programs. *See also* **static**.

Dynamic Data Exchange   *Abbreviated* **DDE**   A system that allows two applications programs to be linked together so that a change made in one application, called the *server,* is immediately reflected in the other, called the *client.* A common example of this process is the use of a communications program to monitor an online service for stock prices and trading information, while a spreadsheet program receives the new data as it comes in, makes changes in its tables, and recalculates its formulas automatically. Applications must be specifically designed as DDE servers or clients for this technique to work. DDE was developed by Microsoft Corporation and IBM.

Dynamic HTML *Abbreviated* **DHTML** Any of numerous technologies that make webpages interactive without sending requests to servers. This is accomplished through the establishment of standards for defining the way in which browsers define webpage properties.

dynamic link library *See* **DLL**.

dynamic RAM *See* **DRAM**

dynamic random-access memory *Abbreviated* **DRAM** *See* **dynamic RAM**.

[E]

Easter egg An embedded surprise, usually a short message or graphic, that is programmed within an application. They are accessed by following a sequence of actions and keystrokes.

EB *Abbreviation of* **exabyte**.

EBCDIC [EBB-see-dik] *Abbreviation of* **Extended Binary-Coded Decimal Interchange Code**. A code used on IBM mainframes and minicomputers to assign numerical values to letters, numbers, punctuation marks, and other characters. *See table. See also* **ASCII**, **extended ASCII**.

TABLE 9 EBCDIC Character Set

Decimal Value	Hexadecimal Value	Character & Meaning	Decimal Value	Hexadecimal Value	Character & Meaning
0	00	NUL Null	14	0E	SO Shift out
1	01	SOH Start of heading	15	0F	SI Shift in
2	02	STX Start of text	16	10	DLE Data length escape
3	03	ETX End of text	17	11	DCI Device control 1
4	04	SEL Select	18	12	DC2 Device control 2
5	05	HT Horizontal tab	19	13	DC3 Device control 3
6	06	RNL Required new line	20	14	RES/ENP Restore/enable presentation
7	07	DEL Delete	21	15	NL New line
8	08	GE Graphic escape	22	16	BS Backspace
9	09	SPS Superscript	23	17	POC Program-operator communication
10	0A	RPT Repeat			
11	0B	VT Vertical tab	24	18	CAN Cancel
12	0C	FF Form feed	25	19	EM End of medium
13	0D	CR Carriage return	26	1A	UBS Unit backspace

TABLE 9 EBCDIC Character Set (continued)

Decimal Value	Hexadecimal Value	Character & Meaning	Decimal Value	Hexadecimal Value	Character & Meaning
27	1B	CUI Customer use 1	59	3B	CU3 Customer use 3
28	1C	IFS Interchange file separator	60	3C	DC4 Device control 4
29	1D	IGS Interchange group separator	61	3D	NAK Negative acknowledge
30	1E	IRS Interchange record separator	63	3F	SUB Substitute
31	1F	IUS/ITB Interchange unit separator/intermediate transmission block	64	40	SP Space
			65	41	RSP Required Space
32	20	DS Digit select	74	4A	¢
33	21	SOS Start of significance	75	4B	.
34	22	FS Field separator	76	4C	<
35	23	WUS Word underscore	77	4D	(
36	24	BYB/INP Bypass/inhibit presentation	78	4E	+
37	25	LF Line feed	79	4F	I Logical OR
38	26	ETB End of transmission block	80	50	&
39	27	ESC Escape	90	5A	!
40	28	SA Set attribute	91	5B	$
41	29	SFE Start field extended	92	5C	*
42	2A	SM/SW Set mode/switch	93	5D	)
43	2B	CSP Control sequence prefix	94	5E	;
44	2C	MFA Modify field attribute	95	5F	¬ Logical NOT
45	2D	ENQ Enquiry	96	60	-
46	2E	ACK Acknowledge	97	61	/
47	2F	BEL Bell	106	6A	¦ Broken pipe
50	32	SYN Synchronous idle	107	6B	,
51	33	IR Index return	108	6C	%
52	34	PP Presentation position	109	6D	_
53	35	TRN Transparent	110	6E	>
54	36	NBS Numeric backspace	111	6F	?
55	37	EOT End of transmission	121	79	` Grave accent
56	38	SBS Subscript	122	7A	:
57	39	IT Indent tab	123	7B	#
58	3A	RFF Required from feed	124	7C	@
			125	7D	´
			126	7E	=
			127	7F	"
			129	81	a
			130	82	b
			131	83	c

TABLE 9 EBCDIC Character Set (continued)

Decimal Value	Hexadecimal Value	Character & Meaning	Decimal Value	Hexadecimal Value	Character & Meaning
132	84	d	201	C9	I
133	85	e	202	CA	SHY Syllable hyphen
134	86	f	208	D0	} Closing brace
135	87	g	209	D1	J
136	88	h	210	D2	K
137	89	i	211	D3	L
145	91	j	212	D4	M
146	92	k	213	D5	N
147	93	l	214	D6	O
148	94	m	215	D7	P
149	95	n	216	D8	Q
150	96	o	217	D9	R
151	97	p	224	E0	\ Reverse slash
152	98	q	225	E1	NSP Numeric space
153	99	r	226	E2	S
161	A1	~	227	E3	T
162	A2	s	228	E4	U
163	A3	t	229	E5	V
164	A4	u	230	E6	W
165	A5	v	231	E7	X
166	A6	w	232	E8	Y
167	A7	x	233	E9	Z
168	A8	y	240	F0	0
169	A9	z	241	F1	1
192	C0	{ Opening brace	242	F2	2
193	C1	A	243	F3	3
194	C2	B	244	F4	4
195	C3	C	245	F5	5
196	C4	D	246	F6	6
197	C5	E	247	F7	7
198	C6	F	248	F8	8
199	C7	G	249	F9	9
200	C8	H	255	FF	EO Eight ones

ecash   Electronic cash. Ecash is advocated as a means of facilitating financial transactions over the Internet, for example, at websites which charge users for each visit.

e-commerce   Commerce that is transacted or conducted electronically, as over the Internet.

ECP   *Abbreviation of* **extended capabilities port.**   A parallel port standard that supports communication between the CPU and peripheral devices. This standard is faster than the Centronics interface. It is similar to the EPP, but was developed by a different group of companies.

edge connector   A set of metal contacts on the edge of a printed circuit expansion board that fits into an expansion slot or a connector on a ribbon cable. *See illustration at* **printed circuit board.**

EDI   *Abbreviation of* **electronic data interchange.**   The set of standards regarding the transmission of business documents and data over networks, especially the Internet. These protocols specify the formats companies use for invoices, orders, and other exchanges of information, reducing paperwork and miscommunication.

editor   A program used to create and edit text files. Editors typically include features such as deleting, copying, and text blocking, but usually do not have the formatting capabilities of word processors. Advanced editor programs also include alternate display modes, comprehensive online help utilities, and features that allow the user to edit several files simultaneously, define keyboard macros, create backup files, and edit such files as the source files for various programming languages. The two basic types of editor are line editors, which only permit one line at a time to be viewed and edited, and full-page or text editors, which allow the user to work with an entire page at once. Programs such as emacs, notepad, and vi are commonly used text editors.

EDO RAM   [ee-dee-OH ram] *Abbreviation of* **Extended Data Out RAM.** A type of DRAM that keeps the last requested data available to the CPU, enabling faster access to the data. The benefits of EDO RAM, which is faster than regular DRAM, became apparent with faster CPUs such as the Pentium microprocessor. However, EDO RAM was later supplanted by innovations such as SDRAM and other newer models of memory chips designed to work at higher speeds.

.edu   In Internet addresses, a top level domain that signifies an address of an educational institution.

EEMS   *Abbreviation of* **Enhanced Expanded Memory Specification**. A version of the original Expanded Memory Specification (EMS), developed by AST, Ashton-Tate, and Quadram, that enabled DOS applications to use more than 1MB of memory. EEMS provided for up to 64 page frames (memory space reserved for blocks, or pages of bytes mapped in from expanded memory) and the storage of executable code in expanded memory. This specification was developed to improve on the capabilities of EMS, and its provisions were subsequently included in EMS version 4.0.

EEPROM   [ee-ee-PROM] *Abbreviation of* **electrically erasable programmable read-only memory**.   A kind of PROM that retains its data even when the power is turned off and that can be erased with an electrical charge and reprogrammed. Most EEPROM can be reprogrammed only with the help of a special peripheral device, but a type of EEPROM called flash memory can be reprogrammed while the chip is in the computer. EEPROM, like other ROM, is slower than RAM and usually has less memory than RAM. EEPROM chips can wear out if they are reprogrammed too many times.

EFF   *Abbreviation of* **Electronic Frontier Foundation**.

EGA   *Abbreviation of* **Enhanced Graphics Adapter**.   A video adapter and video standard developed by IBM and introduced in 1984. EGA is capable of displaying 16 colors from a palette of 64 and has a resolution of 640 horizontal pixels by 350 vertical pixels. EGA, which represented an advance over CGA technology, is now also obsolescent, having largely been replaced by VGA and SVGA.

EIDE   *See* **Enhanced IDE**.

8088   Short for the Intel 8088 microprocessor. *See also* **Intel microprocessors**.

8086   Short for the Intel 8086 microprocessor. *See also* **Intel microprocessors**.

8514/A   A video adapter and video standard developed for IBM Personal System/2 computers. 8514/A has a graphics resolution of up to 1,024 horizontal pixels by 768 vertical pixels and the ability to display 256 colors at a time from a palette of about 262,000. For IBM PC-compatible computers, similar video performance is available through the use of VGA and SVGA adapters. *See table at* **video standard**.

EISA   *Abbreviation of* **Extended Industry Standard Architecture**.   A proprietary standard for bus architecture in IBM PC-compatible computers that takes advantage of the 32-bit data path and multiprocessing capabilities of the Intel 386 processors and beyond. The EISA standard was developed by a group of nine competitors of IBM to compete with the IBM Micro Channel Architecture (MCA). In contrast to the MCA bus, the EISA architecture is backward compatible with the earlier ISA bus, so that 16-bit ISA cards can be used in an EISA machine. *See table at* **bus.**

ELD *Abbreviation of* **electroluminescent display.**

electrically erasable programmable read-only memory *See* **EEPROM.**

electroluminescent display *Abbreviated* **ELD** A type of flat-panel display frequently used in laptop, notebook, and portable computers. A phosphorescent substance is enclosed between two flat panels. Vertical wires run along one panel and horizontal wires along the other so that together they form a grid. When electric voltage is applied to one horizontal wire and one vertical, the point of intersection is changed so that the phosphorescent substance lights up at that point, creating a pixel.

electronic data interchange *See* **EDI.**

Electronic Frontier Foundation An organization working to protect civil liberties in new communication technologies such as the Internet. As well as supporting litigation efforts, the EFF supports educational activities to increase public understanding of civil liberty issues that differ from issues of print-based media.

electronic mail *See* **email.**

ELF emission *See* **extremely low frequency emission.**

elm An early mail program for the Unix platform. Pine has largely replaced elm. Elm stands for *electronic mail. See also* **pine.**

emacs A text editor used primarily in Unix environments. *See also* **vi.**

email or **e-mail** **1.** A feature that lets a computer user send a message to someone at another computer or terminal. The message can be typed directly from the console or uploaded as a file from a disk. Email, also called electronic mail, can duplicate most of the features of paper mail, such as storing messages in in boxes and out boxes, message forwarding, providing delivery receipts, and sending multiple copies, and has the advantage of speed and convenience. Its primary drawback is its lack of security compared with paper documents. Most network systems provide email facilities, as do most online services. **2.** A message sent via email.

email address   The address to which an email message is sent. An email address usually takes the form of username@networkaddress. domain name; for example, JSmith@bigbusiness.com.

embedded command   In word processing programs, a string of characters that is placed directly into a document file and controls the formatting or appearance of the text when it is printed. Entering the command to center a line of text, for instance, usually inserts a code like [Center] or <CTR> in the text. These codes are different for each word processing program, and may appear as uninterpretable characters when a file is viewed or printed using a program different from the one it was created in. Embedded commands are usually invisible in the normal editing mode, but many programs allow you to view them by switching to a separate viewing mode. When a word processing program exhibits erratic or confusing behavior, the problem can often be solved by switching to the reveal mode to search for and remove unnecessary embedded commands.

embedded object   An object inserted into a document in instances where the object was created by a different application than the document; for example, a sound file that is embedded into a text document. By embedding rather than pasting, the inserted document remains in the format in which it was created. *See also* **OLE**.

emoticon   A combination of characters used in email messages to represent a human emotion or attitude. These characters suggest a facial expression when turned sideways. For example, the characters :-) suggest a happy face or humor, and the characters :-(suggest an unhappy face or displeasure.

EMS   *Abbreviation of* Expanded Memory Specification.   A set of documents issued by a collaboration of the Lotus, Intel, and Microsoft corporations (LIM) to standardize the method that programs would use to access expanded memory. EMS was widely used until the release of Microsoft Windows 3.0, which incorporated an XMS memory manager with the operating system. *See also* **XMS**.

emulate   To behave in the same way as another device or program, usually a widely used one. Some word processors, for example, can be set to use the same commands as Microsoft Word or WordPerfect. Most communications programs permit you to choose from different terminal emulations, allowing the computer to access mainframes that expect to see such terminal configurations as the DEC vt-52, vt-100, or vt-200. Software or coprocessor boards that enable one type of computer to emulate another also exist. For example, an Apple Macintosh computer can emulate an IBM PC computer, enabling it to run DOS and Microsoft Windows applications and even to plug into a standard PC network.

Encapsulated PostScript   *Abbreviated* **EPS**   A standard file format for printing high-resolution graphics images stored in the PostScript page description language. EPS images can be created in such graphics programs as Adobe Illustrator or Aldus Freehand. The instructions for printing them on PostScript-compatible printers are stored in a text file. A description of the image is also stored as a bit map for optional screen display. EPS files can also be read by other programs and printed on non-PostScript printers. *See table at* **graphics file format**.

encryption   The process of enciphering or encoding data so that it is inaccessible to unauthorized users. *See also* **decryption, public key cryptography**.

End key   A key on IBM PC and compatible keyboards that moves the cursor to the end of a line, page, or document, depending on which application is running. *See also* **Home key**.

endless loop   A programming error in which code continues to loop back on itself. The only way to break out of such a loop is to shut down the program. Depending on the operating system, this might require shutting down the computer.

end of file   *Abbreviated* **EOF**   A code in a file placed after the final byte of data that indicates there is no more data to follow. In ASCII, the decimal value 26 (hexadecimal 1A) marks the end of a file; in Unix, CTRL-D; and in DOS and O/S, CTRL-Z.

end of line   *Abbreviated* **EOL**   A code in a text file that marks the end of a line of text, including marks for carriage return or new line.

end user   The person who ultimately uses a computer system or software, in contrast with the programmers and developers who troubleshoot programs before they are released. Generally, end user refers to the consumers of computer products.

Energy Star   A set of guidelines introduced by the Environmental Protection Agency that identify the maximum amount of wattage a device, such as a computer, monitor, or printer, can draw in an inactive state or after an amount of time, predetermined by the user, that is spent inactive. To be compliant, a computer, exclusive of monitor, must draw 30 watts of power or less after a predetermined amount of time spent inactive. A computer that includes a monitor in its casing, or from which a monitor is directly powered, must draw 60 watts of power or less after a predetermined amount of time spent inactive. Products that are compliant with the guidelines, which is voluntary, are allowed to display the Energy Star logo.

engine   The part of a software program that performs an important, usually very repetitive task. For example, a word processing program might have an embedded spell check engine. The engine processes the data to ensure correct spelling of words, but the user never sees this part of the software. In calculations software, it is the engine that actually performs the calculations.

Enhanced Expanded Memory Specification   *See* EEMS.

Enhanced Graphics Adapter   *See* EGA.

Enhanced IDE   *Abbreviation of* **Enhanced Integrated Drive Electronics**.   A specification for the drives and interfaces of disks, CD-ROMs, and tapes that locates the majority of the drive control circuitry on the drive circuit and features an interface circuit for the CPU that can support up to four Enhanced IDE drives. It is a successor to the IDE specifications, with increased storage capacity and data transfer speed, and is designed to be comparable to SCSI-2 specifications.

enhanced keyboard   A 101-key keyboard having a row of function keys at the top rather than on the left side and an extra set of cursor control keys between the main typing keys and the numeric keypad.

enhanced parallel port   *See* EPP.

Enhanced Small Device Interface   *See* ESDI.

Enter key   *See* **Return key**.

environment   **1.** The entire set of conditions under which one operates a computer. The term can refer to a number of different aspects of computer operation. In terms of hardware and operating platform, one can work in a mainframe or a microcomputer environment, or a networking environment. With reference to operating systems, one can be in the DOS, Windows, Windows NT, Unix, OS/2, Macintosh, multitasking, or other environment. It also describes different types of user interface, such as graphics or windowing environments.   **2.** An area of a computer's memory that is used by the operating system and some programs to store certain variables that they need frequent access to, such as the command search path, locations of various types of files, and other data. In DOS, the contents of the environment can be viewed with the command SET.

EO *Abbreviation of* **erasable optical disk**.

EOF *Abbreviation of* **end of file**.

EOL *Abbreviation of* **end of line**.

EPIC *Abbreviation of* **Extremely Parallel Instruction Computing**.

EPP *Abbreviation of* **enhanced parallel port**. A parallel port standard that supports communication between the CPU and peripheral devices. This standard is faster than the Centronics interface. It is similar to the ECP, but was developed by a different group of companies.

EPROM [EE-prom] *Abbreviation of* **erasable programmable read-only memory**. A type of ROM (read-only memory) chip that can be erased by exposure to ultraviolet light and then reprogrammed. A special device called a PROM burner or PROM programmer is used to erase and write to an EPROM. EPROMs are useful when developing prototype systems for which the large-scale production of PROM chips is not practical, and in systems where frequent changes are expected to be made in the instructions encoded in ROM. *See also* **EEPROM**. *See table at* **access time**.

EPS *See* **Encapsulated PostScript**.

erasable optical disk *also* **erasable optical disc** *Abbreviated* **EO** A type of optical disk that can be erased and have new data recorded on it. Like CD-ROM and WORM disks, erasable optical disks can store much larger amounts of information than magnetic hard disks, but their access times are considerably slower and they are more expensive. See table at access time.

erasable programmable read-only memory *See* **EPROM**.

erase To remove recorded material from a magnetic tape or other storage medium. Floppy disks containing unnecessary material can be erased and used again.

ergonomics The applied science of equipment design, as for the workplace, intended to maximize productivity by reducing operator fatigue and discomfort. People who use computers benefit from the proper ergonomic design of monitors, keyboards, input devices, and chairs, to prevent muscular discomfort or physical impairment, such as carpal tunnel syndrome.

error message   A message displayed on the screen to inform the user that the system is unable to carry out an operation or that something is not operating as expected.

ESC   *Abbreviation of* **Escape key**.

escape character   **1.** An ASCII character (ASCII 27), generated by pressing the Escape key, that can have different functions depending on which program is running and is often used to cancel the current command or to back up one level in a menu structure. The escape character can be combined with other characters to form an escape sequence.   **2.** A character that functions as an Escape key.

Escape key   *Abbreviated* **ESC**   A key on IBM PC and compatible keyboards that when pressed generates an escape character. On some Apple Macintosh computer keyboards, an Escape key is included for compatibility with IBM PC computers, as when a Macintosh computer is emulating an IBM PC.

escape sequence   A string of characters, typically beginning with an escape character, used to send instructions to a device such as a printer or monitor.

ESDI   An interface standard for connecting hard disk, floppy disk, and tape drives to IBM PC and compatible computers. Although this standard allowed disk and tape drives to transfer data more quickly than previous standards, it has become obsolescent with the rise of SCSI, IDE, and EIDE interfaces. *See also* **SCSI, IDE, EIDE**.

Ethernet   [EE-ther-net]   A widely used local area network protocol developed by Xerox, DEC, and Intel. Ethernet uses a bus topology and provides raw data transfer rates of 10 megabits per second.

Eudora   A popular email program available as freeware or commercially by Qualcomm, Inc. for both Apple Macintosh and Microsoft Windows platforms.

even footer   In word processing, a footer that appears on even-numbered pages.

even header   In word processing, a header that appears on even-numbered pages.

even parity   *See* **parity**.

event   An action or occurrence, such as a keystroke or mouse movement, detected by the computer and usually initiated by a user.

event-driven   Of or relating to software in which the computer remains idle until it is set into motion by an event.

exabyte *Abbreviated* **EB** A unit of measurement of computer memory or data storage capacity equal to 1,152,921,504,608,846,976 (2^{60}) bytes. One exabyte equals 1,024 petabytes. Informally, exabyte is sometimes used to refer to 1,000,000,000,000,000,000 (one quintillion) bytes.

exception An occurrence that may cause a program to interrupt its usual sequence in order to follow another sequence designed specifically for this occurrence. An overflow error is an example of an exception. *See also* **interrupt**.

exclusive OR *See* XOR.

executable file 1. A file containing a program, or part of a program, that has been compiled for fast execution by a computer. Such files are usually written in the computer's machine language, and can include program files, DLL files, and device drivers. 2. A program that can be run by the computer when its name is entered as a command. This includes program files, batch files, and script files, for example. *See table at* **file**.

execute To run a program, carry out a command, or perform a function.

EXE file An executable file with the extension .EXE. *See table at* **file**.

expanded memory In computers using DOS or OS/2, memory added by means of an expansion board to supplement main memory to allow the computer to make use of more than 1 megabyte of memory. Expanded memory cannot be accessed directly, so it is accessed through the technique of mapping blocks of expanded memory, called pages, one at a time into an area of the CPU's usable address space called the page frame. When the computer needs to access data in expanded memory, the desired page is found and inserted into the page frame so that it can be read. For programs to use this extra memory, it must be configured according to the EMS specification, and so is often called EMS memory.

The Intel 80286 microprocessor can address up to 16MB, and the 80386 and later chips can directly address up to 4 gigabytes. Computers using these processors can run in either protected mode, which configures all memory above 1MB as extended memory, or real mode, which emulates the 8086 and configures all memory above 1MB as expanded memory. The software needed for this configuration is called an EMS driver and is built into DOS 4.0 and later versions. *See also* **EEMS, XMS**.

Expanded Memory Specification   *See* **EMS.**

expanded type   A type style that spaces characters farther apart than in ordinary type. Expanded type decreases the number of characters that can fit into a single line.

expansion board   A printed circuit board that can be installed in a computer to provide it with additional features, such as extra memory, better graphics capabilities, or more peripheral devices. Most IBM PC and compatible computers have expansion slots for three to eight expansion boards, one of which is often already filled by a video display adapter. Another is sometimes filled by a disk drive controller. Other slots are available for sound cards, internal modems, or other devices. Full-size cards take up the full width of a 16-bit slot, and half-size cards fit into an 8-bit connector. There are also 32-bit cards for use in machines with EISA architecture. *See illustration at* **printed circuit board.**

expansion bus   The connections between the computer's motherboard and the peripheral devices installed in the system. The IBM Personal Computer AT was based on the 16-bit 80286 processor and so had a 16-bit-wide expansion bus. This became the most widespread industry standard, and is often referred to as the AT bus. Processors such as the 486 can handle data internally over a 32-bit path, but since many peripherals are still 16-bit devices, many systems continue to use a bus of that width. Some, however, do provide one or two 32-bit expansion slots for additional memory boards. Systems that use the EISA bus architecture have 32-bit slots throughout, and so provide more flexibility for future expansion and use of 32-bit peripherals for faster system performance. *See also* **Micro Channel Architecture.**

expansion slot   A long, narrow socket inside a computer cabinet, designed to accept the edge connector on an expansion board. Most IBM PC-compatible computers provide a number of these slots so that additional devices can be connected to the system's expansion bus. Typically the number of expansion slots ranges from three in compact desktop cases to eight in tower-style cases. *See also* **Apple Desktop Bus.**

expert system   A program designed to help solve problems or make decisions in a particular field by using some of the knowledge that would be used by an expert. This knowledge is stored in a component of the program called the knowledge base, in the form of a large number of IF/THEN statements or rules. In interacting with the system, the user typically provides specific information by filling out a questionnaire or answering a series of questions presented by the program. The system then uses a second component, the inference engine, to process the data in a way analogous to human reasoning and present a conclusion. Some expert systems can also justify their conclusions by explaining their procedures. Although unable to rival the complexity of human reasoning in most areas, expert systems are useful in many limited scientific and financial applications.

exponent   1. The amount of times a number is to be multiplied by itself; the power to which a number is to be raised.   2. The digit or digits that indicate the power to which a number is to be raised. In $1,000 = 10^3$, 3 is the exponent of 10.

exponential notation   A system of notation in which numbers are expressed as a number between 1 and 10 multiplied by 10 raised to an appropriate power or exponent. For example, 8,970 in exponential notation is 8.97×10^3; 0.0026 is 2.6×10^{-3}. In effect, the exponent indicates the number of places the decimal point is to be moved to the right (if the exponent is positive) or left (if the exponent is negative). In computing, exponents are generally not written as superscripts, but rather with the symbol E. 8.97×10^3 becomes 8.97E3, 2.6×10^{-3} becomes 2.6 E–3. *See also* **floating-point notation**.

export   To send data created in one program to a second program. The first program performs whatever format conversion is necessary so that the second program can read the data. Many word processing programs can export files created in them to other applications in ASCII or other formats. *See also* **import**.

expression   A string or combination of symbols that represents some value. An expression can consist of a single value, such as a number or variable. More commonly it consists of two or more values, or operands, and one or more operators, which specify what actions are to be performed on the operands. Some examples of expressions are `3.1415`, `pi`, and `2*pi*radius`.

Expressions are used in programming, database management systems, and spreadsheets. *See also* **arithmetic expression, Boolean expression, query**.

extended ASCII   Any of various sets of characters that assign additional ASCII values to numbers from 128 through 255. Extended

ASCII uses 8 bits for each character, yielding a total of 2^8, or 256, codes, 128 more than are available in the standard ASCII set. The additional codes are used to represent foreign characters, mathematical symbols, and symbols for drawing pictures.

While the basic ASCII character set is standardized for all personal computer hardware and software, various sets of extended character codes are used by different computer manufacturers and software developers. IBM uses a set of extended ASCII characters called the IBM extended character set, which became a de facto standard for IBM PC and compatible computers. Apple uses a somewhat different group of extended ASCII characters for Apple Macintosh computers. *See tables at* **ASCII.**

extended attribute Additional information attached to a file by an operating system that tells the system how to edit or display the file. It may include such data as the name of the program that created the file and the names of other files to which it is related. Both OS/2 and Microsoft Windows NT use extended attributes to add advanced features to the FAT.

Extended Binary-Coded Decimal Interchange Code *See* **EBCDIC.**

extended capabilities port *See* **ECP.**

Extended Graphics Array *See* **XGA.**

Extended Industry Standard Architecture *See* **EISA.**

extended memory In IBM PC and compatible computers based on the Intel 80286 microprocessor and its successors, any system memory or RAM that exceeds 1 megabyte and can be accessed directly. The earlier 8086 and 8088, and also the 80286 and later processors running in real mode, can directly address only 1MB of RAM. But by operating in protected mode, the 80286 can have direct access to 16MB, and the 386 and later processors can have up to 4 gigabytes, without resorting to the page-swapping procedure used by expanded memory. The next generation of Pentiums will have a 64-bit address bus which theoretically will allow them to address up to 16 terabytes of RAM directly. This makes extended memory much faster than expanded memory.

Just as the EMS specification allows applications to use expanded memory, extended memory can be used by programs that adhere to the Extended Memory Specification, or XMS. These programs can gain access to extended memory through an extended memory manager device driver. The OS/2 and Unix operating systems can access extended memory directly.

Extended Memory Specification *See* XMS.

extended VGA *See* SVGA.

Extensible Markup Language *See* XML.

extension An optional string of characters following the file name and separated from it by a period. File name extensions can be assigned by programs; for example, .COM and .EXE for executable files, .BAT for batch files, and so on. You can also choose descriptive extensions for your data files, such as .LTR for letters or or .JAN for January. Judicious use of file name extensions is a powerful file management tool, as it permits you to copy or delete whole groups of files at once with wild card characters. For example, if all your memo files in a current directory called MYDIR are labeled with a .MEM extension, they can all be copied quickly to a floppy disk with the command COPY \MYDIR*.MEM A:. *See table at* **file**.

external command In MS-DOS, a program included within the operating system that is not included in the COMMAND.COM file. You execute an external command by entering its name, such as format.com, at the command prompt. *See also* **internal command**.

external modem A modem that is housed in an individual case and is connected to the computer through a cable attached to a serial port. External modems are slightly more expensive than internal modems, they have to be plugged into a separate electrical outlet, and they take up space on top of the computer or on a desk. But they can be easily moved from one computer to another and usually provide a set of status indicator lights that can be helpful in monitoring the progress of a communications link.

extremely low-frequency emission *Abbreviated* **ELF emission** A magnetic field given off by computer monitors and other electrical appliances such as electric blankets and hair dryers. It is unknown whether these emissions pose a danger to humans. The Swedish government has developed a standard for computer monitors, providing consumers with information about the level of ELF emissions from the monitors they use.

Extremely Parallel Instruction Computing *Abbreviated* **EPIC** An instruction set developed by Intel. In contrast with RISC or CISC, EPIC attempts to include the techniques for parallel processing in the processor architecture.

extranet An extension of an institution's intranet that provides outsiders with limited access.

e-zine An electronic magazine, generally one available on the Internet, sometimes for a subscription fee. Some e-zines are merely electronic copies of material that is also available in a printed magazine format, others exists exclusively on the Web.

[F]

F1, F2, F3 . . . *See* **function key**.

face *See* **typeface**.

facsimile *See* **fax**.

fair use The set of copyright law regulations regarding the free use of published material or software for educational and research purposes.

FAQ [fak, ef-ay-CUE] *Abbreviation of* **frequently asked question**. A list of questions that might be asked by newcomers to a website, USENET newsgroup, or other source of information, along with the answers to those questions.

Fast ATA An Internet specification for IDE type drives. Fast ATA is in competition with Enhanced IDE, and provides a maximum transfer rate of up to 13.3 megabits per second.

Fast Ethernet An Ethernet specification that allows for transmission speeds of up to 100 megabits per second, 10 times faster than the regular Ethernet transmission rate. *Also called* **100Base-T**.

FAT *Abbreviation of* **file allocation table**.

FAT32 An updated, 32-bit version of the file allocation table. FAT32 supports disks of up to two terabytes and is more efficient in storage because the size of each cluster is reduced to 4 kilobytes from 32 kilobytes. This smaller size allows, for example, a 42 kilobyte file to to take up 11 4-kilobyte clusters (wasting only 2 kilobytes of cluster space) instead of 2 32-kilobyte clusters (where 22 kilobytes are lost).

fatal error An error in program execution that causes the program to abort.

fat client The client in a client/server architecture in which most of the processing is run on the client. Such a system does not take advantage of the benefits of working on a network, because instead of having programs residing on the server, each computer in the network must have its own copy of every program needed.

fat server   The server in a client/server architecture in which most, if not all, of the processing is run on the server. In this arrangement each individual computer on the network accesses programs on the server rather than requiring extensive memory to store all of the necessary programs on its own hard drive. Similarly, files may be stored on the server instead of each computer's own hard drive.

fault tolerance   A computer system's capability of responding to hardware or software failures without compromising performance or losing data.

fax   *Short for* **facsimile**.   *n.*   **1.** The sending and receiving of data or printed pages over telephone lines or radio by converting them into electronic signals and reconverting and reprinting them at the receiving station.   **2.** Material transmitted by fax.   **3.** A fax machine or fax modem.

v. To send data or printed material by fax.

fax board   *See* **fax modem**.

fax machine   A device that sends and receives printed pages over telephone lines by converting them into electrical signals. The basic components of a fax machine are an optical scanner for digitizing the page, a telephone line for transmitting the information, and a printer for printing received faxes. Fax machines generally send and receive at a rate of 9,600 bps. Most machines use laser or inkjet printers and print on plain paper. Some machines are a combination fax, printer, and copier.

fax modem   A modem that sends and receives fax transmissions to and from a fax machine or another fax modem, rather than another computer, although many fax modems are dual-purpose and can act as regular modems also. Like regular modems, fax modems can be either internal or external. Internal fax modems are called fax boards and are adapters that fit into an expansion slot on a computer. Since fax modems don't have optical scanners, documents they transmit must first be stored as disk files in the computer. Likewise, received documents are written to disk files.

FCC   *Abbreviation of* **Federal Communications Commission**.

FCC certification   A statement that a given make and model of computer falls within the limits set by the Federal Communications Commission with regard to radio frequency interference with other devices. Class A certification signifies that a computer is suitable for use in commercial and industrial environments. Class B certification requires lower levels of radio frequency radiation and is for devices to be used in the home. Class B certification does not guarantee that a computer will not cause interference to nearby radios and television sets, but the levels should be low enough not to be disruptive under normal use for most people.

FDD   *Abbreviation of* **floppy disk drive**.

FDDI   *Abbreviation of* **Fiber Distributed Data Interface**.   A set of standards developed by ANSI for the transmission of data over fiber optic cable, supporting transmission rates of up to 100 megabits per second.

FDHD   *Abbreviation of* **Floppy Drive High Density**.   A disk drive developed by Apple Computer used in Macintosh computers that can accept either double-density or high-density 3.5-inch floppy disks. The FDHD, often called SuperDrive, can also read and format disks in DOS format, enabling Macintosh computers and IBM PC computers to share data.

feathering   In desktop publishing, the process of adding space between the lines of text on a page to force vertical justification.

feature   A functional, desirable, or marketable property of a hardware device or of software.

Federal Communications Commission   *Abbreviated* **FCC**   The United States government agency that regulates interstate and international telephone, telegraph, and radio communications.

female connector   A connector that has one or more receptacles into which pins from a male connector are inserted. *See illustration at* **connector**.

FEP   *Abbreviation of* **front-end processor**.

FF   *Abbreviation of* **form feed**.

Fiber Distributed Data Interface   *See* **FDDI**.

fiber optics   A method of transmitting data in the form of laser light over bundles of glass fibers. This method has numerous advantages over such traditional techniques using wire cables, phone lines, and radio waves, for example. Fiber optics offers greater bandwidth and is virtually insusceptible to electromagnetic interference. It is also far more suited for use by computers, because it can transmit digital data directly without the need to convert it into analog form through a modem. The process of replacing older cable with smaller, lighter fiber optic cable has been under way for some years, and fiber optics is a common method of communications in many parts of the world.

Fidonet **1.** A protocol for sending email and newsgroup posts over telephone lines, begun in 1984 by the Fido BBS, which came to be used by thousands of BBSs. It is now integrated into the Internet. **2.** The network of BBSs and other organizations that use the Fidonet protocol.

field In a database, a space for a single item of information contained in a record. For example, in a database containing records of names, addresses, and account histories for individual clients, one field might hold the Zip code, another the telephone number, and another the date of last contact. When arranged in a table with each record in a single horizontal row, the fields are displayed in vertical columns. In most database management systems, each field is assigned a specific length and data type such as text, date, or currency, as well as other attributes such as optional or required, centered, boldface, and so on.

file A collection of data or information that is stored as a unit in the computer under a single name, called the file name. Files are the basic units that a computer works with in storing and retrieving data. Although a single file is often scattered across many places on a hard disk, the computer retrieves all the pieces and makes them available as a single entity. Table 10 lists various common types of files.

TABLE 10 Common File Types

File Type	Extension	Contents
Backup file	.BAK	Duplicate of a program or data
Batch file	.BAT	Operating system commands
Binary file	.BIN	Data or instructions in binary format
Command file	.COM	Operating system commands
Data file	.DAT	Data
Dynamic link library file	.DLL	Programming routines in executable format
Executable file	.EXE	Programs or commands in executable format
Library file	.LIB	Programming routines or subroutines
Text file	.TXT	Text composed of ASCII characters

file allocation table *Abbreviated* **FAT** An area on a hard disk or floppy disk where information is stored about the physical location of each piece of every file on the disk and the location of unusable areas of the disk. In DOS, OS/2, and some Unix systems, the operating system checks the FAT whenever a request is made to access a file, and uses the information to retrieve the file when reading or to determine where to put it when writing to the disk. If the part of the disk containing the FAT is erased or corrupted, no files on the disk can be read, even though they may be physically intact.

file attribute   *See* **attribute** (sense 2).

file compression   *See* **data compression**.

file compression program   A utility that compresses files so as to minimize the space they take up on a disk or tape. The files are then decompressed as they are needed. File compression programs are used to compress files for long-term storage, as in an archive, and to decompress downloaded files. *See also* **data compression**.

file extension   *See* **extension**.

file format   The format that a program uses to encode data on a disk. Some formats are proprietary, and a file so encoded can only be read by the program that has created the file. Some simple formats, such as ASCII, can be read by many kinds of programs.

file fragmentation   *See* **fragmentation**.

file locking   *See* **lock**.

file management   The placement and organization of files and directories used by an operating system. The operating system has its own file manager, but separate file management programs are also available. These programs provide additional features, such as easier backup procedures. *See also* **directory, hierarchical**.

file name   The name given to a file so that it can be distinguished from other files. Different operating systems have different rules for the length and composition of file names. In DOS, for example, a file name can be up to 8 characters long and must not include these characters:

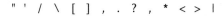

" ' / \ [ ] , . ? , * < > |

Apple Macintosh and Microsoft Windows NT file names can be 31 characters long and cannot include a colon (:).

Many operating systems allow you to put a short extension on each file name to indicate what type of file it is. The extension usually goes after a period at the end of the file name.

file server   *See* **server**.

file sharing network   *See* **peer-to-peer network**.

file system   A combination of software and disk sector configuration that provides an organizational structure for a user's files. A file system such as FAT organizes the files on disk and manages the translation between the structure of files that the user sees on screen and the actual organization of the same files on disk. The way an individual disk's sectors are configured helps determine the ultimate organization of files on disk, as does file size and function. A file system is often part of a computer's operating system. *See also* **file allocation table**.

file transfer   The process of sending files from one computer to another via a modem or network. For example, when you download a file from the Internet, a copy of the file is transferred over the telephone line and written to your hard disk.

file transfer protocol   *Abbreviated* **ftp**   A communications protocol governing the transfer of files from one computer to another over a telephone line or network. Its most important function is to specify how errors are to be detected. It may also specify how file names and data are to be converted when the transfer is between different types of computers. More advanced protocols may specify how to compress or encrypt the data for transmission. *See table 10.*

file type   A designation for a class of files with the same general structure or function. In Microsoft Windows, the file type is usually indicated by the extension.

TABLE 11 File Transfer Protocols

Protocol	Features
Kermit	• Transfers information in blocks of 96 bytes
	• High transmission accuracy
	• Relatively slow
Xmodem	• Transfers information in blocks of 128 bytes
	• Fairly high transmission accuracy
	• Relatively slow (can send only one file at a time)
Ymodem	• Transfers information in blocks of 1,024 bytes (1 kilobyte)
	• High transmission accuracy
	• Supports batch file transfers
Zmodem	• High transmission accuracy
	• Resumes interrupted transmissions at point of interruption, not from the beginning
	• Relatively fast

fill *v.* In graphics programs, to put a color or pattern into an enclosed shape. When you do this, you fill the shape with a color or design.

n. In spreadsheet programs, a command that allows you to fill a range with a series of values once you have provided the starting value, the increment of change between each value, and the ending value.

filter **1.** A command that causes the operating system to read data, manipulate it in some specified way, and output the manipulated data. In DOS and OS/2, the filter commands are FIND, which searches for text in a file; MORE, which displays a file one screenful at a time; and SORT, which alphabetizes the contents of a file. **2.** A set of criteria applied to a database query that causes a subset of the query rows to be returned or displayed.

Finder An interface developed by Apple Computer to the operating system for Apple Macintosh computers. The Finder incorporates windows, icons, and other graphics, and it was the first graphical user interface to gain wide acceptance. The Finder is the Macintosh computer's disk and file management system; it also manages the clipboard and scrapbook. MultiFinder is the multitasking version of the Finder.

finger A program that allows you to determine email address ownership. At the command prompt, typing finger followed by an email address will return the user's name and whether that user is logged on, if you have access to such information. Typing finger followed by a name will return login names of users who have that name. If you are using the finger utility with someone who shares your domain name, you need only to enter his or her login name. Developed originally for Unix, some other platforms now have finger capability.

firewall A network system that isolates a local area network (LAN) from other networks. A firewall typically consists of a single computer system running special security software that connects an organization's LAN to the Internet. The software authenticates all users attempting to connect to the LAN from the Internet before granting them permission. The firewall may also restrict LAN users' access to the Internet. *See also* **authentication**.

FireWire The Apple Computer trade name for IEEE 1394. Apple Computer originally developed this product. *See* **IEEE 1394**.

firmware Programming instructions that are permanently stored in read-only memory (ROM) rather than being stored on disk. ROMs and PROMs that have data or programs written on them are examples of firmware.

fixed disk   *See* **hard disk.**

fixed-frequency monitor   An analog monitor that accepts input signals in only one frequency range. Fixed-frequency monitors come with many inexpensive entry-level computer systems. *See also* **multifrequency monitor, multiscanning monitor.**

fixed-length field   In database systems, a field that stays the same size regardless of how much information it contains. The variable length field grows or shrinks depending on how much data it holds.

fixed pitch   *See* **fixed space.**

fixed-point notation   A mathematical notation in which the decimal point is a permanent placeholder with respect to the whole and fractional number portions of a given number. For some arithmetic operations, such as the addition of two numbers, a computer can process a result quickly if the inputted numbers are in fixed-point notation. For the manipulation of very large numbers and very small numbers, however, fixed-point notation is an inefficient use of computer memory. *See also* **floating-point notation.**

fixed space   The allocation of space of the same width to different characters in a font. Fixed space contrasts with proportional space, which gives each character its own particular width. In a fixed space font, a narrow letter such as *i* is given the same amount of horizontal space as a wider letter such as *w*, while in a proportional space font, *i* would be allocated a smaller amount of space. Many computer display screens show text in a fixed space font, while books, magazines, and newspapers are printed in proportional space. *Also called* **fixed pitch, fixed width.** *See also* **monospace font, pitch.**

fixed width   *See* **fixed space.**

Fkey   A utility on Apple Macintosh computers that is comparable to the function keys on keyboards for IBM PC and compatible computers. To activate a particular command through the Fkey feature, the user presses the Command key, the Shift key, and a number key from 0 to 9. The combination Command-Shift-4, for example, prints the text and images currently on the display screen.

flag   1. A bit or series of bits that serve as a signal to a computer. A flag can mark such items as an unusual piece of data, a possible error, or the beginning or end of a message.   **2.** A boolean field in a database.

flame *v.* **1.** To send an offensive email message or newsgroup posting, especially one containing strong language and personal insults.   **2.** To carry on at great length on a certain topic in an email.   *n.* An email containing such an insulting or overly lengthy message.

flame war A protracted volley of flames among combative participants on an unmoderated mailing list or newsgroup.

flash **1.** To blink or change color in order to get the user's attention. For example, Microsoft Windows will cause an icon or title bar to flash if the printer is out of paper.   **2.** To momentarily hang up a telephone line, as when using a call waiting service. Most modems have a special command to do this.

flash memory A type of electronically erasable programmable read-only memory (EEPROM) chip whose data can be altered. Flash memory chips are a lightweight, fast data storage medium for portable devices and can be rewritten without removing them from the computer's circuit board. The data stored in flash memory remain intact even when the power is shut off.

Modems now use flash memory instead of PROM, making it possible to install new protocols as necessary.

flatbed scanner A type of optical scanner that holds a page stationary while the scanning head moves across the page and converts images and text into digital information. Flatbed scanners are able to scan bound documents that cannot be scanned by a sheet-fed scanner.

flat file *See* ASCII file.

flat-file database A database that contains all of its information in a single file. It imposes very little structure on the data, which makes it flexible and easy to use but slower and less powerful than a relational database.

flat-panel display A thin, lightweight display screen found in laptop and notebook computers. Flat-panel displays do not use conventional cathode-ray tubes. Instead, they use other technologies, such as liquid-crystal, gas plasma, electroluminescent, or thin film transistor displays. *Also called* **flat-screen display**.

flicker *See* screen flicker.

floating-point coprocessor *See* math coprocessor.

floating-point notation A mathematical notation for representing a number, in which there is a set number of digits before and after a decimal point, and the digits are multiplied by a power of some base. In computer memory a number in floating-point notation is often represented as a binary number multiplied by a power of the base 2. The number $60\frac{5}{8}$ can be expressed in base 10 floating-point notation as 60.625 or 6.0625×10^1 or 6.0625E1. In binary floating-point notation this same number is represented as 111100.101 or 1.11100101 (base 2) $\times 2^5$. An arithmetic operation, such as the addition of two numbers, may take longer for a computer to process if the numbers inputted are in floating-point notation, as opposed to fixed-point notation. However, when the numbers that are added together are very large or very small, floating-point notation uses the computer memory more efficiently. *See also* **fixed-point notation, scientific notation**.

floating-point unit A circuit or set of circuits built into a computer with a special set of instructions that enable it to process large mathematical operations very quickly. It may be part of a general processor or a separate unit. There are software emulators for floating-point units. Graphics-intensive software packages may require a floating-point unit (or emulator).

floppy *See* **floppy disk**.

floppy disk A round, flat piece of Mylar coated with magnetic material and covered by a protective jacket, used as a storage medium for personal computers. Originally, floppy disks were the principal storage medium for personal computers, but the development of inexpensive hard disks has diminished their role. Floppy disk drives are slower than hard disk drives, and floppy disks themselves have less storage capacity and are more easily damaged than hard disks. But floppy disks are more portable and considerably less expensive than hard disks, and they are useful for loading some programs into your computer and for backup. Since many large applications are now distributed on CD-ROM, and removable hard disks such as Zip drives are available, floppy disks are losing popularity as a distribution and backup medium.

The 3.5-inch disk is encased in rigid plastic and has a sliding guard that covers the access hole. The drive slides open the guard after you insert the disk into the disk drive. Most newer personal

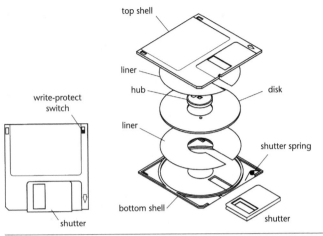

top shell
liner
hub
write-protect switch
liner
disk
shutter spring
bottom shell
shutter
shutter

3.5-INCH FLOPPY DISK   Closed and exploded views of a 3.5-inch floppy disk

computers include only a 3.5-inch floppy disk drive; some models include no disk drive at all.

5.25-inch floppy disks, which have flimsy sleeves and open access holes, were more common than 3.5-inch disks before 1987.

Also called **diskette.** *See illustration.*

floppy disk drive   *See* **floppy disk.** *Also called* **floppy drive.**

floptical disk   An optical disk developed by Insite Peripherals that is the size of a 3.5-inch floppy disk. It can store over 20 megabytes of data magnetically, and the read/write head is aligned by means of a laser.

flowchart   A schematic representation of a sequence of operations, as in a computer program.

flow control   The control of communication between two devices, for example, a computer and a modem, so that the receiving device isn't overwhelmed with data coming in faster than the device can handle.

flush   *adj.* Aligned evenly with a margin. Flush left means that the text is aligned with the left margin, and flush right means that it is aligned with the right margin.

v. In programming, to write the contents of a buffer to disk.

FM synthesis   *Abbreviation of* **frequency modulation synthesis.**   A technique for mimicking the sound of a musical instrument, used by systems that utilize MIDI. FM synthesis creates multiple sine waves for audio transmission and modulates their frequencies according to a predetermined algorithm for a particular musical instrument. Another technique, wavetable synthesis, is considered to produce truer musical sounds than FM synthesis.

Fn *Abbreviation of* **function key**.

folder In graphical user interfaces, an organizing structure that contains multiple files and is analogous to a directory. A folder is usually represented on the screen by the image of a file folder. Like a directory, a folder may contain other folders. *See illustration at* **desktop**.

folio A page number. A folio that appears at the bottom of a page is called a drop folio.

font 1. A complete set of characters of one size and typeface. The height of a font is measured in points (72 points equal one inch). The most common weights are lightface and boldface. Popular styles include roman and italic. Another font specification is pitch, which refers to the number of characters printed per inch. A fixed pitch (or fixed space) font allocates the same amount of space for every character, while a proportional pitch (or proportional space) font gives each character its own particular amount of space.

Screen fonts are the fonts a program uses to display text on a display screen. The screen font usually resembles the printer font, but even a "what you see is what you get" (WYSIWYG) display does not always correspond exactly to the way a document will look in print.

Printers come equipped with a set of resident fonts, also called internal or built-in fonts. Additional fonts can be added to many printers by inserting a font cartridge or by downloading soft fonts from software.

Fonts are produced by computers and printers in two ways. Bit-mapped fonts use a pattern of bits for each character. Every character has its own map, depending on size, weight, and typeface. Outline fonts create a set of mathematical instructions that describe the outline of a font. The same set of instructions can produce different sizes of the same typeface. In outline fonts, a set of instructions called hints are used to improve the quality of fonts at lower resolutions. *See also* **outline font, printer, scalable font**. 2. *See* **font family**.

font cartridge A ROM cartridge that plugs into some printers and enables them to print in fonts other than their resident fonts. The other way to add fonts to a printer is to download soft fonts into the printer's RAM.

font family   A set of fonts in various sizes and weights that share the same typeface. For example, Times 10 point and Times Italic 12 point are in the same font family. *See illustration.*

Times 10 point
Times Italic 10 point
Times bold 10 point

Times 12 point
Times Italic 12 point
Times bold 12 point

Times 14 point
Times Italic 14 point
Times bold 14 point

FONT FAMILY

footer   In word processing, printed information, especially a title, page number, or date, placed in the bottom margin of a page and repeated on every page or every other page of the document. A footer that repeats only on odd-numbered pages is an odd footer. One that repeats only on even-numbered pages is an even footer.

footprint   The amount of space a device occupies on a desk or the floor.

forced page break   An instruction, as in a word processing program, that makes a new page start where you insert it in the document. Such a page break will remain in place even when the document repaginates, until you remove the command. *Also called* **hard page break**.

foreground   **1.** In a multitasking system, the state of accepting data and commands from an input device, such as a keyboard. For example, if your computer is making calculations in a spreadsheet program while you're writing a letter in a word processing program, the word processing program is operating in the foreground.   **2.** On an individual display window, the display of characters and graphics, as opposed to the background, which is the area of the screen behind the characters and graphics.

format   *n.* An arrangement of data for storage, display, or hard copy presentation. Database, spreadsheet, graphics, and word processing programs all have their own formats that can be altered to change the way information is presented.

v. **1.** To arrange the data in a document for display or hard copy presentation. In word processing, for example, setting such attributes in a document as the typeface, point size, margins, headers or footers, line spacing, and justification is referred to as formatting the document. **2.** To run an operating system or utility program that prepares a disk for use by organizing its storage space into addresses that can be recognized and accessed. Reformatting a disk erases only the address tables on the disk, not the actual data. If you accidentally reformat a disk that contains valuable data, you may be able to recover most of the data with a utility program such as PC Tools or Norton Utilities. You can also hire a specialist to try to recover the data. *Also called* **initialize**, especially with reference to Apple Macintosh computers.

form factor The size of a device, measured by its physical dimensions, as opposed to its storage capacity. Often used with respect to hard disks and hard drives, this term is also used to describe the dimensions and layout of a motherboard.

form feed *Abbreviated* **FF** A command that tells the printer to advance to the top of a new page.

formula An expression that instructs an application, such as a database management system or a spreadsheet, to perform a calculation on one or more values. For example, in a spreadsheet program, a formula plugs in the values of a column of cells and performs a calculation on those values.

FORTRAN *Abbreviation of* **formula translator.** The first high-level language, developed in the 1950s by IBM and released in 1957. FORTRAN is designed to handle intensive mathematical calculations and was once used chiefly in mathematics, science, and engineering. Later versions of FORTRAN introduced features that made it useful in other fields as well.

forum In a bulletin board system or other online service, a topical discussion group, especially one that is moderated.

forward compatible *See* **upward compatible.**

486 The Intel 486 microprocessor. *See also* **Intel microprocessors.**

fourth-generation language A user-oriented programming language that is closer to human language than high-level languages are. Fourth-generation languages such as PowerBuilder are often used to structure queries in relational databases.

fps   *Abbreviation of* **frames per second.**   In animation and video, the number of still frames that are displayed each second to create the illusion of a moving picture.

FPU   *Abbreviation of* **floating-point unit.**

fractal   A geometric pattern that is repeated at ever- smaller scales to produce irregular shapes that cannot be represented by classical geometry. Images of natural features, such as landscapes and coastlines, can be generated using fractal geometry. Each portion of a fractal, when magnified, appears identical to the entire image.

fragmentation   **1.** The condition of having different parts of the same file scattered throughout a disk. Fragmentation occurs when the operating system breaks up a file and fits it into the spaces left vacant by previously deleted files. Fragmentation slows down the operating system by making the read/write head search for files over a larger area. *Also called* **file fragmentation.** *See also* **defragment.**   **2.** A similar scattering in a computer's random-access memory (RAM) that takes place when programs and data are repeatedly stored and released.

frame   **1.** A rectangular area in which text or graphics can be shown. In HTML, frames divide a browser's window into segments that are scrolled independently of each other; each frame is a separate HTML document.   **2.** In animation and video, an individual image in a set of images that, when viewed rapidly in sequence, create the illusion of a moving picture. *See illustration.*

frames per second   *See* **fps.**

freeware   Computer programs that are given away free of charge. Freeware remains copyrighted while public domain software does not. The copyright owner of a freeware program may restrict its use or distribution. *See also* **shareware.**

frequency   The number of repetitions, expressed in hertz, of a complete waveform within a specified period of time. One hertz equals one cycle per second; a kilohertz equals 1,000 hertz; and a megahertz equals 1,000 kilohertz.

frequently asked questions   *See* **FAQ.**

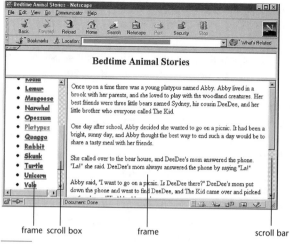

frame scroll box   frame   scroll bar

FRAME

friction feed   A mechanism that draws paper through a dot-matrix printer by pinching it between plastic or rubber rollers. In contrast, a tractor feed mechanism pulls paper through the printer by using two or more toothed wheels. Tractor feeds are able to use only paper with holes on the edges, while friction feeds can adjust to print envelopes and a variety of cut-sheet paper. Most dot-matrix printers are equipped with both types of feed mechanism.

front end   The part of a software program that provides the user interface.

front-end processor   *Abbreviated* **FEP**   A small computer that receives, generates, or handles data before sending it to a larger computer for analysis or further processing. The front-end processor may perform operations such as error checks, format conversions, or sorts. A front-end processor may also act as an interface between the user and the larger computer, which is called the back-end processor.

ftp   *See* **file transfer protocol**.

FTP   A particular file transfer protocol that is commonly used on the Internet.

full backup   A procedure for backing up all the files on a hard disk by copying them to floppy disks, a tape, or another storage medium. It is a good safety measure for frequent users to do full backups once a week. *See also* **differential backup**, **incremental backup**.

full duplex   In communications, a mode of transmission in which data can be sent in two directions simultaneously. In the other mode, half duplex, data can be transmitted in only one direction at a time, and the two senders must alternate their transmissions. Transmission mode is part of the communications protocol that must be established for data to be passed smoothly between two or more computers.

function   In programming and in spreadsheet applications, a procedure or section within a program that returns a single value. Functions can include calculations in finance, mathematics, trigonometry, and statistics, or involve lookup tables or data sorting and comparison. In a spreadsheet, for example, a function may return the amount of compound interest received given the principal, interest rate, and time period.

functional layer   The software layer that contains most of the application logic. For example, the functional layer of a financial application contains all the logic of such tasks as setting up bank accounts and calculating interest.

function key   *Abbreviated* **F** *or* **Fn**   One of a set of computer keys located on the top or the left side of the keyboard on an IBM PC or compatible computer that enters specific commands defined by the program you are running. Keyboards are equipped with either 10 or 12 function keys that are labeled F1, F2, F3, and so on. Function keys execute different commands when they are pressed in combination with the Alt key, the Control key, and or the Shift key.

The equivalent to a function key on an Apple Macintosh computer is the Fkey utility, which executes various commands when you push the Shift key, the Command key, and a number key from 0 to 9.

fuzzy logic   A form of algebra that employs a range of values from *true* to *false* and is used in decision-making with imprecise data. In fuzzy logic the outcome of an operation is assigned a value between 0 and 1 corresponding to the degree of its truth. Fuzzy logic is used, for example, in artificial intelligence systems. *See also* **Boolean logic**.

[G]

G   1. *Abbreviation of* **giga-**.   2. *Abbreviation of* **gigabyte**.

G3   A microprocessor developed by Apple Computer that runs at speeds of up to 266 megahertz per second, used in the Power Macintosh G3 computer line.

G4   A microprocessor developed by Apple Computer that runs at speeds of up to 500 megahertz per second, used in the Power Macintosh G4 computer line.

game port   A port for IBM and compatible PCs into which you connect joysticks and similar input devices for games.

gas plasma display   A type of flat-panel display sometimes used in laptop and notebook computers. Neon is enclosed between two flat panels with vertical wires running along one panel and horizontal wires along the other so that together they form a grid. When an electric current is sent along one horizontal wire and one vertical wire, the point of intersection is charged so that the neon glows reddish orange at the point, creating a pixel.

gateway   1. A device that connects two networks that use different communications protocols. A gateway has a microprocessor capable of converting information from one network into a readable format for a second network that uses a different protocol. For example, gateways are used to link AppleTalk and Ethernet networks.   2. Software or hardware that enables communication between computer networks that use different communications protocols.

Gb   *Abbreviation of* **gigabit**.

GB   *Abbreviation of* **gigabyte**.

Gbps   *Abbreviation of* **gigabits per second**.

GDI   *Abbreviation of* **Graphical Device Interface**.

General Protection Fault   *Abbreviated* **GPF**   A severe failure of a program that usually causes its unexpected termination. General Protection Faults are usually caused by a program that tries to access invalid or inaccessible memory locations.

ghosting   1.   The permanent etching of an image into a display screen when the same image has been left on the screen for a long period of time, a phenomenon that is rarely a problem with modern monitors. Screen savers prevent ghosting either by dimming the screen brightness or by displaying moving images on a screen that has displayed a fixed image for a specified period of time. *Also called* **burn-in.** **2.** The act or process of making a condensed copy of the software and configuration on a computer for rapid recovery from a later software change, as when testing new software.

GIF [jiff or giff]   A bit-mapped color graphics file format. GIF is used by many bulletin board systems and webpages to exchange scanned graphics because it supports efficient data compression. Because there is a patent on the compression algorithm used, PNG was developed. *See also* **PNG.**

giga- *Abbreviated* **G** **1.** A prefix indicating one billion (10^9), as in *gigahertz*. This is also the sense in which *giga-* is generally used in terms of data transmission rates, where a bit is a signal pulse and is counted in the decimal system, which is based on multiples of ten. **2.** A prefix indicating 1,073,741,824 (2^{30}), as in *gigabyte*. This is the sense in which *giga-* is generally used in terms of data storage capacity, which, due to the binary nature of bits, is based on powers of two.

gigabit *Abbreviated* **Gb**   One billion (1,000,000,000) bits, used as a unit for expressing the rate of data transmission per unit of time (usually one second). In highly techincal contexts involving data storage capacity, it can refer to 1,073,741,824 (2^{30}) bits.

gigabyte *Abbreviated* **G** or **GB**   A unit of measurement of computer memory or data storage capacity, equal to 1,073,741,824 (2^{30}) bytes. One gigabyte equals 1,024 megabytes. Informally, the term is sometimes used to refer to one billion (1,000,000,000) bytes.

gigaflop   A measure of computing speed equal to one billion floating-point operations per second.

glitch **1.** A false or spurious electronic signal caused by a brief, unwanted surge or loss of electric power, especially one that causes a computer or other hardware to function **2.** A small programming error that generally goes unnoticed and does not have an impact on usability.

global **1.** Of or relating to an entire program, document, or file. A global format for a spreadsheet, for example, is a format that applies to every cell in that spreadsheet. **2.** Of or relating to all the users in a computer network.

glossary   In word processing, a storage utility for holding text that you would ordinarily have to type over and over again. When you access a glossary it inserts the appropriate text into your document and saves you the trouble of typing it again.

Gnu   [noo]   A software organization dedicated to the free exchange of software. Gnu has built its own version of the Unix operating system, known as Linux, as well as a complete set of tools, all of which are free to the general public.

.gov   In Internet address, a top level domain that signifies an address of a United States government agency at the federal level. Many agencies at the state level have addresses ending in the two-letter postal abbreviation of the state plus *.us* as in *mo.us* for Missouri or *nv.us* for Nevada.

GPF   *Abbreviation of* **General Protection Fault**.

Gopher   A software tool that lets the user search for and access files on the Internet. Gopher presents a menu of files for the user to choose from; these files may be text files or may include sound or images.

gppm   *Abbreviation of* **graphics pages per minute**.

grabber   **1.** A device that captures an image from a video camera or other video source and converts it to digital form.   **2.** An onscreen cursor, often represented by an icon of a hand, that grabs onscreen objects and allows you to move them around.

graphical device interface   *Abbreviated* **GDI**   A Microsoft Windows standard for displaying or printing bitmapped text and graphical images with a consistent style.

graphical user interface   *Abbreviated* **GUI**   An interface that enables you to choose commands, start programs, and see lists of files and other options using images rather than plain text. Choices can be made with keyboard commands, by using the mouse to move an onscreen pointer, or by selecting an image on a touchscreen.

   Graphical user interfaces take full advantage of the bit-mapped graphics displays of personal computers. GUIs are easier for most people to learn to use than command-driven interfaces. Also, a GUI uses a standard format for text and graphics, so that different applications running under a common GUI can share data.

   A graphical user interface is used on all Apple Macintosh computers. Many applications for IBM PC and compatible computers use GUIs, most of them based on Microsoft Windows. Unix systems such as X-Windows also use GUIs.

graphics   The display and manipulation of pictorial information by computers. The two basic methods of creating computer graphics are object-oriented graphics and bit-mapped graphics.

In object-oriented graphics, each pictorial object is represented by a mathematical description. Programs that use object-oriented graphics, such as draw programs, can manipulate one object without affecting surrounding objects. Objects can be enlarged or reduced without introducing scaling distortions.

In bit-mapped graphics, pictures are represented as patterns of dots or pixels. The patterns are stored in memory as arrays of bits called bit maps. Bit-mapped graphics cannot be resized easily without distortion. Paint programs use bit-mapped graphics.

Many graphics-based applications exist, including desktop publishing software, presentation graphics, and CAD (computer-aided design) software.

graphics accelerator   An expansion board that includes a graphics coprocessor. The coprocessor is a microprocessor specially designed for fast graphics processing. The graphics accelerator frees the CPU (central processing unit) from graphics processing, resulting in significant improvement in a system's ability to run graphical user interfaces, such as Microsoft Windows, and their related applications. *Also called* **video accelerator**.

graphics adapter   *See* **video adapter**.

graphics-based   Of or relating to programs and hardware that display images as bit maps or geometrical objects, as opposed to the ASCII or extended ASCII characters used by character-based systems. Examples of graphics-based software include presentation graphics and desktop publishing programs. Graphics-based applications usually require a large amount of memory, a powerful CPU, and a monitor with graphics capability, and support a graphics standard such as VGA.

graphics file format   The way in which a program reads and stores information so as to create and manipulate graphics images. There are numerous proprietary graphics file formats, with little standardization among them. Table 12 compares various common graphics file formats.

TABLE 12 Common Graphics File Formats

File Format	Data Storage Format	Characteristics
BMP	Bit-mapped	Used by Microsoft Windows
CGM (Computer Graphics Metafile)	Object-oriented	Used by many software and hardware products
EPS (Encapsulated PostScript)	Object-oriented	Used by the PostScript language
GIF	Bit-mapped	Used by almost all systems; most common format
HPGL (Hewlett-Packard Graphics Language)	Bit-mapped	Used by many IBM PC-based graphics products
JPEG (Joint Photographic Experts Group)	Bit-mapped	Used to compress full-color natural images
PCX	Bit-mapped	Used by many graphics programs, optical scanners, and fax modems
PICT	Object-oriented	Used by almost all Macintosh graphics programs
PSD	Object-oriented	Used by Adobe Photoshop
TIFF (Tagged Image File Format)	Bit-mapped	Used for storing scanned images
WMF (Windows Metafile Format)	Object-oriented	Used for transferring graphics between Microsoft Windows applications

graphics mode A mode of resolution on a video adapter that allows the screen to display both text and graphics. In graphics mode, both text and images are treated as illuminated patterns of pixels. Programs that run totally in graphics mode are called graphics-based programs. In character mode, the screen is split into larger units, or boxes, each one able to hold one ASCII character.

graphics pages per minute *Abbreviated* **gppm** The speed at which a printer, especially a laser printer, can print pages of graphics images, as opposed to pages per minute (ppm), the speed at which a printer prints pages of text. Given the relative complexity of graphics versus text, a printer's graphics pages per minute rating is always considerably slower than its pages per minute rating.

graphics tablet *See* **digitizing tablet**.

gray scale A series of shades from pure white to pure black. In computer graphics, the number of gradations within this scale varies depending on the number of bits used to store the shading information for each pixel. Typically, current hardware and software can represent from 16 to 256 shades of gray.

gray scaling A computer's use of shades of gray to represent a graphics image. Gray scaling usually involves converting a continuous tone image — an image with thousands of different shades of gray, such as a black and white photograph — into an image with a much smaller number of gray shades that can be stored and manipulated by a computer. Gray scaling differs from dithering in that dithering creates the illusion of shades of gray by alternating black and white dots. In gray scaling, each dot is a particular shade of gray.

greeking In desktop publishing, the use of gray bars or garbled text to simulate how text will appear on a page. Greeking is used when one is evaluating the layout and design of a document rather than its content. *See also* **preview, thumbnail**.

Green Book The set of specifications, developed by the Philips Corporation and the Sony Corporation, that lays out the standards for CD-I technology.

grep A tool, originally developed for the Unix platform, that allows you to search text files for specific text patterns.

Group 3 Protocol An international standard developed by the ITU for fax machines and fax modems.

Group 4 Protocol An international standard developed by the ITU for the technology involved in transmitting faxes over ISDN lines.

groupware Software that helps organize the activities of users in a network. Examples of groupware include schedulers that help employees plan meetings; electronic newsletters; and software designed to make collaborative writing projects easier.

GUI [GOO-ee] *Abbreviation of* **graphical user interface**.

gutter In a bound document, the blank space formed by the inner margins of two facing pages. In desktop publishing and word processing, you should allow for additional margin space on the side of a page that will be bound in order to accommodate the gutter. *Also called* **offset**.

[H]

H.323   An international standard developed by the ITU for audio and video conferencing and telephony in real time over the Internet.

hacker   **1.** A person who is proficient at using or programming a computer; a computer buff.   **2.** A person who breaks into a computer system to view, alter, or steal restricted data and programs. Some former hackers have become professional designers of sophisticated computer security systems. In this sense, *also called* **cracker**.

half duplex   A mode of transmission in which data can be sent in only one direction at a time, so that two senders must alternate their transmissions. *Also called* **local echo**. *See also* **communications protocol, full duplex**.

half-height drive   A disk drive for current IBM PC and compatible computers that is roughly half as tall as older drives, which were about three inches high. Half-height drives are now standard for IBM PC and compatible computers.

halftone   A photograph or other continuous tone image in which the gradation of tones is simulated by the relative darkness and density of tiny dots. In traditional printing, halftones are created by photographing an image through a fine screen. In desktop publishing, photographs are scanned and then converted electronically into patterns of black and white dots. Dark shades are reproduced by dense patterns of large dots, and lighter shades by less dense patterns of smaller dots. *See also* **dithering**.

hand-held   Of or relating to a computer or device small enough to be held in one hand and operated with the other. Hand-held devices are often used for maintaining daily planners and address books.

hand-held scanner   A compact, portable scanner whose scan head is moved over text or images by hand. Most software for hand-held scanners automatically combines two half-page scans into a single image. The hand-held scanner, dependent on the steadiness of your hand to accurately render an image, is generally less expensive because it doesn't require a mechanism to move the scan head or paper.

handle   **1.** In object-oriented graphics programs, one of the squares that appears around an object that you have selected. You use the handle to drag, enlarge, reduce, or reshape the selected object. *See illustration at* **Bézier curve.** **2.** A nickname used in an online chat room.

handshaking An exchange that takes place between two devices so that communications can begin. Hardware handshaking occurs over a special communications line between a computer and a peripheral, such as a serial printer, before a transfer of data takes place. In software handshaking, codes are exchanged through modems to establish a file transfer protocol for the exchange of information.

handwriting recognition The ability of a computer to accept handwritten text as input by recognizing handwritten characters and converting them into text that can be edited onscreen. Many handheld PDAs, for example, use this technology. The user writes onto the screen with a stylus using a modified alphabet system that allows each letter to be written without lifting up the stylus. However, since many people type faster than they are able to write, keyboards may remain preferable to handwriting as a means of input. *See also* **speech recognition.**

hang To halt operations in such a way that the computer system does not respond to any input devices, such as the keyboard or mouse. A hung system usually requires rebooting. *See also* **crash.**

hanging indent In word processing, an indentation of every line in a paragraph except the first. *Also called* **hanging paragraph, outdent.**

hard **1.** Existing physically as opposed to intangibly. For example, a hard copy is printed output that exists physically on paper, as opposed to existing electronically in a disk file. **2.** Permanently wired or fixed, as a hard disk, which is usually permanently installed in a computer. *See also* **soft.**

hard card An expansion card containing a hard disk drive. The hard card fits into an expansion slot instead of a disk drive bay. Hard cards are easy to install and often faster than conventional disk drives, but may have less storage capacity.

hard-coded Using an explicit number, character, or word in a software program as opposed to using a variable that is set to that value. Hard-coded software can usually be written faster, but it is usually harder to modify.

hard copy A printed version of data stored on a disk or in memory.

hard disk A rigid magnetic disk fixed within a disk drive and used for storing computer data. Hard disks offer considerably more storage

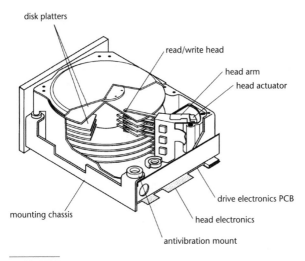

disk platters

read/write head

head arm

head actuator

drive electronics PCB

mounting chassis

head electronics

antivibration mount

HARD DISK

and quicker access to data than floppy disks do. Hard disks for many new personal computers have storage capacities of up to 16 gigabytes and have access times of about eight milliseconds. Although most hard disks are permanently installed, it is possible to buy removable hard disks in the form of disk packs or removable cartridges.

A single hard disk consists of several disk platters. Each platter has two read/write heads, one for each side of the platter, that float on a thin sheet of air just above a magnetized surface. All the read/write heads are attached to a single head arm so that they don't move independently. Each platter has the same number of tracks, and the group of tracks in corresponding locations on all the platters is called a cylinder.

There are several interface standards for connecting hard disks to computers. These include SCSI (Small Computer System Interface), SCSI-2, IDE (Integrated Drive Electronics), and Enhanced IDE interface. *Also called* **fixed disk.** *See illustration. See table at* **access time.**

hard disk drive *See* **hard drive.**

hard drive A disk drive that contains a hard disk. *Also called* **hard disk drive.**

hard hyphen In programs with hyphenation, a hyphen that you manually add to a word, as in the word user-friendly or a hyphenated last name. Soft hyphens are added automatically by the program to break words that would otherwise extend too far into the right margin. Many programs will also break a line at a hard hyphen, but if the text is later reconfigured, the hyphen will remain even if the word then fits on one line.

hard page break   *See* **forced page break**.

hard return   An instruction that moves the cursor or printer to the beginning of the next line. Since many word processing programs have word wrap, soft returns are automatically inserted at the end of each line. A hard return is inserted not by the program but by the user, typically to end a paragraph. *See also* **carriage return**.

hardware   A computer, its components, its peripherals, and other associated equipment. Hardware includes chips, disk drives, display screens, cables, expansion boards, modems, speakers, and printers—in short, any physical object that is part of a computer system. Software consists of the programs and data that control the functioning of the hardware. *See also* **firmware**.

hardware address   *See* **MAC address**.

hard-wired   **1.** Connected by electrical wires or cables.   **2.** Implemented through logic circuitry that is permanently connected within a computer and therefore not subject to change by programming.

hash   A value generated by performing a hash function on a string of data. The hash value is generally, but not always, shorter than the original value. Hashes are often used to ensure the accuracy of transmissions. The sender encrypts data and a hash of the data, and the receiver decrypts both, and also generates a hash of the data. If that hash and the decrypted hash are the same, it's almost assured that the data wasn't altered in transmission.

Hashes can also be used to create an index of values assigned to data to facilitate searches. Compilers use hashes to create symbol tables, and databases use them to store data to disk.

hash function   An operation performed on a string, such as a data record, that generates a smaller string that is used as the index designating where to store the original string in an array or table. A good hash function generates a uniform distribution across the array. The modulo operator is often used as a simple effect has function.

Hayes command set   *See* **AT command set**.

Hayes compatibility   The ability of a modem to use a standardized set of commands developed by Hayes Microcomputer Products. Most modems are Hayes compatible, as are many popular communications software programs.

HDTV   *Abbreviation of* **high-definition television**.   A television system that has twice the standard number of scanning lines per frame and therefore produces pictures with greater detail.

head   The device in a magnetic disk or tape drive that enables it to read data from and write data to the disk or tape. Inside the head are one or two small coils through which electric current can pass. When the head writes data to the disk or tape, current passes through the coils toward the magnetic fields on the disk or tape and causes the magnetic particles directly beneath the head to align either north-south or south-north. When the head reads the data, the magnetic particles directly beneath the head send a current back through the coils that is to be translated into binary code. The direction in which the particles are aligned determines whether the bit will have a value of 0 or 1. *Also called* **read/write head**. *See illustration at* **hard disk**.

head crash   The sudden dropping of the read/write head onto the surface or platter of a hard disk or, more rarely, onto a floppy disk. When this happens, the oxide coating on the disk or platter is scratched off or burned, and the data stored on that part of the disk is destroyed. If this occurs, both the disk and the head will probably have to be replaced. A head crash can be caused by rough handling of the drive, by dirt particles in the drive, or by mechanical failure. Most new hard disks station the head over an unused area on the platters when the power is shut off, making data loss less likely in the event of a crash. Programs to perform this action on older hard disks can also be purchased as part of certain utility packages. *Also called* **disk crash**.

header   **1.** In word processing, printed information, such as a title or name, placed in the top margin of a page and usually repeated on every page or every other page of the document.   **2.** Data stored at the beginning of a file or other unit of memory to provide information about a given file, program, or device or about the memory. Headers usually contain information for use by the operating system or the program the information concerns, and therefore you usually cannot access this information very easily.

heap   An area of memory set aside by a program to store program components whose size or structure vary or aren't known until the program is running. The heap is generally used for components where memory is allocated dynamically at run time. *See also* **stack**.

heat sink   A device designed to prevent the overheating of computer components, such as integrated circuits or microprocessors, by absorbing and dissipating heat, often through metal fins.

help   Information about an application that can be accessed from within the application. This information usually includes instructions on using the program correctly. It may also contain version and licensing software. On some applications, the information called up on the screen varies according to where you are in the program. *See also* **context-sensitive help**.

help key   A key that calls up help from within a program. Some keyboards have a special help key, but each individual program must designate either this or a function key as its own help key.

Hercules Graphics Adapter   A video adapter for IBM-compatible computers introduced in 1982 by Hercules Computer Technology. This system, which offered a resolution of 720 x 348 pixels on a monochrome monitor, became obsolete with the advent of color monitor standards such as VGA.

hertz   *Abbreviated* **Hz**   A unit of frequency equal to one cycle per second.

heterogeneous network   A network comprising computers and other devices from different manufacturers, possibly including IBM PC and compatible computers, Apple Macintosh systems, Unix systems, and even mainframes.

heuristic   A method of solving problems through knowledge derived from experience rather than relying on static algorithmic formulas. Heuristics are used when the computation time required for an exhaustive evaluation of all possibilities is too large to be practical, such as in a computerized chess game.

Hewlett-Packard Graphics Language   *See* **HPGL**.

hex   *Short for* **hexadecimal**.

hexadecimal   Of, relating to, or based on the number 16. The hexadecimal system uses the digits 0 through 9, and then the letters A through F to represent the decimal numbers 10 through 15. Programmers often use the hexadecimal system instead of the binary system that computers use because binary numbers can be overly long, requiring four digits for every hexadecimal digit. For example, hexadecimal C is 12 in decimal numbers and 1100 in binary. *Hexadecimal* was coined in the early 1960s to replace *sexadecimal. See table at* **binary**.

hidden file   A file that is not ordinarily shown in a directory listing. In DOS, for example, the system files IO.SYS and MSDOS.SYS are hidden so that you won't accidentally delete or corrupt them. *See also* **attribute**.

hierarchical   Being organized pyramidally into general groups that divide into more specific subgroups. Folders on Apple Macintosh computers and directories on IBM PC and compatible computers are organized hierarchically, so that at the top level there is a small number of folders or root directories and at the bottom level there is a large number of files. *See also* **directory, folder**.

High Definition Television   *See* **HDTV**.

high-density disk   A floppy disk with more memory than a double-density disk. High-density 5.25-inch disks for IBM PC and compatible computers can store up to 1.2MB of data, and 3.5-inch high-density disks can store 1.44MB. *See also* **density**.

high-end workstation   A workstation that has better performance characteristics, such as processor speed, memory, and storage, than the average computer. High-end workstations are usually used for complex scientific applications involving many variables, such as predicting the weather and modeling human behavior.

high-level language   A programming language, such as C, C++, Java, or Pascal, that uses words and some form of syntax, bringing it much closer to natural language than assembly language or machine language, and in which each instruction or statement corresponds to several instructions in machine language. High-level languages are much easier for people to learn and faster to use than assembly language. A high-level language must be translated into machine language by a compiler or an interpreter. *See also* **assembly language, low-level language**.

highlight   To make displayed text appear in reverse video or in some other manner different from normal text. Highlighting often indicates that the text is ready for some other operation, such as deletion. It is also used to draw attention to a particular segment of text.

high memory   In DOS-based computers, the range of memory between the first 640 kilobytes and 1 megabyte of extended memory. This range is sometimes referred to by the abbreviation **HMA**, which stands for **high memory area**.

high resolution   *See* **resolution**.

hints   1. A set of software instructions for improving the print and screen quality of fonts at low resolutions. Hints are especially useful when working with small point sizes.   **2.** A display that appears when a user accesses a particular area of an application screen. The display contains a brief description indicating how that area is to be used.

HMA   *See* **high memory**.

home computer   A personal computer designed and marketed specifically for use in the home rather than the office.

Home key   The key that moves the cursor to the beginning of the line, the screen, or the file.

homepage   The first screen containing information you see when you arrive at a website. The homepage usually contains general information about an organization and information about using the website.

host   A computer containing data or programs that another computer can access over a network or by modem. For example, if your computer is part of a network, the computer it connects to when you log on is the host. *See also* **server**.

HotBot   A proprietary Internet search engine and portal.

hot key   A key or sequence of keys that when pressed accesses a memory resident program, such as a calculator or a notepad. Some programs or applications let you choose your own hot keys and select the features they will access. *Also called* **shortcut key**.

hot link   A connection between two files that allows one to be updated automatically every time you update the other. For example, you may have a graph illustrating information in a database. If you establish a hot link between them, every time you make a change in the database the graph will change accordingly.

HP-compatible printer   A laser printer for IBM PC and compatible computers that understands the language developed by Hewlett-Packard for its laser printer drivers.

HPGL *Abbreviation of* **Hewlett-Packard Graphics Language**. A printer control language developed by Hewlett-Packard and used by Hewlett-Packard's original LaserJet printer. HPGL has since become a standard printer control language.

HTML *Abbreviation of* **hypertext markup language**. A coding system used on the World Wide Web to format text and set up hyperlinks between documents. HTML is built on top of SGML.

HTTP *Abbreviation of* **hypertext transfer protocol**. A client-server protocol used on the World Wide Web to govern the transfer of data.

hub A device to which many others are connected and through which they communicate. For example, in a star-topology network, the central device to which all the computers are connected is the hub.

HyperCard A hypertext program developed by Apple Computer for Macintosh computers that features cards organized into stacks and uses buttons to allow interaction. A card may have both text and graphics. You can scroll back and forth through the cards in a stack much the same way you can with a card file. HyperCard can be used to form databases, educational programs, and games, among other things. HyperCard can also be used to customize the desktop. *See also* **HyperTalk, hypertext**.

hypercube A class of network topologies used for parallel processing with several computers in which an n-dimensional hypercube features 2^n nodes, a computer at each node, and n paths from each computer to its nearest neighbor. Its name comes from the resemblance of the network topology to the outline of an n-dimensional cube.

hyperlink In a hypertext document, a cross-reference that takes you directly to another related document or to another location within the same document. Hyperlinks are indicated on screen by a font or color change or by bold or underlined type, for example. You may choose to follow a hyperlink by clicking on it or selecting it in some other specified way. Hyperlinks are used to connect documents on the Web.

hypermedia Information that is presented via computer-controlled displays so that readers can navigate easily and quickly between the distinct but integrative components or elements of text, graphics, video, and sound.

HyperTalk The programming language for HyperCard that lets you write a script to go with any object, such as a button or a field, on your card. HyperTalk is a high-level language designed for easy programming. *See also* **HyperCard**.

hypertext   A format for presenting text that is heavily cross-referenced through hyperlinks. A document presented in hypertext may have links to other text documents or to graphical images, sound, or video as well. You can read the text of a book in hypertext, for example, and use a mouse to click on words or sections to access more detailed information about a subject.

hypertext markup language   *See* **HTML**.

hypertext transfer protocol   *See* **HTTP**.

hyphenation program   A program to insert hyphens into a document to keep the right margin relatively even and keep the lines as long as possible. Many word processing programs include hyphenation. Hyphenation programs may use an internal dictionary, a set of rules, or both to determine where hyphens can be inserted. Whichever process they are using, however, they tend to make mistakes, for you are bound to use a word that their dictionary does not include and that does not follow the rules. Most hyphenation programs allow you to override their decisions as necessary.

[I]

I-beam pointer   A cursor when it has the shape of the letter I, usually indicating the place where text will be inserted on the screen as you type.

IBM PC   **1.** The first personal computer made by International Business Machines in 1981, using the Intel microprocessor 8088 and having 16 kilobytes of RAM but expandable to 64KB.   **2.** Any of the personal computers made by IBM, including the original IBM PC, the IBM PC/AT, the IBM PC/XT, the IBM PS/1 and the IBM PS/2. For the most part, all IBM PC computers can use the same software, which allows them to share files. They all use DOS, but some of the PS/2 computers can also use OS/2.

IBM PC-compatible   A computer that can run all or most of the software and use many of the peripheral devices, such as printers and keyboards, designed to run on an IBM PC.

IC   *Abbreviation of* **integrated circuit**.

icon   In graphical user interfaces, a picture on the screen that represents a specific file, directory, window, or program. By clicking on the icon, you can open the file, directory, or window, or start the program. For example, if you have a folder called *word processing,* you can click on it to see what word processing programs you have on your disk, and then click on the icon for word processing to start up that program. *See illustration at* **desktop.**

IDE   *Abbreviation of* **Integrated Drive Electronics.**   A specification for disk drives and disk drive interface circuits that locates the majority of the disk drive control circuitry on the disk drive circuit. IDE specifications feature an interface circuit for the CPU that can support up to two IDE disk drives. The interface circuit is often located directly on the motherboard. *See also* **Enhanced IDE.**

identifier   A character or string of characters that identifies a file, record, variable, or other data. A file name, for example, is the identifier for a file.

IEEE   *Abbreviation of* **Institute of Electrical and Electronic Engineers.** An international organization of engineers. The IEEE has developed and set many hardware and software standards used in the computer, telecommunications, and electronics industries.

IEEE 802   A set of standards developed by the IEEE involving the operation and management of local area networks.

illegal character   A character that your computer won't accept in a particular command or statement, usually because it is reserved for another use. For example, in Microsoft Windows file names "." always separates the name of the file from the extension, and for this reason you cannot have a file called "ETC...." In this case, the period would be an illegal character.

iMac   A Macintosh computer developed by Apple Computer and released in 1998. iMac models have from 350 to 400 megahertz G3 processor, include a 56 Kbps modem, have 6 to 13 gigabytes of disk storage, and are known for their sleek design, which includes a translucent casing available in bright colors.

image map   A graphic that is encoded with multiple HTML links. The link that you select depends on the portion of the map you click. Examples of image maps include a map of the United States in which clicking on the individual states will link you to data specific to that state, or a picture of a skeleton in which clicking on an individual bone will link you to data specific to that bone.

image processing   The use of a computer to analyze, manipulate, or modify images. Examples include changing the contrast of a picture, removing wrinkles from the photograph of a face, or adding color to a black and white image.

imagesetter   A typesetting device that produces very high-resolution output directly from a computer file, as for camera-ready copy. *Also called* **typesetter**.

ImageWriter   A dot-matrix printer developed by Apple Computer for Macintosh computers. Some models are letter-quality printers.

IMAP   *Abbreviation of* **Internet Message Access Protocol**.   A protocol developed by Stanford University for retrieving and storing incoming email. With IMAP, rather than downloading email onto your computer, the email is stored on a mail server, allowing you access to it from remote locations. The most recent version, IMAP4, is supported by most browsers and email programs. *See also* **POP**.

impact printer   A printer that prints by striking a pin or a character against an ink ribbon, which in turn hits the paper, leaving a mark. Dot-matrix printers are impact printers. Daisywheel printers are impact printers that print like a typewriter. Impact printers are rarely used now for anything but printing multipart forms. *See table at* **printer**.

import   To bring data or a file from one program or system to another. The format of the data or file you wish to import must be compatible with the program you are importing it into. Otherwise, you will have to use a conversion program. Many programs are designed to be compatible with each other in order to allow importing and exporting. For example, a graphics file in PICT of TIFF formats can be imported into most desktop publishing programs. *See also* **export**.

inclusive OR   *See* **OR**.

increment   *n.* The amount by which a variable is increased.
   v. To add one value to another; to increase in value. *See also* **decrement**.

incremental backup   A procedure for backing up only the files that you have changed or added since doing your last backup. It is good practice to do an incremental backup from your hard disk onto a floppy disk or a tape whenever you finish working at your computer. *See also* **differential backup, full backup**.

index   A list of keywords that identify a record, used for efficient data retrieval and sorting.

indexed sequential access method   *Abbreviated* ISAM.   An efficient method of data storage to and retrieval from a hard disk in which data is both stored sequentially and indexed. The index allows you to search on a field quickly instead of searching chronologically.

Industry Standard Architecture   *See* ISA.

information   Facts, such as figures, words, or graphs, especially when output by the computer into a form that conveys meaning to you and other humans. For example, when you type a document into the computer, the computer stores your document as data in machine language, but when you call up your document on the screen, your computer returns it to you as information. *See also* **data**.

information services   *See* IS.

information systems   *See* IS.

information technology   *Abbreviated* IT.   The technology involved with the transmission and storage of information, especially the development, installation, implementation, and management of computer systems and applications within companies, universities, and other organizations.

INI file   In Microsoft Windows, an application-specific file that contains information about the initial configuration of the application. For example, an INI file for a word processing program might contain information about default settings for such items as margins, line spacing, and font. The extension for INI files is *.INI*.   INI files are often used to store user defined settings. Under Windows NT most of the information previously stored in INI files has been moved to the registry.

INIT   A utility program for Apple Macintosh computers that is executed whenever you start or restart your computer. INITs sometimes cause crashes by interfering with the memory for another program. *See also* **terminate and stay resident**.

inline graphic   A graphics file embedded in a webpage or other HTML document. Since it is embedded, it doesn't need to be opened separately from the rest of the document; therefore, the webpage or HTML document is loaded more efficiently and quickly.

initialize   1. To prepare a disk or printer for use. *See also* **format**. 2. In programming, to set a variable to a starting value.

ink-jet printer A nonimpact printer that prints by spraying ink onto paper. Ink-jet printers can print with a resolution of up to 1,200 dots per inch (dpi). Work printed on an ink-jet printer looks very similar to that printed by a laser printer, but the ink from an ink-jet printer tends to be less stable. Ink-jet printers are usually somewhat slower than laser printers, but usually cost significantly less. Color ink-jet printers are reasonably priced as well. *See table at* **printer**.

input *n.* Information put into a computer for processing, such as commands typed from a keyboard, a data file read from a disk, or a bit map of a scanned image.

v. To enter data or a program into a computer. *See also* **output**.

input device A machine that enables you to put information into a computer. Keyboards, modems, mice, and scanners are examples of input devices. *See also* **output device**.

input/output *See* I/O.

Ins *Abbreviation of* **Insert key**.

insertion point **1.** In some graphical user interfaces, such as Microsoft Windows and those on Apple Macintosh computers, the cursor appearing as a blinking vertical bar to show the point where characters that you insert will go. **2.** The point so indicated by the cursor.

Insert key *Abbreviated* **Ins** A key that you press to toggle between insert mode and overwrite mode.

insert mode In word processing, a mode in which you can insert new characters without writing over what you have already typed in. *See also* **overwrite mode**.

Institute of Electrical and Electronic Engineers *See* IEEE.

instruction A command, especially one in assembly language or machine language. *See also* **statement**.

instruction set The set of available commands that a processor can recognize and perform.

integer A member of the set of positive whole numbers (1, 2, 3,...), negative whole numbers (–1, –2, –3,...), and zero (0). Integers have no decimal points. They are used in many programming languages.

integrated Combining two or more tasks into one program, especially offering word processing, spreadsheets, communications, and database management in one program.

integrated circuit *Abbreviated* **IC** **1.** An electronic circuit whose components, such as transistors and resistors, are etched or imprinted on a single slice of semiconductor material. Integrated circuits are categorized by the number of electronic components they contain per chip. Table 13 lists various types of integrated circuits. *Also called* **microchip.** **2.** *See* **chip**.

TABLE 13 Types of Integrated Circuits

Type	Electronic Components per Chip
Small-scale integration (SSI)	<100
Medium-scale integration (MSI)	100–3,000
Large-scale integration (LSI)	3,000–100,000
Very large-scale integration (VLSI)	100,000–1,000,000
Ultra large-scale integration (ULSI)	>1,000,000

Integrated Drive Electronics interface *See* **IDE interface.**

Integrated Services Digital Network *See* **ISDN.**

Intel microprocessors A group of microprocessors made by Intel. Intel microprocessors are mass-produced and used in many affordable IBM PC-compatible computers. Intel has continually evolved their product line, maintaining the ability to run programs originally developed for the first 8086 processors. See Table 14 on pages 142–3 for information about individual kinds of Intel microprocessors. *See also* **microprocessor, Motorola microprocessors, Pentium.**

interactive Being a program or a kind of processing in which you interact directly with the computer. For example, if you are running an interactive program, you enter a command and the display indicates a result. If the result is not what you wanted, you can enter a different command to obtain a different result. Computer games are interactive; you make a move, the computer responds, and you make your next move based on the response. Most processing is now interactive, but batch processing used to predominate.

interface **1.** The devices, graphics, commands, and prompts that enable a computer to communicate with any other entity, such as a printer or the user. For example, the ports and connector are the interface between a computer and a printer. The interface that lets a user communicate with the computer is called a user interface. *See also* **user interface.** **2.** *See* **port.**

interlacing A method of increasing a monitor's resolution by having the cathode-ray tube send electrons across every other line of the

TABLE 14 Intel Microprocessors

Microprocessor	Data Bus Width (bits)	Maximum Clock Speed (MHz)	Characteristics
Intel 8080	8	2	• Forerunner of current Intel line
Intel 8088	8	8	• Used in the original IBM PC/XT
Intel 8086	16	10	• 8MHz version used in IBM PS/2 models 25 and 30
Intel 80286 also known as 286	16	12.5	• Real mode (compatible with MS-DOS; limited to 1MB of memory) • Protected mode (can access up to 16MB of memory • Used in IBM PC/AT, AT&T PC 6300, Hewlett-Packard Vectra PC, and Tandy 3000 computers
Intel 386DX also known as Intel 80386DX, Intel 30386, 386	32	40	• Can access up to 4GB of memory in protected mode • Supports multitasking • Used in Compaq Deskpro 386 computers
Intel 386SX also known as Intel 80386SX	16	33	• Lower-cost alternative to the faster 386DX • Compatible with both the 80286 and the 386DX
Intel 486DX also known as Intel 80486DX, Intel 80486 i486DX, 486	32	100	• Built-in math coprocessor • Built-in memory cache • "DX2" version available: indicates the internal clock speed is twice the clock speed of the rest of the computer
			• "DX4" version available: indicates the internal clock speed is three times the clock speed of the rest of the computer
Intel 486SX also known as Intel 80486SX, i486SX	32	33	• Lower-cost alternative to the faster 486DX • Does not include the built-in math coprocessor

TABLE 14 Intel Microprocessors (continued)

Microprocessor	Data Bus Width (bits)	Maximum Clock Speed (MHz)	Characteristics
Intel Pentium family:			
—Pentium Pro	64	366	• Up to five times faster than the 486DX microprocessor
—Pentium MMX			
—Pentium II			• Can execute multiple instructions each clock cycle • Suitable for processor-intensive applications, such as spreadsheets, CAD, and multimedia
—Pentium III	64	1,000	• 70 new instructions
—Pentium III Xeon		(1 GHz)	• Designed to enhance Internet usage and multimedia • Suitable for multiprocessor servers for increased performance and redundancy
Celeron family	64	700	• Inexpensive alternative to Pentiums • Designed for workstations under $1000 • 128KB Level 2 cache • Integrated MMX technology • Reduced power consumption for longer battery life in notebooks
Itanium	64	1,000	• IA-64 processor using Explicitly Parallel Instruction Computing (EPIC) • Advanced features for parallel instruction processing • Designed to enhance data intensive applications to promote e-business

screen each time it refreshes the screen. This allows for greater resolution than would otherwise be possible at a comparable cost, but the lines sometimes flicker while they are waiting to be refreshed.

interleaving 1. A method of letting the disk drive access the sectors on a disk faster. The disk or platters spin around so rapidly that the head cannot read every sector on each round. If data is stored contiguously so that each chunk of data is physically right next to the data it should follow, the head may miss a chunk of data and have to wait a round to catch it. You can figure out how many sectors go by while the head is still reading the first one, and then format your disk drive so that it will skip that many sectors when writing data to the disk. That way, the head will be able to read an entire sequence of data on each round without missing any sectors. **2.** A similar method of speeding up access to RAM. Ordinarily, the rows of chips that make up RAM are organized so that odd and even chips follow each other in one row. On any cycle through the row, the memory will have time to read only one chip. The CPU usually needs access to odd and even chips alternately, and it can read them much more quickly than the memory. Interleaving establishes two or more rows of chips that alternate all odd with all even. The memory then sends data from each one of these alternating rows of chips to the CPU at one time.

internal cache *See* **Level 1 cache**.

internal command In MS-DOS, a command included within the operating system that is also included in the COMMAND.COM file. Examples include DIR and COPY. Since it is available in memory, you can execute an internal command by entering its name at the command prompt. *See also* **external command**.

internal font *See* **resident font**.

internal modem A modem that goes into an expansion slot inside the computer instead of sitting outside the computer in a separate box. An internal modem requires one cable to connect it to a telephone jack. *Also called* **on-board modem**.

International Organization for Standardization *See* **ISO**.

International Telecommunication Union *See* **ITU**.

Internet Message Access Protocol *See* **IMAP**.

Internet Protocol *See* **IP**.

Internet A matrix of networks that interconnects millions of supercomputers, mainframes, workstations, personal computers, laptops, and hand-held computers. The networks that make up the Internet all use a standard set of communications protocols, thus allowing computers with distinctive software and hardware to communicate. Some of the most popular features of the Internet are email, file transfer, remote login, and the World Wide Web. *See also* **World Wide Web**.

Internet Explorer A web browser developed by Microsoft Corporation.

Internet Relay Chat *See* IRC.

Internet Service Provider *See* ISP.

interpreter A program that translates each instruction in its source program into machine language when the code is executed. The interpreter is run every time the program is executed and makes the translation every time the program is executed. Thus, execution of interpreted programs is generally slower than execution of compiled programs because those are translated when the program is compiled, not when it is run. *See also* **compiler.**

interpretive Of or relating to an interpreter. An interpretive programming language does not require a program to be compiled before it is run. BASIC is an example of an interpretive programming language.

interprocess communication *Abbreviated* IPC The ability for two applications running on a computer or two networked computers to share data. Dynamic Data Exchange is an example of an interprocess communication. *See also* **Dynamic Data Exchange.**

interrupt A signal to a program that demands an immediate response. The program may stop temporarily so that another action can be performed. It may also decide to ignore the interrupt. If it stops running, it saves its current work before executing whatever instructions are interrupting it. As soon as this is over, the program resumes. Interrupts may come from the hardware or the software. *See also* **exception.**

interrupt handler A program that runs when an interrupt takes place.

interrupt request *See* IRQ.

intranet A private network that provides services similar to those found on the Internet. A typical example of an intranet would be a company's internal network that provides web servers and browsers.

inverse video *See* **reverse video.**

invoke To activate or start a software program.

I/O *Abbreviation of* **input/output.** Designating a program or device, such as a mouse or printer, that is used to input or output data rather than to process it. A modem, for example, both inputs and outputs data but does not process it.

IP *Abbreviation of* **Internet Protocol.** A protocol that specifies the way data is broken into packets and the way those packets are addressed for transmission. This protocol is generally used in conjunction with the Transmission Control Protocol. *See also* **TCP, TCP/IP.**

IP address *Abbreviation of* **Internet protocol address.** The unique numerical sequence that serves as an identifier for an Internet server. An IP address appears as a series of numbers separated by dots or periods, as 192.135.174.1.

IPC *Abbreviation of* **interprocess communication.**

IRC *Abbreviation of* **Internet Relay Chat.** A network of Internet servers worldwide through which individual users can hold real-time online conversations. In an IRC, users can communicate with each other as part of a group discussion on any of a number of specified topics.

IRMA board An expansion board for Apple Macintosh computers and IBM PC and compatible computers that lets them emulate terminals. This means that if you have an IRMA board, you can connect your computer to a mainframe for certain tasks while still using it as a personal computer for others.

IRQ *Abbreviation of* **interrupt request.** A hardware line by which a device transmits an interrupt to the CPU. Each device attached to the computer has its own IRQ, and each IRQ has a number. The lower the number, the higher the ranking over other devices. When you add a new peripheral and it tries to use an IRQ that is assigned to another device, you will have to reconfigure the IRQ settings.

IS *Abbreviation of* **information services** *or* **information systems.** The department of an organization that is responsible for computer systems and data management.

ISA *Abbreviation of* **Industry Standard Architecture.** The bus architecture used for IBM PC/XT computers and IBM PC/AT computers. The ISA bus was originally created for the IBM PC/XT and had an 8-bit data path. The version created for the IBM PC/AT, known as the AT bus, has a 16-bit data path but remains downward compatible with the older version. The AT bus has become the industry standard because of the large number of peripherals and expansion boards designed to connect to it. *See also* **EISA, Micro Channel Architecture.** *See table at* **bus.**

ISAM *Abbreviation of* **indexed sequential access method.**

ISAPI A CGI-like standard developed by Microsoft that defines the methods for passing arguments and running programs on a web server. The ISAPI was developed for Microsoft Internet Information Server.

ISDN   *Abbreviation of* **Integrated Services Digital Network.**   A standard for transmitting digital data over standard telephone lines. In order to transmit digital data over a normal, analog telephone circuit, a modem must convert the digital signal into an analog one. Another modem must undo the translation on the other end. ISDN allows digital data to be transferred over the line without such conversion. This, in turn, allows transfer speeds high enough to carry real-time video and voice as well as other data.

In North America, an ISDN circuit is divided into B (or bearer) channels (2 for copper phone wires, 23 for fiber optic lines) carrying voice and data and a single D (or data) channel that carries control information. The B channels, running at 64 kilobits per second each, can be combined to yield a throughput of 128 kilobits per second for standard phone lines.

Availability of ISDN in the United States is currently limited to those areas where the local phone company has installed new equipment in its central offices, but these areas are growing. Incompatibilities between different vendors' interpretations of the standard are being resolved, and the cost of required hardware is falling. Since the monthly cost for an ISDN line is comparable to that for an analog line, it is becoming the connection method of choice for telecommuting. *See also* **circuit switching, packet switching.**

ISO   An organization, the International Organization for Standardization, that sets standards in many businesses and technologies, including computing and communications. The term ISO is not an abbreviation, but instead derives from the Greek word *isos*, meaning *equal.*

ISO Latin 1   A standard character set developed by the ISO, containing the characters found in most Western European languages. It is HTML's and HTTP's default character set.

ISP   *Abbreviation of* **Internet Service Provider.**   An organization that provides other organizations or individuals with access to the Internet. America Online and Prodigy are examples of ISPs.

IT   *Abbreviation of* **information technology.**

italic   A font style in which characters slant to the right. Italic is based on a Renaissance script. *See illustration at* **font family.**

Itanium   A microprocessor developed by Intel that has advanced features for parallel instruction processing. *See table at* **Intel microprocessor.**

iteration   The act of reprocessing one or more statements or instructions in a loop until a given condition is true. *See also* **loop.**

ITU   *Abbreviation of* the **International Telecommunications Union.** An international organization and United Nations agency that sets standard for the telecommunications industry.

[J]

jaggies   In computer graphics, jagged distortions that appear where there should be smooth curves or diagonals. *See also* **aliasing.** *See illustration at* **antialiasing.**

Java   An object-oriented programming language developed by Sun Microsystems. Java is similar to C++ without some of the more complex features of C++. Java is designed to run over the Internet, and it provides a secure environment for writing and executing World Wide Web applications. One of the major advantages of Java is that it is platform-independent. A program written in Java, known as an applet, can be run on almost any computer.

JavaBean   An object created according to specifications developed by Sun Microsystems for use in Java. You can create a Java application by combining JavaBeans. JavaBeans are similar to ActiveX components, except that they can run on any platform.

Java Database Connectivity   *Abbreviated* **JDBC**   An application program interface developed by JavaSoft, a subsidiary of Sun Microsystems, that enables Java programs to retrieve data from SQL-compliant databases.

JavaScript   A scripting language developed by Sun Microsystems that allows lines of code to be inserted into an HTML file. JavaScript has a simplified C-like syntax.

Jaz   A disk drive developed by Iomega that is capable of transferring data at a rate of 330 megabytes per second to a removable 1GB disk. The Jaz drive is based on standard hard disk technology, and can be installed either internally or externally using either a SCSI or parallel port.

JDBC   *Abbreviation of* **Java Database Connectivity**.

job   A specified action or group of actions that the computer carries out as a single unit. For example, when an IBM PC or compatible computer prints a document, the process is considered a print job.

join   A procedure used in a relational database to extract information from two separate database tables into a single query. For example, if you have one database with the phone numbers and addresses of all students and another with the names of all students in each class, you can do a join to yield the names and addresses for all students in a particular class.

Joint Photographic Experts Group   *See* **JPEG**.

joystick   A pointing device consisting of a long stick attached to a plastic base. When the stick is moved in any direction, a pointer on the screen will move in the same direction. A joystick usually comes with control buttons that are set by the program to activate certain commands in much the same way control characters are. The joystick is a popular user control device for computer games and some CAD/CAM systems.

JPEG   *Abbreviation of* **Joint Photographic Experts Group**.   The standard algorithm for image compression. JPEG can compress color or black-and-white digital images using lossy compression.

Jscript   The version of JavaScript developed by Microsoft Corporation, used in the Microsoft Internet Explorer browser. It is not fully compatible with Javascript.

jumper   A plug consisting of two or three metal slots, usually enclosed in a small plastic box, and designed to fit over pins in a circuit board to close an electric circuit. You can configure your circuit board by selecting which circuits to close and putting jumpers over them.

justification   The adjustment of spacing within a document so that lines end evenly at a straight margin. Newspaper articles and other typeset copy, for example, are usually justified both left and right, so that both the left and right margins of each column are even. Copy that is typed using a typewriter, on the other hand, is usually justified only at the left, so that the left margin is even but the right margin is uneven, or ragged.

[K]

K *Abbreviation of* **kilobyte.**

Kb *Abbreviation of* **kilobit.**

KB *Abbreviation of* **kilobyte.**

Kbps *Abbreviation of* **kilobits per second.**

Kermit In telecommunications, an asynchronous protocol developed to govern the transfer of files between computers by modem. Kermit works by transferring groups of up to 96 bytes at a time and then checking each group for transmission errors. Kermit translates all control characters into ASCII characters. Because Kermit is known for accuracy, it is used by many modems and communications programs. Super Kermit is a newer and faster version of Kermit that uses full duplex transmission. *See also* **Xmodem, Ymodem, Zmodem.** *See table at* **communications protocol.**

kernel An operating system's core that interacts directly with the hardware. It usually processes tasks unseen by the user. These tasks may include memory management, allocation of resources, and interrupt response.

kerning The adjustment of space between pairs of characters, usually in display type, so that the overall spacing of the letters appears even. Kerning makes certain combinations of letters, such as *WA, VA, TA, YA,* and *MW,* look better. Some page layout programs have an automatic kerning feature. Manual kerning can be performed with most page layout programs and some word processing programs. *See illustration.*

WAVY   WAVY

without kerning   with kerning

KERNING

key *n.* A button on a keyboard that is pressed to enter data or a command.

v. To enter data into a computer by pressing buttons on the keyboard.

keyboard A set of keys arranged as on a typewriter that is the principal input device for most computers. All keyboards include a set of alphanumeric keys, usually in the standard layout of conventional typewriters. Most also have a numeric keypad to one side. All keyboards include a number of keys for special characters. These special keys include the Control, Alt, and Shift keys on keyboards for IBM PC and compatible computers and the Command, Option, and Shift keys on Apple Macintosh keyboards. These keys are used to change the function of other keys hit at the same time. Some other special keys are the function keys, which have different functions depending on which program is running, and the Arrow keys, which enable you to move the cursor right, left, up, or down.

Keyboards are not standardized, although many manufacturers imitate the IBM PC keyboards. All Macintosh keyboards are called ADB keyboards because they connect to the Apple Desktop Bus (ADB). Because of repetitive motion and stress-injury problems that many people develop as a result of typing on a keyboard, keyboards are often designed to focus on safety features such as built-in wrist rests and adjustable height for each hand. *See also* **Dvorak keyboard, QWERTY keyboard**.

keyboard buffer   A memory buffer for storing keystrokes until the CPU can act on them, allowing fast typists to continue typing even if the characters don't appear immediately on the screen.

keyboard template   A piece of paper or plastic that is placed on top of or next to keys, especially function keys, with written information as to what each key does in a particular program.

keypad   *See* **numeric keypad**.

keystroke   An instance of pressing a key. Some programs require more keystrokes than others to do the same tasks, so that you have to press more keys to get the same result.

keyword   **1.** In programming, a reserved word that is built into the syntax of the programming language.   **2.** In word processing programs and database management systems, a word, code, or phrase that identifies a record or document and can be used in sorting or searching.

KHz or **kHz**   *Abbreviation of* **kilohertz**.

kill   **1.** To stop or end a process.   **2.** To erase or delete a file permanently.

killfile   A file containing lists of character strings, usually the names of authors or titles of threads, associated with Usenet news articles that you don't want to read. When you open a Usenet newsgroup, it will automatically run the killfile you've created for that newsgroup, deleting posts that match the items you've placed in the killfile. This is a handy method of avoiding people or topics that you don't want to deal with.

killer app An application that becomes so popular that it forces out the competition or causes the competition to conform to it.

kilo- *Abbreviated* **k, K** **1.** A prefix indicating 1,000 (10^3), as in *kilohertz*. This is also the sense in which *kilo-* is generally used in terms of data transmission rates, where a bit is a signal pulse and is counted in the decimal system, which is based on multiples of ten. Some people abbreviate this decimal *kilo-* with a lowercase *k* to avoid confusion with the binary *kilo-,* which they abbreviate with an uppercase *K.* **2.** A prefix indicating 1,024 (2^{10}), as in *kilobyte*. This is the sense in which *kilo-* is generally used in terms of data storage capacity, which, due to the binary nature of bits, is based on powers of two. Some people abbreviate this binary *kilo-* with an uppercase *K* to avoid confusion with the decimal *kilo-,* which they abbreviate with a lowercase *k.*

kilobit *Abbreviated* **Kb** One thousand (1,000) bits, used as a unit for expressing the rate of data transmission per unit of time (usually one second). In highly techincal contexts involving data storage capacity, it can refer to 1,024 (2^{10}) bits.

kilobyte *Abbreviated* **K, KB** A unit of measurement of computer memory or data storage capacity, equal to 1,024 (2^{10}) bytes. Informally, the term is sometimes used to refer to one thousand (1,000) bytes.

kilohertz *Abbreviated* **KHz** *or* **kHz** A unit of frequency equal to 1,000 hertz.

kludge A workable but poorly designed, often makeshift piece of hardware or software. Kludges are patched together from mismatched elements or elements designed for other uses. A kludge offers a sloppy or inelegant solution to a problem.

[L]

L1 cache *See* **Level 1 cache.**

L2 cache *See* **Level 2 cache.**

label **1.** Generally, a name identifying the contents of memory or of a file, tape, disk, or record. **2.** In data storage, one character or a sequence of characters by which the operating system identifies a floppy disk, tape, or part of a hard disk, such as the name of a volume. Each operating system has its own restrictions on labels, typically limiting the number or kinds of characters allowed.   **3.** In spreadsheets, descriptive text or a heading, such as *Net Income,* that is placed in a cell.   **4.** In programming, a name identifying a section of a program, such as a particular routine or line of code.   **5.** A small piece of paper with an adhesive backing that can be written on and attached to a floppy disk or piece of equipment to identify it.

LAN   *Abbreviation of* **local area network**.

landscape   Of or relating to a mode in which a page is oriented so that it is wider than it is tall. Spreadsheets are typically in landscape mode. Many word processing and page layout programs can also display or print text in this mode. Not all printers, however, are capable of printing in landscape mode. *See illustration. See also* **portrait**.

landscape   portrait

LANDSCAPE Landscape and portrait orientations

language   A system for communicating thoughts and feelings through the use of voice sounds and written symbols representing these sounds in organized combinations and patterns. Each sound or combination of sounds, along with its written representation, that communicates a meaning is called a word. All the words in a language constitute its vocabulary. The language's semantics define the meanings of words and word combinations. The language's syntax comprises the rules whereby words are combined into grammatical sentences.

In computer science, such human languages are called natural languages. We cannot yet communicate efficiently with computers using natural languages, although research in this area continues to show promise. Instead, we must use specially constructed computer languages. Such languages, in order of increasing closeness to natural languages, include machine languages, programming languages, and fourth-generation languages. *See also* **artificial intelligence, translation software**.

laptop   A portable computer that fits on one's lap. A laptop usually weighs between 3 and 8 pounds, and when folded shut is about the size of a textbook. Laptops can be plugged in or run on batteries, although the batteries must be recharged every few hours.

Laptop computers use a thin, lightweight display screen called a flat-panel display, rather than the cathode-ray tube technology of larger personal computers. Laptop displays vary widely in quality. Typically, their display screens show fewer lines than displays on larger computers and can be difficult to read in bright light. Laptops are self-contained units, having their own central processing units, memory, and disk drives. *See also* **notebook**.

large-scale integration   *Abbreviated* **LSI**   The technology for placing up to 100,000 electronic components on a single integrated circuit. *See table at* **integrated circuit**.

laser font   *See* **outline font**.

laser printer   A nonimpact printer that uses a laser to produce an image on a rotating drum before transferring the image to paper. Signals, in the form of commands in a page description language, are sent from the operating system or application software to control the laser beam, rapidly turning the beam on and off and moving it across the drum. The drum is coated with an electrically charged film. Where each point of light hits the drum, the charge is reversed from negative to positive or from positive to negative, depending on the laser printer's design. As the drum rotates, it comes into contact with a bin of toner, a black powder charged oppositely to the charges created by the laser on the drum. Because oppositely charged static particles attract each other, the toner sticks to the drum in a pattern of black dots. Meanwhile, gears and rollers send a sheet of paper past an electrically charged wire, charging the paper, which is then pressed against the drum. The toner is electrostatically transferred to the paper. Finally, heat and pressure fuse the toner to the paper by melting and pressing a wax contained in the toner. Some printers use arrays of light-emitting diodes or liquid-crystal displays rather than a laser to charge the drum, but otherwise they work like a laser printer.

Regarding page description languages, two are de facto standards for laser printers. Hewlett-Packard's PCL (Printer Control Language) is the mainstay in IBM PC and compatible computers. PostScript, developed by Adobe Systems, is the standard for Apple Macintosh computer printers.

Laser printers transfer the page as a whole to the drum, treating a page and the text it contains as one large graphic image. For this reason, they are sometimes referred to as *page printers*. Laser printers are relatively fast and quiet and produce sharp, high-quality text and graphics.

Laser printers come with one or more fonts built into their hardware. These are called resident fonts, or internal or built-in fonts. You are not limited to your laser printer's resident fonts, however. You can print with a virtually unlimited number of fonts by downloading fonts into your laser printer or by inserting font cartridges, ROM boards hardwired with one or more fonts.

All laser printers contain some RAM; often the amount can be increased by adding memory cards. Fonts can be downloaded from disk to the printer's RAM. A downloaded font is called a soft font. Hard fonts are built into font cartridges, which are inserted into slots in the laser printer. *See table at* **printer**.

LaserWriter   A line of laser printers developed by Apple Computers used with Macintosh computers.

latency   **1.** In a network, the amount of time that elapses in the transmission of a packet from its source to its destination.   **2.** In disk drives, the amount of time that elapses in the rotation of the proper disk sector to a position under the read/write head.

LaTeX   A page description language having intuitive commands that allow you to concentrate on content in contrast to appearance when typesetting.

launch   To start a program.

LAWN   *Abbreviation of* **local area wireless network**.

layer   In a hierarchical architecture, a set of functions that have a common purpose and a well-defined interface to functions above and below them in the hierarchy. For example, ISO specifies a seven-layer communications protocol in which the lowest layer defines how the physical connections are made between devices, and the higher layers define how applications can use the protocol to communicate. As long as a particular layer meets its defined functionality and interface, you can swap different implementations of the same layer without affecting the performance of the system.

layout   **1.** In desktop publishing and word processing, the art or process of arranging text and graphics on a page. Layout covers the overall design of a page, including elements such as page and type size, typeface, and the placement of graphics, titles, and page numbers. *See also* **page layout program, WYSIWYG.   2.** In database management systems, the arrangement of fields, leaders, and other elements when information is displayed in a report.

LCD   *Abbreviation of* **liquid-crystal display.**

LCD printer   *Abbreviation of* **liquid crystal display printer.**

leader   A row of dots or sometimes dashes leading the eye across the page, as from an index or table of contents entry to a page number. Most word processing programs allow you to define tab stops that automatically insert leaders when you press the Tab key.

leading   The vertical spacing between lines of text, measured in points. The measure includes the size of the font, so that 8-point type with 2-point spacing between lines is a leading of 10 points. Most word processing and all desktop publishing applications allow you to set the leading. *Also called* **line spacing.**

leading zero   In the display of numbers, a zero that is added as a placeholder to make a number fill up a field with a required amount of characters. For example, in 003.14159, the initial two zeroes are both leading zeroes.

leaf   An element at the lowest level of a hierarchical tree structure. Leaves have no other elements branching from them. A file in a hierarchical file system is a leaf; a directory is a node. *See also* **node.**

leased line   A phone line that is leased from a telecommunications company for dedicated use between two points. *See also* **dedicated link.**

least significant bit   In a byte sequence, the bit having the least amount of significance, usually the rightmost bit of a binary number.

least significant character   In a string, the character having the least amount of significance, usually the rightmost character.

least significant digit   In a number, the digit having the least amount of significance, usually the rightmost digit.

LED   *Abbreviation of* **light-emitting diode.**

LED printer *Abbreviation of* **light-emitting diode printer**.

left justify To align text so that each line is flush against the left margin, but leaving the right margin ragged, or uneven.

legacy Of or relating to data produced or manipulated by an earlier or obsolete version software or hardware that has since been upgraded or discontinued.

legacy application 1. Software designed with older technology that is hard to maintain due to obsolete design or older coding practices. 2. An existing application that is being replaced by a completely new system rather than a version upgrade, especially a proprietary system.

legend An explanatory table or list of the symbols appearing on a map or chart.

letter-quality *Abbreviated* **LQ** Of or producing printed characters similar in clarity to those produced by a conventional typewriter. Computer printers are classified according to those that produce letter-quality type, such as laser and ink-jet printers, and those that do not, such as most dot-matrix printers. Typically, dot-matrix printers produce near-letter quality type and draft-quality type; that is, type suitable for printing drafts of documents. In reality, laser printers produce type that is significantly better than that produced by typewriters, making the term *letter-quality* a misnomer. *See illustration.*

J J J

LETTER-QUALITY   Common type qualities

Level 1 cache *Abbreviated* **L1 cache** Cache memory that is built into the microprocessor's circuitry, as opposed to that of the motherboard. *Also called* **internal cache, primary cache**.

Level 2 cache *Abbreviated* **L2 cache** The second level of cache memory in a microprocessor, which is larger and slower than the primary cache but smaller and faster than main memory.

lex A software tool for parsing text according to specified rules.

lexicographic sort A sort, such as a dictionary sort, for which the user may define a sequence for the items being sorted. The user is thus not limited to the ordering implied by the character-encoding system used by the operating system. *See also* **dictionary sort**.

LF   *Abbreviation of* **line feed**.

library   **1.** In programming, a collection of standard routines or subroutines, each performing a specific task that a program can use. Libraries save time because a programmer can insert a library routine into a program without rewriting the instructions each time they are needed. Library routines do not have to be explicitly linked to every program that uses them. The linker automatically checks libraries for routines that it does not find elsewhere. *See also* **DLL**. **2.** A collection of information, as in data files.

license   A legal agreement between the developer and the user of software that specifies the conditions for distributing, storing, and using that software.

light-emitting diode   *Abbreviated* **LED**   An electronic semiconductor device that emits light when an electric current passes through it. LEDs need more power than liquid-crystal displays, and they are not usually used for display screens. They are used for indicator lights, as on the front of a disk drive, and in some printers they serve the same function as a laser beam in a laser printer.

light-emitting diode printer   *Abbreviated* **LED printer**.   A printer that produces high-quality text and images.   Like a laser printer, toner is electrostatically fused to the paper, but instead of using a laser, the source of light is a panel of light-emitting diodes.

light pen   A light-sensitive input device shaped like a pen, used to select objects on a video display screen. Light pens are used for tasks that involve a lot of updating, such as tracking inventory or filling out forms, since the user can move a light pen quickly and accurately across the screen. *Also called* **light stylus**.

line   **1.** A wire or system of wires connecting communications systems. **2.** A string of characters in a horizontal row.   **3.** A single statement in a computer program.

line art   An illustration consisting solely of lines, without shading. An example of line art is the illustration at **floppy disk**.

line editor   A simple program for editing text in which you can only edit or write one line at a time. Most line editors are obsolete.

line feed   Abbreviated **LF**   **1.** On a display screen, a signal that advances the cursor to the same position one line below. The Enter or

Return key, which moves the cursor to the beginning of the following line, uses both the line feed and carriage return signals.   **2.** A signal that tells a printer to advance the paper one line.

line noise   Unwanted electronic signals on a phone line that interfere with data transfers. Static is an example of line noise.

line printer   A high-speed impact printer, primarily used in data processing, that prints an entire line of type as a unit. The line printer differs from the dot-matrix printer, which prints each character individually, and the laser printer, which prints each page as a unit. Line printers usually serve more than one user and tend to be fast (up to 3,000 lines per minute) and loud. *See table at* **printer**.

line spacing   *See* **leading**.

link   *v.*   **1.** To connect two files in such a way that a change in the data of one file is reflected in the other. For instance, a customer database could be linked to an inventory database so that entering a sale of an item into the customer database would automatically update the inventory database. In some cases, linked files do not have to be from the same program; a spreadsheet can be linked to a word processing document, and a change in the spreadsheet will then affect the corresponding part of the document. Although they are connected, the two files remain separate entities. A connection between two documents that automatically makes changes is sometimes known as a hot link. A cold link needs to be activated with a command to update. *See also* **Dynamic Data Exchange, OLE.**   **2.** To insert a link in a webpage.   **3.** In programming, to bring together all the modules and libraries and build an executable file. Linking is one of the final stages in the assembly of a software program.

n.   **1.** A connection between computers, devices, programs, or files over which data is transmitted.   **2.** *See* **hyperlink.**   **3.** *See* **hot link.**

linker   An executable program that joins modules (small blocks of code) so that data can be passed between them. Modules can be added or replaced individually. *See also* **compile, library**.

Linux   A version of the Unix operating system developed by Linus Torvalds and Gnu. Unlike other versions of Unix, Linux and its source code is offered free of charge. It can run on many hardware platforms. *See also* **operating system, Unix**.

liquid-crystal display   *Abbreviated* LCD   A low-power flat-panel display used in many laptop computers and also in devices such as calculators and digital watches. Most LCDs in laptops are monochrome, with blue or dark gray images on a light gray background, and use backlighting to enhance image contrast.

An LCD is made of liquid crystals sandwiched between two layers of glass filters. Liquid crystals are rod-shaped molecules that flow like a liquid but have a crystalline order in their arrangement. Electric currents can be used to control the alignment of the molecules and therefore their transmission of light through the filters. Cells of liquid crystals are arranged in an array to form pixels, each cell acting as a tiny electronically controlled shutter.

There are two basic ways to produce color LCDs. Active-matrix technology produces exceptionally sharp color images but is very expensive. Passive-matrix technologies are cheaper but are difficult to read at an angle and produce washed-out color.

liquid-crystal display printer   A high-quality printer that resembles a laser printer. Instead of using a laser to create images on the print drum, it shines a light beam through a liquid-crystal panel. Individual pixels in the panel act as tiny shutters, blocking or transmitting the light to form a dot pattern on the drum. *See table at* **printer**. *Also called* **liquid-crystal shutter printer**.

LISP   *Abbreviation of* **list processor**.   A programming language that is widely used in artificial intelligence research. Developed in the 1960s by John McCarthy at MIT, LISP is made up of expressions that constitute lists of instructions to the computer. These lists establish relationships between symbolic values, and the computer performs computations based on those relationships. Since each list yields a value that can be used in other lists, there is no distinction between data and instructions within a LISP program.

list   An ordered series of data with an organizational structure that allows data to be input or deleted in any order.

listing   A printout of a program in source code.

list processor   *See* **LISP**.

LISTSERV   A mailing list manager owned by L-Soft International, used for distribution of email among the list's members. It was originally developed for BITNET, and versions are available for Unix and Microsoft Windows platforms.

list server   A system that maintains mail distribution lists related to specific subjects. By subscribing to a particular list server, a user will get email every time someone sends a message to that list. Similarly, anyone can send email to the whole group by sending a message to that particular list.

literal   A letter or symbol that stands for itself as opposed to a feature, function, or entity associated with it in a programming language. For example, $ can be a symbol that refers to the end of a line, but as a literal, it is a dollar sign.

lithium-ion battery   A rechargeable battery for portable computers. Although more expensive than NiCad and NiMH batteries, it has greater storage capacity, is lighter, and is free of poisonous metals such as lead and mercury.

load   *v.*   **1.** To transfer a program from a storage device into a computer's memory. Before a program on a disk can be executed, it must be loaded into the computer's RAM (random-access memory).   **2.** To transfer data into a computer's memory for processing.   **3.** To mount an external storage device, such as a tape, floppy disk, or CD into its drive.   **4.** To import a large amount of data into a database.

n. An amount of work that a computer undertakes at one time.

loader   A computer program that transfers data from offline memory into internal storage.

local area network   *Abbreviated* **LAN**   A network that links together computers and peripherals within a limited area, such as a building or group of buildings. Each computer or device in LAN is known as a node. The computers in a LAN have independent CPUs (central processing units), but they are able to exchange data and files with each other and to share such resources as laser printers.

The three principal LAN organizing structures, called topologies, are bus, ring, and star. In a bus topology, all computers and other devices are connected to a central cable. In a ring topology, the computers are joined in a loop, so that a message from one passes through each node until it reaches its proper destination. In a star topology, all nodes are connected to one central computer, known as the hub.

Additionally, LANs are organized as either peer-to-peer networks, in which all computers are similarly equipped and communicate directly with one another, or client/server networks, in which a central computer, the server, provides data and controls communication between all nodes.

Every LAN has a protocol that governs the exchange of data between nodes, and a network operating system (NOS), software that allows communication between devices to take place. *See also* **AppleTalk, Ethernet**.

local area wireless network   *Abbreviated* **LAWN**   A local area network that uses high-frequency radio waves or infrared beams to link together computers and other devices.

local bus   An expansion bus that transmits data many times faster than the ISA bus found in most personal computers. Some new personal computers have both a local bus and an ISA or EISA bus for connecting older peripherals.

local echo   *See* **half duplex**.

lock   **1.** In networking and other multi-user systems, to make a file or other unit of data inaccessible. The operating system locks a file or database record after one user has begun to work on it so that subsequent users cannot work on it at the same time. A locked file can usually be viewed by other users, but they can not modify it until it is unlocked. This is also known as write locking. Another type of locking, read locking, prevents other users from reading the data until the change is completed. This is useful when changing a large amount of data, such as when loading data from tape.   **2.** To write-protect a floppy disk.

log   **1.** A log file.   **2.** *Abbreviation of* **logarithm**.

logarithm   *Abbreviated* **log**   The power to which a base, such as 10, must be raised to produce a given number. If $n^x = a$, the logarithm of a, with n as the base, is x; symbolically, $\log_n a = x$. For example, $10^3 = 1,000$; therefore, $\log_{10} 1,000 = 3$. The common logarithm (base 10), the natural logarithm (base e), and the binary logarithm (base 2) are used most often. Common and natural logarithms are often used in programming.

log   file A file that lists the activities of a machine or program or users on a computer system.

logic   The nonarithmetic operations performed by a computer — for example, sorting, comparing, and matching — that involve decisions with only one of two possible outcomes, such as yes/no or true/false.

logical   Of or relating to the way the user perceives the organization of an element such as a database or a file. To the user, a file may be a discrete unit, but it is likely that the file is stored in pieces scattered throughout a computer's memory or a disk. The term physical is used when referring to the actual location and structure of an element.

logical operator   *See* **Boolean operator.**

logic gate   A mechanical, optical, or electronic system that performs a logical operation on an input signal. Logic gates are a component of microchips, allowing the computer to execute instructions.

log in   *See* **log on.**

login name   *See* **username.**

log off   *See* **log out.**

log on   To identify yourself to a multiuser computer system so that you can begin working on it. Logging on typically consists of giving your username and a password; it protects a network or system from unauthorized users and allows the network or system to keep track of usage time.

log out   To end a session with a multiuser computer system. Logging off signals the system that you have finished communicating with it.

look-and-feel   The general appearance and functioning of the user interface of a software product. Programs with the same look-and-feel appear essentially the same on-screen, and the user who knows one such program can run the others without learning new commands and menus. The look-and-feel of software, as opposed to its internal structure, has been a consideration in several legal cases concerning software copyright violations.

lookup   A function in which the computer consults a previously assembled table of values until a specified value is found. This table, known as the lookup table, typically contains a series of values that are frequently needed. For example, a lookup table may contain the sales tax rates for different cities and states.

loop   In programming, a sequence of instructions that repeats either a specified number of times or until a particular condition prevails.

lossless compression   Data compression that can be achieved with no loss of information.

lossy compression   Data compression with some loss of information. Lossy compression can occur, for example, when data is prepared for transmission over a relatively small bandwidth. A common form of data that undergoes lossy compression is audio and video data, and the data that is lost is usually fine-resolution data whose absence is not noticeable.

lowercase   Of, related to, or being a noncapitalized letter. *See also* **case-sensitive.**

low-level language A computer language, such as an assembly language or machine language, in which each line of code is an individual instruction that can be directly carried out by the CPU (central processing unit). A high-level language, on the other hand, often combines several CPU instructions in each statement and is closer to human language.

low-resolution *See* **resolution**.

LPT Originally an abbreviation for *line printer terminal,* it is now the logical device name that an operating system uses to identify a printer.

LQ *Abbreviation of* **letter-quality**.

LSI *Abbreviation of* **large-scale integration**.

lurk To read but not participate in ongoing discussions on a newsgroup or mailing list or in a chatroom. Proper netiquette dictates that newcomers to a newsgroup lurk for a while to get an understanding of the people and issues to avoid sending unwanted, irrelevant, or redundant messages.

Lycos A proprietary Internet search engine and portal.

LYNX A web browser that displays text but not graphics for Unix platforms.

[M]

m *Abbreviation of* **milli-**.

M *Abbreviation of* **mega-**.

Mac The Apple Macintosh computer. *See* **Macintosh**.

MAC Address *Abbreviation for* **Media Access Control address**. The address of the network card of the machine at the hardware level. This address is six bytes and is issued by the hardware manufacturer. *Also known as* **hardware address**.

machine address *See* **absolute address**.

machine code *See* **machine language**.

machine-dependent Of or relating to software that can be used only with a particular model of computer. Machine-dependent software often makes optimal use of the special features in a specific piece of hardware.

machine-independent Of or relating to software that can be used with a variety of computers.

machine language The language used and understood by the CPU (central processing unit) of a computer. Each different type of CPU has its own machine language. Each instruction and piece of data in machine language is made up of a series of 0s and 1s, representing bits. Machine language is the lowest-level language, and programs in high-level languages must be converted to machine language before they can be run or stored by a computer. Such a conversion is made by a compiler, which translates the entire program into machine language, or an interpreter, which translates and executes each instruction before moving on to the next. *Also called* **machine code**.

machine-readable In a form that can be fed directly into a computer, as data on a disk. For example, with technology such as optical character recognition, typed documents are machine-readable to a properly equipped computer.

Macintosh A popular line of personal computers introduced in 1984 by Apple Computer. Macintosh computers were the first to have a graphical user interface (GUI) that employs windows, icons, and onscreen menus. A mouse can be used to control a pointer on the screen that chooses commands, selects files, and executes programs. The popularity of Macintosh computers is due in part to this interface, which is often regarded as more intuitive than command-driven interfaces.

   Since the GUI is built into the operating system of Macintosh computers, there is consistency in the look and operation of different Macintosh software applications. Other GUIs, such as Microsoft Windows, developed for the IBM operating environment, and Gnome for the Linux environment, have incorporated many of the visual tools of the Macintosh. Macintosh devices and software are usually incompatible with IBM PC and compatible computers. However, with the development of USB devices, this conflict has been considerably reduced.

MacOs Apple Computer's name for the Macintosh operating system.

macro A set of stored commands that are executed when a simple key combination is pressed. Macros are helpful when you frequently perform a task that requires several commands. For example, a macro can be used to get into a particular file without going through several menus or directories. Macros can also be used as glossaries, to record and output a series of frequently used keystrokes, such as a letter heading. Operating systems and many applications allow the user to create personal macros. Add-in programs are available for applications without macro capabilities. Macros can be vulnerable to viruses because of the way they work with programs.

macro virus   A computer virus that is spread by being embedded in a document file within an application. If you open the document, the macro virus is automatically run, infecting your computer. Depending on your mail reader, it can also send copies out to addresses in your address book.

magnetic disk   *See* **disk**.

magnetic-ink character recognition   *Abbreviated* **MICR**   A technique for making printed characters machine-readable by printing with ink containing a magnetic powder. A character-recognition device compares the magnetic pattern produced by a character with patterns produced by known shapes. The matched character is then converted into digital information. MICR differs from optical character recognition, in which an optical scanner recognizes characters by detecting patterns of light and dark. MICR systems are used by banks to read the codes printed along the bottom edge of checks.

magnetic media   Any type of mass storage that holds information magnetically. Floppy disks and tapes are magnetic media.

magnetic tape   *See* **tape**.

magneto-optical disk *also* **magneto-optical disc**   A high-density erasable disk that is encoded by magnetically aligning crystals that have been heated in the focus of an intense laser. The alignment of the crystals is stable at room temperature, and the disk is read by using the polarization of a reflected laser beam to determine this alignment. The focus of the laser beam can be made small, which allows a high density of data to be stored.

mail   *See* **email**.

mail bomb   To send someone an extremely large amount of email, often enough to crash their mail system. Mail bombing is one of several forms of online harassment.

mailing list   A service that sends an email sent to a mail server to everyone who is subscribed to that list. Generally mailing lists are focused around a particular topic or social group. If a group of people wish to correspond, it is efficient to set up a mailing list, because subscribers can send one message to a central address instead of to each member.

mail merge   A feature in many word processing programs that creates "personalized" form letters. The main document contains the text of the form letter, along with codes or symbols that indicate where personalized information (such as names and addresses) goes. This information is usually contained in a separate text file whose fields correspond to the codes or symbols in the form letter. Some word processors allow you to use Boolean operators, such as AND or OR, to specify conditions for merging information. *Also called* **merge**.

mainframe   A large, powerful computer, capable of serving hundreds of connected terminals and frequently used for large jobs, such as printing invoices. Mainframes are used to meet the computing needs of large organizations. First developed in the 1950s, they have largely been supplanted by client/server networks for general office use. *See also* **supercomputer**.

main memory   Memory that is internal to the computer and directly accessible to the CPU (central processing unit); RAM (random-access memory).

Majordomo   A freeware mailing list server for managing mailing lists on the Unix platform.

male connector   A connector that has one or many exposed pins. *See illustration at* **connector**.

man page   *A short form for* **manual page**. A page of online documentation for Unix systems. At the Unix prompt, if you type in *man* and the name of a command, documentation about that command, including the syntax one should use in executing it, will be displayed.

management information system   *See* **MIS**.

map   *n.* A representation of the structure or location of something. A memory map describes where data and programs are stored in memory; a bit map represents every dot of a graphic image in memory.

v. To translate or be translated from one value or form to another. A programming language, such as C, maps onto machine language. In computer graphics, a three-dimensional object, such as a sphere, can be mapped onto a plane. The computer maps a virtual address onto a physical address when it swaps data from disk to RAM under a virtual memory system.

MAPI   *Abbreviation of* **Messaging Application Program Interface.** An interface developed by Microsoft Corporation by which various applications, such as email and fax capabilities, work together using one client. *See also* **API.**

maximize   To make a window in a GUI as large as possible.

mass storage   The storage devices and techniques used to supplement the main memory of a computer, including hard disks, floppy disks, magnetic tape, and optical disks. Mass storage devices can accommodate larger amounts of data than main memory, and they retain data when power is turned off. Mass storage capacity is expressed in kilobytes (1,024 bytes), megabytes (1,024 kilobytes), or gigabytes, (1,024 megabytes). *Also called* **secondary storage.**

master page   In desktop publishing, a template used for all the individual pages in a publication.

math coprocessor   A coprocessor that performs mathematical operations for the CPU (central processing unit). Math coprocessors use floating-point representation and can perform calculations many times faster than the CPU alone, making them particularly useful with calculation-intensive applications, such as spreadsheets and programs that employ object-oriented graphics. Most Motorola and Intel microprocessors have companion math coprocessors, which are built in, or can be added to, computers. *Also called* **floating-point coprocessor, numeric coprocessor.** *See also* **floating-point notation.**

matrix   *Plural* **matrices.**   A rectangular array of elements of the same kind, arranged in rows and columns. Matrices are used in a variety of computer operations. A matrix may contain numbers or text in table form, as in spreadsheets or lookup tables. A bit map of a monochromatic image, such as a character on a display screen, is stored in memory as a matrix of 0s and 1s (bits). Dot-matrix printers produce characters and images as matrices of ink dots.

Mb   *Abbreviation of* **megabit.**

MB   *Abbreviation of* **megabyte.**

Mbps   *Abbreviation of* **megabits per second.**

MCA   *Abbreviation of* **Micro Channel Architecture.**

MCGA   *Abbreviation of* **MultiColor Graphics Array.**   A video adapter, now obsolete, that was included in low-end models of the IBM PS/2. It had more graphics capabilities than CGA but was not as powerful as EGA or VGA.

MDA   *Abbreviation of* **monochrome display adapter**.   A monochrome video adapter used with some of the earliest PC models. The MDA can display text but not graphics.

MDI   *Abbreviation of* **multiple document interface**.   A user interface in Microsoft Windows in which a single running application allows several documents to be active concurrently. MDI restricts the borders of the active document windows to the region within the borders of the application window. An example of an MDI application is Microsoft Word in Windows. *See also* **SDI**.

mean time between failures   *See* **MTBF**.

Media Access Control address   *See* **MAC address**.

medium   *See* **storage medium**.

meg   *Abbreviation of* **megabyte**.

mega-   *Abbreviated* **M**   **1.** A prefix indicating 1 million (10^6), as in *megahertz*. This is also the sense in which *mega-* is generally used in terms of data transmission rates, where a bit is a signal pulse and is counted in the decimal system, which is based on multiples of ten. **2.** A prefix indicating 1,048,576 (2^{20}), as in *megabyte*. This is the sense in which *mega-* is generally used in terms of data storage capacity, which, due to the binary nature of bits, is based on powers of two.

megabit   *Abbreviated* **Mb**   One million (1,000,000) bits, used as a unit for expressing the rate of data transmission per unit of time (usually one second). In highly technical contexts involving data storage capacity, it can refer to 1,048,576 (2^{20}) bits.

megabyte   *Abbreviated* **MB, meg**   A unit of measurement of computer memory or data storage capacity equal to 1,048,576 (2^{20}) bytes. One megabyte equals 1,024 kilobytes. Informally, the term is sometimes used to refer to one million (1,000,000) bytes.

megaflop   *Abbreviated* **MFLOP**   A measure of computing speed, equal to one million floating-point notation calculations per second. Workstations, minicomputers, and mainframes are rated in megaflops.

megahertz   *Abbreviated* **MHz**   A unit of frequency equal to 1,000,000 hertz.

membrane keyboard   A keyboard having pressure-sensitive areas in place of keys covered by a thin, transparent plastic. Membrane keyboards are often used in factories, restaurants, and other environments that have a lot of dirt and dust which would damage regular keyboards.

memory   1. *See* **RAM.**   2. The capacity of a computer, chips, and storage devices to preserve data and programs for retrieval. Memory is measured in bytes   3. A system for preserving data and programs for retrieval. Volatile memory, or RAM, stores information only until the power is turned off. Nonvolatile memory stores memory even when the power is off. Nonvolatile memory includes ROM, PROM, EPROM, and EEPROM, as well as such external devices as disk drives and tape drives. *See also* **expanded memory, extended memory, flash memory, main memory,** *and* **virtual memory.**

memory card   A storage device that uses a variety of types of chip, including RAM, ROM, EEPROM, and flash memory. Since the data stored in a memory card remains intact even when the power is turned off and you can rewrite data without removing the card from the computer's circuit board, the memory card functions as a substitute for a hard disk. Memory cards are often used in handheld devices, such as PDAs and digital cameras.

memory effect   A property of NiCad batteries in which the amount of charging they accept at one time fixes the maximum amount of charging they can accept in subsequent recharges. NiCad batteries are used, for example, in laptop computers. The memory effect is related to the recharging of a battery that is not 100% drained. If a battery is only 90% drained, it will only require 10% of the full power to recharge. Because of the memory effect, in the future that battery will only accept a maximum of 10% recharging.

memory management unit   *See* **MMU.**

memory-resident   Designating a program that remains permanently in a computer's RAM. The CPU (central processing unit) must load a file or program into RAM before it can be processed. Other data or programs are copied or swapped from RAM onto disk to make room for the program that you are running, but a memory-resident program will not be moved from RAM. Central parts of the operating system are memory-resident, as are utilities or accessory programs such as calendars, calculators, and spell checkers. These memory-resident programs are activated when you press a simple key sequence known as a hot key. *Also called* **RAM-resident.**

menu   An onscreen list of available options or commands. Usually the options are highlighted by a bar that you can move from one item to another. You can choose a menu item by keying in its code or by

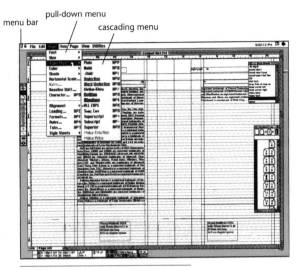

MENU On an Apple Macintosh computer

pointing to the item with the mouse and clicking a mouse button. Choosing often leads to a submenu, called a cascading menu, or to a dialog box containing options that further refine the original menu selection. *See illustration. See also* **menu bar, pull-down menu, tear-off menu.**

menu bar A horizontal bar that runs across the top of the screen or of a window and holds the names of available menu options. When you choose an option from the menu bar, another list of commands or options drops down below the bar. *See also* **menu.**

menu-driven Of or relating to a type of user interface in which the user issues commands by making selections from on-screen menus. Menu-driven programs are easier to use than command-driven programs, which require you to learn and type in commands, because in a menu-driven program, the command choices are all there in front of you.

merge *v.* **1.** To combine two files into one so that the resulting file has the same structure as each of its components. If you merge two files, each containing an alphabetically arranged list of names, the resulting file will contain all of the names from the two files in alphabetical order. In contrast, if you were to append the same files, the first list of names would simply be followed by the second. **2.** To generate form letters by doing a mail merge. *n. See* **mail merge**.

message box   *See* **alert box**.

Messaging Application Program Interface   *See* **MAPI**.

metalanguage   A language that is used to define another language.

metaphor   An interface technique of expressing abstract or soft entities, such as computer functions, programs, or data, as everyday objects such as desktops, paintbrushes, file folders, or trash cans. Graphical user interfaces, such as the one used by the Apple Macintosh computer, are based on these metaphors.

metatag   An HTML or XML tag for setting off descriptive information about a document. The information in a metatag does not appear when the webpage is displayed in a browser. You can put information about yourself or the document in a metatag. Because some search engines search on information in the metatag, adding keywords that describe the document will increase the chances of a web engine returning your webpage if that word is searched on.

MFLOP   [EM-flop] *Abbreviation of* **megaflop**.

MFM   *Abbreviation of* **Modified Frequency Modulation**.

MHz   *Abbreviation of* **megahertz**.

MICR   [MY-ker] *Abbreviation of* **magnetic-ink character recognition**.

micro   *Short for* **microcomputer** *or* **microprocessor**.

micro-   **1.** A prefix indicating something very small.   **2.** A prefix indicating one millionth (10^{-6}), as in microsecond.

Micro Channel Architecture   *Abbreviated* **MCA**   The bus architecture once used in high-end IBM PS/2 computers, characterized by a 32-bit data path. Although many computers use a 32-bit bus structure on the motherboard to connect the RAM and the microprocessor, the 16-bit ISA bus was formerly the standard for expansion boards. MCA's 32-bit expansion slots did not accommodate the many peripherals and adapters that were designed for the ISA bus, so it was not accepted as the standard for expansion bus architecture and is now obsolete.

microchip   *See* **integrated circuit**.

microcode The lowest-level code for translating each instruction of machine code into an elementary circuit operation, such as the computing, memory, or input/output operation, of a computer. Since it is usually stored in a computer's ROM, microcode is considered firmware, and can be used as an alternative to hardwiring a circuit.

Microcom Networking Protocol One of a group of communications protocols developed by Microcom, Inc., used by high-speed modems for data compression and error detection.

microcomputer *See* **personal computer**.

microkernel In programming, the part of an operating system's code that must be rewritten for each different platform on which the system is intended for use. Keeping all the hardware-dependent parts of operating system code together in the microkernel makes an operating system more easily portable.

microprocessor An integrated circuit that contains the entire CPU (central processing unit) of a computer on a single chip. When referring to personal computers, the terms *microprocessor* and *central processing unit* are often used synonymously. Microprocessors manufactured by Intel are generally used in IBM PC and compatible computers. Motorola microprocessors are used in Apple Macintosh computers and in Hewlett-Packard workstations.

Microprocessors are distinguished on the basis of power and speed. Power is measured by data width; that is, the number of bits of data the microprocessor can process at one time. Often, it is useful to distinguish between register width, or the number of bits of data the computer can process within its CPU (central processing unit) at one time, and bus width, the number of bits of data than can be transferred between the CPU and other components, such as expansion boards, printers, or disk drives, at one time. Speed is specified by the clock speed given in megahertz (MHz) or gigahertz (GHz). A microprocessor that runs at 1GHz executes 1 billion cycles per second. Clock speed determines how fast a computer can execute instructions. The higher the clock speed and the bigger the data width, the more powerful the microprocessor. Table 14 (pages 142–3) and Table 15 (page 180) compare the features of various microprocessors. *See also* **Intel microprocessors, Motorola microprocessors**.

microsecond A unit of time equal to one millionth (10^{-6}) of a second.

Microsoft Internet Explorer *See* **Internet Explorer**.

Microsoft Windows *See* **Windows**.

microspacing The insertion of spaces of various sizes between characters to achieve justification, the alignment of text with respect to left and right margins.

middleware Software that serves as an intermediary between systems software and an application — for example software that provides a single API through which an application can interact with several different database programs.

MIDI *Abbreviation of* **Musical Instrument Digital Interface**. A protocol for the exchange of information between computers and musical devices such as synthesizers. Computers with a MIDI interface can read encoded data representing sounds and can manipulate it in many different ways, as by changing pitch, tempo, or volume. These computers can also translate data representing sounds into a musical score.

millennium bug *See* **Year 2000 Problem**.

milli- *Abbreviated* **m** A prefix indicating one thousandth (10^{-3}), as in millisecond.

million instructions per second *See* **MIPS**.

millisecond *Abbreviated* **ms** A unit of time equal to one thousandth (10^{-3}) of a second.

MIME *Abbreviation of* **Multipurpose Internet Mail Extensions**. An extension of simple mail transfer protocol (SMTP) that allows for the transmission of many forms of data, such as binary, video, and audio data.

MIME attachment A document or file that is not part of the body of an email message but is sent along with it. Most email programs support this mechanism of sending files.

mini *Short for* **minicomputer**.

minicomputer A computer, usually fitting within a single cabinet, that has more memory and a higher execution speed than a personal computer, but is less powerful than a mainframe. A minicomputer can process input and output from many terminals simultaneously. A minicomputer is often used as the server in a client/server network. However, these have become less common as the processing power of Intel and AMD central processing units has increased.

minimize To hide a window on your desktop. When you minimize a window, usually an icon or button will appear on the desktop so that you can click on it in order to restore the window.

minitower *See* **tower**.

MIPS *Abbreviation of* **million instructions per second.** A measure of computing speed. MIPS refers to the number of instructions a computer's CPU (central processing unit) can carry out in 1 second. For example, a computer rated at 50 MIPS executes, on the average, 50,000,000 instructions per second.

MIPS is not the only variable to consider when judging a computer's speed. Other factors include the rate of data transfer between memory and the CPU and the speed of peripherals such as disk drives. *See also* **throughput**.

mirror site A server that contains a duplicate of another server. Mirror sites are often at different locations in order to ensure the availability of data in case of a power failure or heavy data traffic.

MIS *Abbreviation of* **management information system.** A computer system designed for an place of business. The nature of the system can vary from an expensive mainframe to a local area network, and allows managers to organize, manipulate, and access data efficiently and effectively.

MMU *Abbreviation of* **memory management unit** Hardware that allows virtual memory addresses to map to physical memory addresses. An MMU can be part of the CPU (central processing unit), or it can be a separate chip. In some older systems, the MMU was separate from the processor.

MMX A technology introduced by Intel that enhances its CPU (central processing unit) architecture in order to handle multimedia and communications more efficiently. MMX-based CPUs are designed to speed image processing, motion video, speech synthesis, telephony, and 3D graphics. The MMX technology is incorporated into all Intel Pentium chips.

MNP *Abbreviation of* **Microcom Networking Protocol.**

mode An operating state for a program or device, especially one that can be selected by the user. In many word processing programs, you can choose between the insert mode, which inserts whatever you are typing without deleting text, and the overwrite mode, which replaces existing text with whatever you are typing. In some programs the actions carried out by the function keys change if you change modes.

modem *Abbreviation of* **modulator/demodulator**.   A device that converts data from digital signals to analog signals and vice versa, so that computers can communicate over telephone lines, which transmit analog waves. A modem encodes digital information as analog waves in order to transmit it. At the other end, a modem must change analog waves back into digital code so that they can be understood by the receiving computer.

A number of different communications protocols govern digital-to-analog conversion, data compression, and error detection. There are so many different protocols, with so many variations, that newer modems must engage in a complicated discussion at the start of each connection in order to choose a common set to use. This process, called handshaking, is also governed by protocol.

Noise on telephone lines can corrupt the data passing between modems. Not all communications protocols detect such errors, so file transfer protocols use checksums to ensure that files are not corrupted when they are uploaded or downloaded. Communications software can hide most of the complexity of controlling the modem and choosing file transfer protocols. It can also automate log-on procedures and perform other tasks to make access to online services easy and efficient.

Modems are serial devices; that is, they transmit data one bit at a time rather than sending several bits simultaneously. The speed at which modems transmit data is measured in bps (bits per second), although baud rate is also used. Internal modems are on an expansion board that is plugged into a computer; external modems are connected by a cable to the computer's serial port. *See tables at* **communications protocol, file transfer protocol**.

moderated newsgroup   A newsgroup for which posts are first seen by a moderator, who can choose which posts are actually posted, thus keeping the discussions on topic and comparatively free of flaming and spam.

moderator   A person who oversees a forum for discussion, such as a newsgroup, mailing list, or chatroom, to ensure that the rules of that forum are followed, for example, by blocking people who are harassing others from entering a chat room or by preventing spam from being posted to a newsgroup.

modified frequency modulation   *Abbreviated* **MFM**   A method for encoding data on a magnetic storage device, now used primarily by floppy disk drives. Since twice as much data can be stored over an earlier encoding method, disks using the modified frequency modulation method are generally called double-density disks. For hard disk drives, this technology is being supplanted by the run length limited method of encoding data, which is faster. *See also* **run length limited**.

modular architecture   A hardware or software system in which each component, or module, can be replaced independently of all the other modules. The opposite of modular is integrated; in a system with integrated architecture, no clear distinction exists between components. *See also* **integrated circuit**.

modulation   **1.** The variation of a property of an electromagnetic wave or signal, such as its amplitude, frequency, or phase.   **2.** The process of changing a digital signal to analog so that a modem can send the signal can be sent over telephone lines.

module   **1.** In software, a portion of a program that carries out a specific function and may be used alone or combined with other modules to compose a program. Modules can be copied and used in many programs, and new programs can be created by combining existing modules in different ways with a linker. *Also called* **object module**. *See also* **link**.   **2.** A self-contained hardware component that is installed as a unit.

moiré effect   The perceived flickering or distortion of printed or displayed high-contrast images. You can often rectify this optical illusion by altering the image's size or resolution.

monitor   The display screen of a computer and the case in which it is contained. Monitors come in a variety of screen sizes. A typical monitor has a screen that measures anywhere from 15 to 21 inches, with 17-inch and 19-inch models being the most common.

Monochrome monitors, now rarely used with computers, are able to display only one color against a background; color monitors are capable of displaying many colors. The more bits a monitor uses to represent each pixel, the greater the number of colors the monitor can display. Analog monitors accept a continuous, or analog, signal that allows them to display an infinite variety of colors, while digital monitors can display only a fixed number of colors. Some monitors can accept either analog or digital signals.

The video adapter sends signals to the monitor and determines, within the limits imposed by the monitor's structure, what the display will look like. The video standard supported by a video adapter determines the resolution and colors that a monitor can display. *Also called* **video display terminal**. *See also* **fixed-frequency monitor, multifrequency monitor, multiscanning monitor**.

monochrome   Of, relating to, or being a computer screen capable of displaying only one color on a dark or light background.

Monochrome Display Adapter   *See* **MDA**.

monospace font   A font in which each character is given the same pitch, or width. *See also* **fixed space, proportional font**.

MOO   A MUD having an object-oriented language allowing the players to create objects, especially personalized characters and situations. The first of these went online in the early 1980s. MOOs were among the first virtual communities created on the Internet.

Moore's Law   In the mid-1960s, Gordon Moore, one of the founders of Intel Corporation, observed that the density of transistors on integrated circuits had been doubling every year. Although the pace slowed slightly in the following years, Moore's law is the observation that the density of transistors doubles every 18 months. This has resulted in smaller and less expensive chips. This pattern has held true; however, technology is approaching the point where the circuits are only a few atoms wide. If circuits reach a width of just one atom, new technologies will need to be developed in order to make transistors more dense.

morphing   The transformation of one image into another by computer.

Mosaic   A public-domain web browser developed by the National Center for Supercomputing Applications. Mosaic has largely been supplanted by Netscape Navigator and Microsoft Internet Explorer.

most significant bit   In a byte sequence, the bit having the greatest amount of significance, usually the leftmost bit of a binary number.

most significant character   In a string, the character having the greatest amount of significance, usually the leftmost character.

most significant digit   In a number, the digit having the greatest amount of significance, usually the leftmost digit.

motherboard   The main printed circuit board in a personal computer. It contains the CPU (central processing unit), main system memory, controllers for disk drives and other devices, serial and parallel ports, and sometimes expansion slots. The motherboard is easy to recognize because it is typically the largest printed circuit card inside the computer's case, and the large CPU chip is usually clearly labeled. It usually lies flat against one end, and cards and chips are inserted into it. An effective way to upgrade the performance of an older computer is to replace the motherboard. By replacing the CPU, ROM, memory, and support circuits all at once, a user ensures that these key components of the system will continue to work together, and creates a new computer in the old case. This allows you to keep all of the data and cards from your old computer while increasing the computer's speed and performance. *Also called* **system board**, especially on an IBM PC.

Motorola microprocessors   A family of microprocessors made by Motorola Corporation and used most notably in Apple Macintosh computers. The early, 8-bit 6800 model was succeeded by the 68000, which had a 16-bit bus and was the basis for the original Macintosh computer. Later models include the 32-bit 68020 with a clock speed of 16MHz used in the original Macintosh II, the 68030, versions of which had clock speeds of up to 50 megahertz, and the 68040, which had a built-in math coprocessor. In the mid 1990s, Motorola began producing microprocessors based on the PowerPC architecture jointly developed with IBM and Apple. Some models have 64-bit data busses. The PowerPC 740 and 750 have clock speeds of up to 400 megahertz and provide high performance levels for desktop and workstation computer systems. See Table 15 on page 180 for information about individual kinds of Motorola microprocessors. *See also* **Intel microprocessors**.

mount   To put a floppy disk into a floppy disk drive. Used especially of Apple and Unix environments.

mouse   *Plural* **mice** *or* **mouses**.   A hand-held, button-activated input device that when rolled along a flat surface controls the movement of a cursor or pointer on a display screen, largely freeing the user from the keyboard. With menu-driven applications you simply point to a command choice and click a button on the mouse. With draw or paint programs the mouse can be used like a pen or brush. Mice are distinguished by the way they work internally and by how they connect to the computer.

  A mechanical mouse has a rubber-coated ball on its underside that rotates as you move the mouse. Optical sensors detect the motion and move the screen pointer correspondingly. You can roll the mouse over almost any surface, but using a mousepad gives the best results.

TABLE 15 Motorola Microprocessors

Microprocessor	Data Bus Width (bits)	Maximum Clock Speed (MHz)	Characteristics
Motorola 68000	16	8	• Can access up to 16MB of memory • Used in original Apple Macintosh computer and certain laser printers
Motorola 68020	32	33	• Can access up to 4GB of memory • Used in Macintosh II and LC computers
Motorola 68030	32	50	• Can access up to 4GB of memory • Used in certain Macintosh II and SE/30 computers
Motorola 68040	32	33	• Built-in math coprocessor • Used in Macintosh Quadra and Centris computers
Motorola MPC601	64	80	• The first microprocessor available with PowerPC architecture • Can execute three instructions each clock cycle • Used in Power Macintosh computers
Motorola PowerPC 603e	64	300	• Can execute three instructions each clock cycle • Designed for systems with low power requirements, such as laptops
Motorola EC603e	64	266	• Can execute three instructions each clock cycle • Offers workstation-level performance • Optimized for embedded applications
Motorola PowerPC 604e	64	350	• Can execute four instructions each clock cycle • Provides high performance levels for desktop, workstation, and symmetric multiprocessing computer systems.

An optical mouse uses reflections from an LED (light-emitting diode) to track the mouse's movement. An optical mouse requires a special mat to reflect the light properly. The mat is marked with a grid that acts as a frame of reference for the optical device.

For Macintosh computers, mice connect to the computer through the Apple Desktop Bus. For IBM PC and compatible computers, most mice connect to the computer through a special mouse port. A serial mouse, however, connects to a standard serial port. Newer models of mice are connected via a USB port, which allows you to change devices while using the computer.

mousepad   A flat piece of material, such as specially coated foam rubber, designed to provide an optimum surface on which to use a mouse.

Moving Picture Experts Group   *See* **MPEG**.

MP3   **1.** An MPEG standard used especially for digitally transmitting music over the Internet. Most songs encoded in this popular format are copyrighted versions of recordings released in other formats; however, some artists make their works available over the Internet using MP3 technology. Several programs are available to facilitate the transfer of these files between users, including Napster, Gnutella, and Freenet. There are numerous legal issues regarding the swapping of files and the violation of copyright laws. Many of these issues are as yet undecided.   **2.** A file containing a song or other audio data that is encoded using this standard.

MPEG   *Abbreviation of* **Moving Pictures Expert Group**.   The standard, set by a committee of the International Standards Organization, for the compression of digital video and audio data. MPEG-1 is a compression standard for video CDs, and MPEG-2 is a compression standard used for broadcast video.

ms   *Abbreviation of* **millisecond**.

MS-DOS   The DOS operating system developed by Microsoft Corporation for IBM.

MS-Windows   *See* **Microsoft Windows**.

MTBF   *Abbreviation of* **mean time between failures**.   A measure of the reliability of electronic and mechanical devices. The MTBF for a component reports its average working life, as tested under ideal conditions, before its first failure requiring service. MTBFs for electromechanical components such as disk drives are usually expressed in thousands or tens of thousands of hours. The higher the number, the more reliable the product.

MUD   *Abbreviation of* **Multi-User Dungeon**.   A computer program, usually running over the Internet and often text-based, that allows multiple users to participate in virtual-reality role-playing games.

MultiColor Graphics Array *See* MCGA.

multidimensional database A database system that organizes data in forms other than a matrix of rows and columns. Multidimensional database systems allow the users to retrieve information based on complex search criteria. *See also* **database management system, query, report, report generator.**

MultiFinder A version of Finder developed by Apple Computers that allows more than one program to be loaded into memory at a time so that the user can switch quickly from one program to another. It differs from a true multitasking system in that it uses the technique known as context switching or task switching, in which all background applications are halted and only the one in the foreground runs.

multifrequency monitor A monitor that can respond to a fixed number of different video signal frequency ranges. This allows it to support different resolutions and video standards, such as VGA. *See also* **multiscanning monitor.**

multimedia *adj.* **1.** Designating a type of computer application that can combine text, graphics, full-motion video, and sound into an integrated package. For example, a multimedia encyclopedia can allow you to look up the entry for *Mozart,* click on a button, and hear a selection from a Mozart symphony while looking at the score. Because graphics and sound files require large amounts of storage space, multimedia applications only became practical with the development of sufficiently fast microprocessors and CD-ROM technology. Minimum requirements for a personal computer to run multimedia applications include an Intel Pentium or equivalent processor, 16 megabytes of RAM, VGA graphics, a mouse, a sound card, and a multimedia-compatible CD-ROM drive. **2.** Designating a computer or a computer system on which such applications may be run.

n. **1.** The combined use of such media as text, graphics, video, and sound, as on a computer system. **2.** The capability to use such combined media.

multiplex To combine more than one analog or digital signal for transmission over a common line.

multiplexer *Abbreviated* **mux** A hardware device that allows data signals from several sources to be transmitted over a common line.

multiprocessing A method of computing in which different parts of a task are distributed between two or more similar CPUs (central processing units), allowing the computer to complete operations more quickly and to handle larger, more complex procedures. *See also* **coprocessor, multitasking, parallel processing**.

Multipurpose Internet Mail Extensions   *See* MIME.

multiscanning monitor   A monitor that can automatically detect and respond to a signal from a video adapter at any frequency within a wide range. This allows it to work with adapters for any video standard from monochrome to SVGA. *See also* **multifrequency monitor**.

multisession drive   A drive capable of reading from a CD data that was appended after the first writing session occurred. A multisession drive can recognize the extended header format that is used when data is appended to a CD. Multisession drives are commonly used in conjunction with Photo CD technology.

Multisync monitor   A multiscanning monitor developed by NEC, Inc.

multitasking   A mode of operation in which a single CPU (central processing unit) works on more than one task simultaneously. Multitasking differs from task switching in that a program can continue to run in the background while the user's attention is on another process in the foreground. This can be done either by having the operating system parcel out fixed slices of CPU time to each program in succession or by allowing the programs themselves to turn over control of the CPU to other programs in the intervals when they do not need it. Although the processor can only perform one operation at a time, it switches from one to the other so quickly that it seems to the user as if all the programs are running together. Most current operating systems were developed to enhance multitasking. *See also* **multiprocessing, operating environment, parallel processing**.

multithreading   A mode of operation in which a single program concurrently executes more than one task. Synonymous with single program multitasking, multithreading is useful for the synchronous processing of audio and video data.

multi-user   Of, relating to, or being a computer system intended to be used by more than one person at a time. Most multi-user systems are built around mainframes or minicomputers, typically using an operating system such as Unix that is designed for this purpose.

Multi-User Dungeon   *See* MUD.

Musical Instrument Digital Interface   *See* MIDI.

mux   *See* **multiplexer**.

[N]

n *Abbreviation of* **nano-**.

NAND A Boolean operator that returns the value TRUE if either or both of its operands are FALSE. Table 16 shows the results of the NAND operator.

TABLE 16 Results of NAND Operator

a	b	a NAND a
FALSE	FALSE	TRUE
FALSE	TRUE	TRUE
TRUE	FALSE	TRUE
TRUE	TRUE	FALSE

nano- *Abbreviated* **n** A prefix indicating one billionth (10^{-9}), as in nanoseconds.

nanosecond *Abbreviated* **ns** A unit of time equal to one billionth (10^{-9}) of a second.

National Television Standards Committee *See* **NTSC**.

natural language In computer science, human language as opposed to a programming language or machine language. One of the long-standing goals of computer science, particularly in the field of artificial intelligence, has been to develop computer systems that can interact with human beings in natural language. Computers work well with programming languages such as BASIC or C because their syntax is finite, well-defined, and relatively small, but natural language presents problems because it is exactly the opposite. Human language is such a complex phenomenon that linguists have found it impossible even to agree on a theory that adequately explains what language is, much less a comprehensive description of the rules that make it work. *See also* **language**.

near-letter quality *Abbreviated* **NLQ** Of, related to, or being a print mode of dot-matrix printers that is better than draft-quality mode but not as good as letter-quality mode. *See illustration at* **letter-quality**.

nest To embed one subroutine, set of data, or word processing document sequentially within another. In a database, for example, a nested record is a record containing a field that is itself a record. A nested table is a table within another table.

net   *A shortened form of* **network**. *See also* **Net**.

Net   *A shortened form of* **Internet**. Net is usually capitalized when referring to the Internet, as opposed simply to computer networks of any type. Thus you can speak of *one of the most frequently visited sites on the Net* but *tools for net navigation*, since the latter might include tools that are designed for use on networks other than the Internet.

NetBEUI   *Abbreviation of* **NetBIOS Extended User Interface**.   A protocol originally developed by IBM that is an enhanced version of NetBIOS. NetBEUI is used by Microsoft Corporation's network operating and local-area network systems.

NetBIOS   *Abbreviation of* **NetBIOS Extended User Interface**.   An API whose programs regulate the transmission of data among a network's nodes. NetBIOS is used on Microsoft- and IBM-based local-area networks. *See also* **BIOS**.

NetBIOS Extended User Interface.   *See* **NETBEUI**.

netiquette   A set of unofficial rules for good behavior and politeness that were developed for use in Usenet on the Internet, and later expanded to relate to email, chat rooms, and similar modes of online communication. For example, it is considered good netiquette to refrain from posting messages to inappropriate newsgroups. An important netiquette rule is to read the FAQ before posting a question to a newsgroup.

Netscape Navigator   A web browser developed by Netscape Corporation.

NetWare   A local-area network operating system developed by Novell Corporation that runs on numerous kinds of different hardware, configurations, and communications protocols, providing a consistent interface. Versions of NetWare are available for both the Apple and Microsoft Windows platforms.

network   A system of computers, and often peripherals such as printers, linked together. The smallest networks are local area networks (LANs), in which as few as 2 or as many as 500 computers are connected by cables within a small geographic area, often within the same building. Larger networks, called wide area networks (WANs), use telephone lines or radio waves to link computers that can be thousands of miles apart.

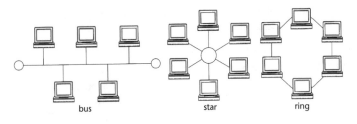

bus   star   ring

NETWORK   Three common network configurations

The geometric arrangement of the computers is called the topology of the network. Common topologies include the star, bus, and ring. LANs can also be connected to a backbone to build a larger LAN or WAN. The protocol standardizes the rules and signals that computers on a network use to communicate. AppleTalk, a protocol suitable for small networks, is built into all Apple Macintosh computers and laser printers. Popular protocols for LANs include Ethernet, and, specifically for IBM PC computers, the IBM token-ring network. *See illustration. See also* **client/server network**, **extranet**, **intranet**, **peer-to-peer network**.

network administrator   A person who is responsible for maintaining and repairing a computer network, including its software.

Network Basic Input/Output System   *See* **NetBIOS**.

Network File System   *Abbreviated* **NFS**   A utility developed by Sun Microsystems that allows people to access files that are located on another computer in the network. The Network File System is available on Unix and Microsoft Windows platforms.

network interface card   *Abbreviated* NIC   A printed circuit board or an adapter that allows a computer to be connected to a network. Network interface cards permit the network connection to be made directly to the computer's internal bus, rather than through the much slower serial port. Interface cards are usually made for a single type of network. The most common kind is an ethernet card, which provides high speed data transmission. Ethernet cards are now commonly installed in laptops and some desktop systems.

network operating system   *Abbreviated* **NOS**   An operating system that provides the features necessary to operate a local-area network. Network operating systems are often regarded as software that extends or enhances the functionality of basic operating systems.

network server   *See* **file server**.

network topology   *See* **topology**.

neural network   A computing system modeled after a biological nervous system that attempts to approximate the workings of the human brain. Interconnected processing elements play the role of neurons (nerve cells). Each processing element has a limited number of inputs, corresponding to the impulses a neuron receives. Its inputs determine each element's output, which corresponds to the nerve impulse that travels to the next neuron. Rather than being programmed, the processing elements "learn" from the kinds and patterns of input they receive.

Neural networks are either built from hardware circuits or simulated on a computer through software. Although commercial applications of neural networks are limited at this point, they are beginning to be used in areas such as voice and pattern recognition and speech synthesis. *See also* **artificial intelligence**.

newbie   A person who is a novice at something, such as one who has just started using an online service, is learning how to use a particular kind of software, or has just begun participating in a newsgroup. In Usenet newsgroups, the term is often used negatively in reference to new users who ask questions that are found in the FAQ. Proper netiquette dictates that when you begin participating in a newsgroup that you read the FAQ before you begin asking questions.

newsgroup   An area on a computer network, especially in Usenet on the Internet, devoted to the discussion of a topic. Newsgroup names consist of a string of words separated by periods, indicating the topic, as in rec.pets.cats.

newsreader   An application that allows users to read Usenet newsgroups. Microsoft Internet Explorer and Netscape Communicator include newsreaders. Popular newsreaders in Unix platforms include *tin* and *trn*.

news server   A server that allows users to access Usenet newsgroups.

NFS   *Abbreviation of* **Network File System**.

nibble   Half a byte; four bits. *Also spelled* **nybble**.

NIC *Abbreviation of* **network interface card**.

NiCad battery [NYE-cad] A type of rechargeable battery widely used with portable electronic equipment, including laptop and notebook computers. NiCad batteries are made up of cells containing nickel and cadmium and can be recharged up to about 1,000 times under ideal conditions. The most significant characteristic of NiCad batteries is the so-called memory effect, in which a battery that is recharged after being only partially drained soon loses its ability to hold a full charge.

nickel-metal-hydride battery *Abbreviated* **NiMH** A type of rechargeable battery similar to a NiCad battery but using nickel metal hydride rather than cadmium. Besides avoiding the problems of using and disposing of cadmium, which is toxic, NiMH cells provide higher power density than NiCads, allowing batteries to be much smaller for a given storage capacity or to last longer for a given size.

NLQ *Abbreviation of* **near-letter quality**.

node 1. In a local area network, a workstation, server, printer, or another device that is connected to the network and able to process data. 2. In a tree structure as used in directory or database management and programming, a point where two or more lines or branches of the tree meet.

noise A random electrical signal on a communications channel that interferes with the desired signal or data. Noise can either be generated by the circuitry of the communications device itself or come from one of a variety of external sources, including radio and TV signals, lightning, and nearby transmission lines.

nonimpact printer A printer that does not rely on mechanical force to transfer ink or wax to the page, such as a laser printer, an ink-jet printer, or a thermal printer. Nonimpact printers are considerably quieter than impact printers, but they cannot be used for printing multipart forms. *See table at* **printer**.

noninterlaced Designating a type of monitor that does not use the technique of interlacing when scanning the display screen, but instead scans every line on every refresh cycle. Although noninterlaced displays are more expensive than interlaced ones for the same level of resolution, they allow the screen to be redrawn faster for graphics and video images and avoid the flickering of interlaced displays. *See also* **interlacing, raster scanning**.

nonvolatile memory Memory whose contents are not lost when the system power is shut off. Nonvolatile memory is used in calculators, printers, and other devices whose programming does not need to be changed, and in personal computers for the BIOS and other instructions the computer needs to read during the boot sequence. Disk storage and ROM are both nonvolatile memory, as opposed to the volatile memory held in RAM.

no parity *See* **parity**.

NOR A Boolean operator that returns the value TRUE if and only if both of its operands are FALSE. Table 17 shows the results of the NOR operator.

TABLE 17 Results of NOR Operator

a	b	a NOR b
FALSE	FALSE	TRUE
FALSE	TRUE	FALSE
TRUE	FALSE	FALSE
TRUE	TRUE	FALSE

NOS *Abbreviation of* **network operating system**.

NOT A Boolean operator that returns the value TRUE if its operand is FALSE, and FALSE if its operand is TRUE.

notebook A portable computer that is about 1 foot wide, generally weighs from 3 to 7 pounds, and is powered by rechargeable batteries. They usually contain a single 3.5-inch floppy disk drive, CD, or DVD drive. Despite their small size, many notebook computers offer nearly the same capabilities as desktop models, but they are more expensive. All notebook models now have some multimedia capabilities.

notepad A desk accessory in the Microsoft Windows and Apple Macintosh operating environments. Notepad is a text editor that allows the user to jot down notes, write short memos, and create and edit batch files.

ns *Abbreviation of* **nanosecond**.

NSAPI A CGI-like standard developed by Netscape that defines the methods for passing arguments and running programs on a World

Wide Web server. The NSAPI was developed for the Netscape Navigator Server.

NTSC   *Abbreviation of* **National Television Standards Committee**. An organization that sets standards for television and video in most of North and South America, including the United States. Televisions that follow the NSTC standards have 525 lines per frame that refresh 60 times per second. Most European and Asian countries follow PAL standards. *See also* **PAL**.

NuBus   A high-speed expansion bus developed by Apple Computers and used in Macintosh II computers. NuBus expansion slots accept 96-pin expansion boards.

null character   A data control character that fills computer time by adding nonsignificant zeros to a data sequence. The null character can be used, for example, to pad data fields, terminate character strings, or separate blocks of data. In the ASCII character set, the null character is symbolized by NUL and represented by the character code 0.

null-modem cable   A cable that allows two computers to be connected directly together through their serial ports without using a modem. A null-modem cable is used, for example, to connect a portable computer with a larger computer so that they can exchange data.

number cruncher   A program or computer, such as a supercomputer, that is able to perform complex, lengthy calculations.

numeric coprocessor   *See* **math coprocessor**.

numeric keypad   A group of keys, separate from and usually to the right of the typing area on a keyboard, that consists of the numbers 0–9, a decimal point, and mathematical operators. Numeric keypads are designed for entering large amounts of numeric data. A numeric keypad may also have function keys and an Enter key.

Often, as on keyboards for IBM PC and compatible computers, the keys on the keypad do double duty. In numeric mode, the keys represent numbers. In cursor control mode, they function as arrow keys. The Num Lock key is pressed to toggle between modes.

Num Lock key   A key on IBM PC and compatible computers that toggles the numeric keypad between numeric mode and cursor control mode.

nybble   *Alternate spelling of* **nibble**.

[O]

object **1.** In object-oriented programming, a discrete item that consists of data and the procedures necessary to operate on that data. **2.** A discrete item that can be selected and maneuvered, such as an onscreen graphic.

object code The code that is produced by a compiler from the source code. Source code consists of the instructions written by the programmer in a high-level programming language such as C or FORTRAN. The object code is most often in the form of machine language that can be directly executed by a computer. It may, however, be in assembly language, an intermediate code that is then translated into machine language by an assembler or a linker.

object linking and embedding *See* **OLE.**

object module *See* **module.**

object-oriented Describing and handling data as a set of objects rather than as a collection of elements, bits, or points. Each object in an object-oriented system not only contains data but is individually responsible for knowing how to manipulate that data.

object-oriented graphics A method of representing graphics images by mathematical description rather than as a series of points. This allows you to move, resize, rotate, stretch, or copy a design element in one operation without having to redraw all the points on the figure that are to be changed, as must be done with a bit-mapped graphic. Even overlapping objects can be handled in this way without being confused or interfering with other objects. Also in contrast with bit-mapped graphics, an object-oriented image can be viewed or printed at whatever resolution is available to the monitor or printer. *Also called* **vector graphics.** *See also* **raster graphics.**

object-oriented interface A user interface in which actions are performed by manipulating symbols on the screen. Each item on the screen has one or more menus or dialog boxes associated with it, usually accessed through a mouse click or a special key combination. These menus and dialog boxes can be used to modify or manipulate the object in some way. For example, clicking with the right mouse button in a cell on many spreadsheets brings up a menu of formatting commands for that cell. Right-clicking on the header for the cell's column may bring up formatting commands for all the cells in the column. This type of interface makes it appear that each object controls its own appearance and behavior.

object-oriented programming *Abbreviated* OOP A paradigm for programming that is schematic rather than linear. In conventional programming, the programmer lists the procedures to be performed on the data in order to accomplish a task. In object-oriented programming, the concepts of procedure and data are replaced by the concepts of objects and messages. An object includes both a package of data and a description of the operations that can be performed on the data. A message specifies one of the operations but, unlike a procedure, does not describe how the operation should be carried out. C++ is an example of an OOP language.

Programmers can send messages to objects and create relationships between objects. New objects can take on all relevant features of existing objects. Since objects are self-contained, they function as modules and can be copied and combined to create new programs. Object-oriented programming meshes naturally with graphical user interfaces. An object can be represented on-screen by an icon, and the user can copy or reposition the object by dragging its icon around the screen with a mouse. The internal complexity of the object is completely hidden from the user.

oblique A simulated italic type style created by slanting the roman characters of a font. Oblique letters lack the cursive appearance of italic letters.

OCR *Abbreviation of* **optical character recognition**.

octal Of or relating to a number system having a base of 8. In contrast with the decimal (base 10) system most of us use everyday, in which each place in a number represents a successive power of 10, each place in an octal number represents a power of 8. Thus the decimal number 1,165 is written in octal notation as 2215, which stands for $(2 \times 8^3) + (2 \times 8^2) + (1 \times 8) + (5 \times 1)$ or $1,024 + 128 + 8 + 5$. Octal notation is used in computer programming because three-digit binary numbers are readily converted into one-digit octal numbers from 0 to 7. *See also* **binary**, **hexadecimal**.

octet A byte with exactly eight bits.

OCX A Microsoft-based technology using OLE custom controls. The components allow programmers to design controls that can be embedded in other applications, respond to events, and generate events. The name is derived from the file extension of these controls.

ODBC *Abbreviation of* **Open Database Connectivity**. A standard that allows different applications to communicate with different database servers. An ODBC server translates standardized database requests from an application to a format that a particular database server understands. ODBC was developed by a consortium of companies and is supported on Microsoft Windows, Windows NT, and Unix platforms.

odd footer In word processing, a footer that appears on odd-numbered pages.

odd header In word processing, a header that appears on odd-numbered pages.

odd parity *See* **parity**.

OEM *Abbreviation of* **original equipment manufacturer**. The company that actually manufactures a piece of computer equipment, which is then modified or repackaged and sold to the consumer. The term is often applied to value-added resellers (VARs), who purchase separate components in bulk from large manufacturers and package them as complete computer systems. Although technically not OEMs, these VARs are the first to create a working computer out of separate parts and therefore they are sometimes considered to be entitled to the designation.

office automation The use of computers, computer networks, and related equipment to perform the tasks necessary to managing or operating an office efficiently.

offline Not connected to a computer or computer network.

offset **1.** A value that specifies the distance of an address from a reference point known as the base address. If A is the address 100, then A + 7, where 7 is the offset, specifies the address 107. **2.** *See* **gutter**.

OLAP *Abbreviation of* **Online Analytical Processing**. OLAP software allows users to analyze large amounts of complex data quickly and interactively. OLAP software must support sophisticated logical and statistical processing using very few commands.

OLE *Abbreviation of* **Object Linking and Embedding**. A Microsoft Windows technology for linking documents and establishing how updates to the data of one document affect the data in other documents. Whether linked or embedded, one document appears to be part of another; for example, a graph may be placed in a spreadsheet, which in turn may be part of a word processing document. Sound and video may also be embedded. Linked documents are stored in separate files but updates in one are automatically reflected in the other. The data for an embedded document is actually stored in the same file as the enclosing document and is not identifiable as a separate entity. In either case, the applications responsible for editing all the different pieces cooperate to make it easy to move among them and unnecessary to start each explicitly.

on-board   Located on a circuit board.

on-board modem   *See* **internal modem**.

100Base-T   *See* **Fast Ethernet**.

online   Connected to or accessible by means of a computer or computer network.

online help   The onscreen help that a network or an application provides when a user requests it.

online service   **1.** A commercial service that provides access to the Internet for a subscription fee. The access may be through telephone, cable, or wireless service. The provider often supplies email, ftp, conferencing, and other services.   **2.** Access to large databases and other electronic information provided through a computer network. This access may or may not involve a fee, and may or may not include additional access to the Internet. For example, many libraries have their card catalogs set up as online services. Other examples include LEXIS-NEXIS and the Dow Jones News/Retrieval Service.

OOP   *Abbreviation of* **object-oriented programming**.

open   **1.** To make a file ready for reading or writing.   **2.** In a graphical user interface, to expand an icon into a window. *See also* **close**.

open architecture   **1.** A system design whose specifications are publicly available. Open architecture is exemplified by the IBM PC computer design, which can be copied by anyone and for which any third party is free to design and distribute add-on products. This approach allows for more flexibility in the design of new devices and techniques, but risks incompatibility. *See also* **closed architecture**, **proprietary**.   **2.** A computer design that includes expansion slots for additional printed circuit boards to enhance or customize a system.

OpenDoc   An application programming interface (API) developed by Apple Computer, IBM, and other companies. OpenDoc allows you to embed application features, such as graphics and audio, that use different platforms into a single compound document.

Open Software Foundation   *See* OSF.

operand   **1.** A number or variable on which a mathematical operation is performed. In the expression *8 + x, 8* and *x* are the operands, and the operation is addition.   **2.** In programming, the data on which a single instruction acts.

operating environment   The type of interface and command structure under which one operates a computer. For example, the Apple Macintosh computer environment is a graphical user interface that uses icons and menus. The term is often used to make a distinction between a true operating system such as Microsoft Windows NT and a program such as Microsoft Windows 3.1, which seems to function as an operating system but in fact relies on DOS. *See also* **environment**.

operating system   *Abbreviated* OS   Software designed to control the hardware of a specific computer system in order to allow users and application programs to employ it easily. The operating system mediates between hardware and applications programs. It handles the details of sending instructions to the hardware and allocating system resources in case of conflicts, thus relieving applications developers of this burden and providing a standard platform for new programs. Common operating systems for personal computers are DOS, OS/2, Mac OS X, Unix, Windows ME, and Windows 2000.

operation   **1.** An action performed on one or more numbers or variables. Addition, subtraction, multiplication, and division are common arithmetic operations. *See also* **operand, operator.**   **2.** In programming, an action resulting from a single instruction.

operator   A symbol or character that represents an operation. In computing, the following symbols are used as common mathematical operators: + (addition), − (subtraction), * (multiplication), / (division), and ^ (exponentiation). In programming, spreadsheets, and database query languages, one encounters Boolean operators such as AND, OR, and NOT, and relational operators, such as > (greater than) and < (less than).

optical character recognition   *Abbreviated* **OCR**   The use of a light-sensitive device, such as an optical scanner or reader, to identify and encode printed or handwritten characters. The scanner matches the patterns of light and dark on a printed page against patterns stored in memory to determine the letter of the alphabet, numerical character, or punctuation mark. Once a page has been processed using OCR, it can be stored as computer text instead of as a graphic. A page that is scanned into the computer or received over a fax modem can be converted into a computer file using and then edited.

optical disk   A plastic-coated disk that stores digital data, such as music or text, as tiny pits etched into the surface to be read by a laser. Optical disks provide much higher storage density than magnetic disks, but the data may take longer to retrieve and optical disk technology is still expensive. Some optical disks are used for read-only data storage, others are erasable.

optical fiber   *See* **fiber optics**.

optical mouse   A mouse that senses motion by reflecting the light from a pair of light-emitting diodes (LEDs) off a special pad marked with a grid of colored lines. Optical mice are more precise than mechanical ones but are also more expensive. The optomechanical mouse is a hybrid that uses a rolling ball as in a mechanical mouse but replaces the mechanical motion-encoder wheels with optical encoders. The optical encoders consist of a pair of slotted wheels that periodically interrupt the signals sent from two LEDs to a pair of light-sensitive transistors. The optomechanical mouse provides some of the precision of the optical mouse but does not require a special pad.

optical resolution   The resolution at which a scanner or other video device can digitize images without being enhanced by software, measured in dots per inch.

optical scanner   A device that converts images and text printed on paper into digital information that can be stored as a computer file and processed by graphics software. Optical scanners work by sensing the light and dark areas on a page and digitizing the lightness values, converting them into numerical values that are recorded in electronic form as a bit-mapped graphic.

There are currently 3 main types of optical scanners. Sheet-fed scanners, which operate much like fax machines, require the manual insertion of single sheets of paper. A flatbed scanner works like an office copying machine and can scan books and other printed material. Hand-held scanners are relatively inexpensive and can also be used on books but can only scan part of a page at a time. When using a hand-held scanner, scanning a whole page requires multiple passes and a steady hand. Scanners also vary in their resolution, which ranges from 300 to 1,200 or more dots per inch, and in their ability to perform gray scale scanning; however, gray scale scanners are being phased out now that high-resolution color scanners are also available.

Scanners are often used to insert graphics or text copied from other sources into a document. Because all images are stored in bitmap form, however, it is important to remember that text copied by a scanner cannot be edited in a word processing program; this can only be done if the text is read and converted to ASCII characters by an optical character recognition program.

optimization 1. The process of increasing the computing speed of a task on a machine without losing any vital elements of the task. For example, the optimization of a program that is to run on a parallel processor can be performed by analyzing and flagging for the processor steps in the program that do not rely directly upon each other and can be performed simultaneously. 2. The process of improving something based on the importance of some criteria. For example, a design may be optimized for reuse by using generic names and functions.

option 1. A character or string that may be added to a command at the user's discretion to change the way the command works, but is not required. For example, the DOS command DIR, issued by itself, brings to the screen a list of files in the current directory, in their order on the disk and with subdirectory names first. The use of command line options, however, lets you issue a command such as DIR /P /A:-R, which yields a directory with pauses when the screen is full (/P) and does not list any files marked with the attribute read-only (/A:-R). In DOS, command options are usually preceded by a forward slash or a hyphen. *Also called* **switch**. *See also* **argument**. 2. In graphical user interfaces, a choice that can be made within a dialog box.

Option key A key on Apple Macintosh computer keyboards that when pressed in combination with another key generates a number of special characters or alternate commands.

OR A Boolean operator that returns the value TRUE if either or both of its operands are TRUE. Table 18 shows the results of the OR operator. *Also called* **inclusive OR.**

TABLE 18 Results of OR Operator

a	b	a OR a
FALSE	FALSE	FALSE
FALSE	TRUE	TRUE
TRUE	FALSE	TRUE
TRUE	TRUE	TRUE

Oracle A database management system developed by Oracle Corporation that runs on Unix and Microsoft Windows.

ordinal number A number indicating position in a series or order. The ordinal numbers are first (1st), second (2nd), third (3rd), and so on.

orientation The presentation of a page so that it is wider than it is tall or taller than it is wide. *See illustration at* **landscape.** *See also* **landscape, portrait.**

original equipment manufacturer *See* **OEM.**

orphan In word processing, a first line of a paragraph that appears as the last line on a page. *See also* **widow.**

OS *Abbreviation for* **operating system.**

OS/2 An operating system for personal computers originally developed by IBM and Microsoft Corporation to be the successor to DOS. OS/2 requires an Intel 80286 or later microprocessor, and unlike DOS it can use protected mode. This allows it to offer such features as virtual memory and multitasking. Versions of OS/2 after version 1.0 provide a graphical user interface called Presentation Manager. Versions 2.0 and 2.1, developed by IBM alone, are major advances that make full use of the 32-bit architecture of the 80386 and later processors. Version 2.1 supports the multitasking of DOS programs. Its successor, version 3.0, also known as OS/2 Warp, requires 4MB of RAM to operate, which is less than the 6MB required to run version

2.1. OS/2 Warp supports a plug and play capability that automatically installs and configures PCMCIA cards.

OSF   *Abbreviation of* **Open Software Foundation.**   A foundation created by nine computer companies to create a common operating system and interfaces based on Unix and the X Window System. The goal of the foundation is to develop a single software operating environment that would run on a number of different hardware platforms. The nine companies are Apollo, DEC, Hewlett-Packard, IBM, Bull, Nixdorf, Philips, Siemens and Hitachi.

outdent   *See* **hanging indent.**

outline font   A printer font or screen font in which the outlines of each character are defined by a mathematical formula. The printer then fills in the outlines at its maximum resolution. TrueType is a popular page description language for defining outline fonts.

Unlike bit-mapped fonts, outline fonts are scalable; that is, they can be adjusted in size without becoming distorted. Because mathematical formulas adjust the lines and arcs of the outline, you need only one font in the printer's memory to print or display any type size from 2 to 127 points. However, fonts that are scaled at low resolutions may not look very good or even readable on screen, and may benefit from hints. *Also called* **scalable font, vector font.** *See illustration.*

OUTLINE FONT   Bit-mapped and outline fonts

output   *n.* Information produced by a computer, such as the results of processing data input to the computer. Output can be printed, displayed on a screen, written to disk, or transferred via networks to other computers.

v. To send output to a printer, display screen, storage device, modem, or other output device. *See also* **input.**

output device   A machine that enables you to get information out of a computer. Printers, display screens, and speakers are examples of output devices. *See also* **input device.**

OverDrive   An Intel microprocessor that is an upgrade for some 486 chips. Generally you can upgrade the 486 quickly by inserting the

OverDrive chip into an empty socket designed for it or into the socket that the chip you're replacing came from.

overflow error An error that results, for example, when a calculation produces a unit of data too large to be stored in the memory location allotted to it. An overflow error may also occur when a modem receives data too fast for the CPU (central processing unit). *Also called* **buffer overflow**.

overlaid windows A display mode in which windows overlap each other, with only the topmost window displayed in full. Overlaid windows are also called cascading windows, especially if the windows overlap in such a way that the title bar remains visible in each window. *See also* **tiled windows, zoom**. *See illustration at* **desktop**.

overstrike mode **1.** In word processing, a mode in which you can type two characters in the same position so as to create or simulate another character that may not be available, such as o and / for the character ø. **2.** *See* **overwrite mode**.

overwrite To record new data on a disk where other data is already stored, thus destroying the old data.

overwrite mode In word processing, a mode in which you can type over an existing character and replace it with a new character. Most word processors allow you to select either overwrite mode or insert mode. In insert mode, typing inserts new characters but does not delete old ones. *Also called* **overstrike mode, typeover mode**.

[P]

p *Abbreviation of* **pico-**.

pack To store data in compressed form by either compressing a file or eliminating the space between files on a disk. A packed file is a file in a compressed format. Some modems pack data before transmission. Since fewer bytes need to be sent, the data can be transmitted in less time. The receiving modem must then be able to unpack or uncompress the data. *See also* **data compression**.

packaged software Software not designed for a specific client but written for mass use and commercially distributed through dealers and other channels. *Also called* **shrink-wrapped software**.

packed file A file that has undergone data compression so as to take up less memory. There are various programs available for packing files, and each employs its own set of codes to represent data. This means that you usually need a copy of the program used to pack a file in order to uncompress it. Most files available for downloading from bulletin board systems have been packed. Many people pack all files they don't need on a regular basis. The most popular packing software is *Zip, PKZip, and WinZip*.

packet A short block of data transmitted in a packet switching network. *See also* **datagram**.

Packet Internet Groper *See* PING.

packet sniffer A program that intercepts data transmitted over the Internet and translates it back into human-readable text. Network administrators use packet sniffers to help locate and relieve network congestion. Unencrypted transmissions are insecure and are liable to be read by people running packet sniffers. Packet sniffers are also used for illicit purposes such as obtaining passwords or credit card numbers. *Also called* **sniffer**.

packet switching A strategy for the transmission of data over a network in which the data is divided into packets; each packet is independently provided with a path between the origin and the destination. This strategy is commonly used in local area networks (LANs) and wide area networks (WANs), and capitalizes on the increase in efficiency that is obtained when there are many paths available and there is a large volume of traffic over these paths.

page A fixed quantity of memory. In graphics programs, for example, a page of memory corresponds to one screen's worth of images. In virtual memory, a page is a set amount of memory, usually 256, 512, or 1,024 bytes, that can be moved as a block between RAM and a disk.

page break In word processing, a separation between pages of text. Most word processing programs create a page break automatically when you have entered enough text to fill a page. *See also* **forced page break**.

page description language *Abbreviated* **PDL** A programming language for controlling the layout and contents of printed pages with instructions indicating, for example, what fonts and margins are to be used. A page description language gives descriptions of characters and graphics that a printer can process according to its own capabilities, so that the same page description language description will yield different results from printers with different resolutions. This means that although you don't have to change the printing codes in your document every time you use a different printer, you can use only a printer with some processing capabilities of its own. Two popular laser printer page description languages are Adobe PostScript and Hewlett-Packard PCL (Printer Control Language).

Page Down key   *Abbreviated* **PgDn**   A key that moves the cursor down a screenful of lines in most word processing programs but may have other uses in other applications.

page fault   An error that occurs when there is an attempt to read or write data that is not available in random access memory (RAM). When this happens, the system gets the data from a storage device and places it in the RAM.

page file   A file on a hard disk that contains portion of the memory data required by programs. A page file is used for the temporary storage of data in memory that is not currently in use. The process of writing data to a page file and reading data from a page file is called paging. Paging allows large applications to run using relatively small amounts of memory.

page frame   An area of the CPU's usable address space to which a page of virtual memory may be mapped from disk.

page layout program   An application that allows you to arrange text and graphics from various files together on a page. Page layout programs let you change fonts, crop graphics, create text columns, and adjust the size of text and images. The page design you are creating is displayed as a graphics image onscreen. Two popular page layout programs are PageMaker from Aldus Corporation and QuarkXPress, developed by Quark, Inc. *See also* **desktop publishing**.

page preview   *See* **preview**.

page printer   A printer, such as a laser printer, that processes all the data for one page at the same time. Such printers require comparatively larger amounts of memory than others because the data for each page must be placed in memory before it is printed.

pages per minute   *Abbreviated* **ppm**   A measure of the speed of certain printers, especially laser printers. A printer's ppm rating is calculated by its manufacturer and is usually based on how fast it can print a page that has text in a single typeface and no graphics or other special elements. Therefore, this rating is not a reliable measure if you use many typefaces or lots of graphics. In the latter case, the graphics pages per minute (gppm) rating is more meaningful.

Page Up key *Abbreviated* **PgUp** A key that moves the cursor up a screenful of lines in most word processing programs but may have other uses in other applications.

pagination 1. The dividing of a document into pages, as in word processing. Most programs do this automatically. 2. The numbering of the pages of a document at the top or bottom of each page.

paging In virtual memory systems, the transfer of pages of data between RAM and an auxiliary memory device, such as a hard disk. Paging allows virtual memory to seem larger than actual physical memory. When you ask the computer for a page of data not on hand in RAM, the operating system exchanges a page of data in RAM for the requested data residing elsewhere. This can greatly increase the apparent amount of RAM available. *See also* **page**, **virtual memory**.

paint program A graphics application whose images are stored as bit maps. A paint program lets you select a tool, such as a paintbrush or a can of spray paint, from a group of icons and paint with that tool in the shape and width it permits. Whatever area you cover with that tool will be shaded with the solid or patterned background you have chosen. You can also select an icon that guides you in drawing circles, curves, or straight lines. Table 19 shows some common paint program tools. *See also* **draw program**.

TABLE 19 Common Paint Program Tools

Tool	Function
Pencil	Draws a line one pixel thick
Eraser	Erases black or colored areas
Paintbrush	Paints areas with the selected fill pattern
Paint Bucket	Pours the selected fill pattern into an enclosed area
Airbrush	Sprays the selected fill pattern with adjustable rates of flow, spray area, and dot size
Dropper	Sets the writing color to the color of the selected pixel
Freehand	Paints freeform shapes
Grabber	Moves the document in the window
Text	Enters text

palette **1.** The group of colors that a given monitor is capable of displaying. **2.** The selection of colors available in a given graphics program. In general, fewer colors can be displayed on-screen at one time than are available in the palette overall. **3.** The group of patterns, widths, and drawing tools, such as paintbrushes and pencils, available in a paint or draw program.

palmtop A computer that is small enough to fit in the palm of your hand and usually features a PIM (personal information manager). *See also* **PDA**.

Pantone Matching System *Abbreviated* **PMS** A standard system developed by Pantone, Inc. for identifying approximately 500 ink colors, each assigned a specific number. PMS also allows you to mix colors. Many graphics and desktop publishing programs use PMS, as do traditional print shops.

paper feed The mechanism that feeds paper through a printer. For example, some dot-matrix printers use a tractor feed. *See also* **friction feed, tractor feed**.

paperless office An office in which the use of computer technology has eliminated the need for the use of paper as the medium on which information is transmitted and stored. Although the use of paper can be reduced, as by sending email instead of paper memos, in reality few offices have significantly reduced their use of paper.

paper-white display A monochrome monitor that displays characters and graphics in black against a white background.

parallel **1.** Relating to or used in the simultaneous transmission of several bits of data over separate wires within a cable or over separate communications lines. *See also* **parallel interface, parallel port, serial**. **2.** Relating to or carrying out the simultaneous performance of separate tasks. *See also* **parallel processing**.

parallel interface A system for the transmission of data along several parallel wires. The interface itself consists of these wires, their connectors, and the parallel ports in each of the devices being connected. Each wire transmits one bit at a time so that together they transmit several bits simultaneously. In a Centronics interface, there are eight of these wires, so that data is transmitted in bytes. The remaining wires send information telling one device that the other is ready to receive or send data. A printer is usually connected to a personal computer by a parallel interface. *See also* **serial interface**.

parallel port   A port with multiple pin holes for use in a parallel interface. Each pin in the input/output connector connects to a parallel wire. Most computers have at least one parallel port, usually used by a printer. *See also* **serial port**.

parallel processing   The simultaneous processing of different tasks in a program by two or more microprocessors. Parallel processing is usually carried out by a single computer with more than one CPU (central processing unit), but it can also be carried out by several computers (each with a single CPU) connected together in a network. Sophisticated software is required to distribute tasks among the microprocessors. In multiprocessing, a program is broken down into sequential tasks so that, for example, one microprocessor sorts data, another analyzes it, and a third sends the results to a display screen. Parallel processing contrasts with multitasking, in which one CPU runs several programs at once.

parameter   1. One of a group of adjustable factors that distinguish an environment or determine how a system will work. For example, when you determine what color will represent what on your display screen, or when you set the margins and page length in a word processing document, you are setting parameters.   2. A specification that you add or change in giving the computer a command. For example, if you give the DOS command COPY, you must specify what you want copied and where you want the copy to go. If you enter COPY A:\DFILE.RUR, the file name "DFILE.RUR" is a parameter that tells the computer what to copy.   3. In programming, a value that is passed to a function or routine so that it can be operated on to produce a result. *See also* **argument**.

parameter RAM   *Abbreviated* **PRAM**. In Apple Macintosh computers, a section of RAM that is powered by a battery and stores information about the system configuration, including date and time.

parent directory   A directory in which a subdirectory is located. For example, if you work in a directory called MYSTUFF and have a subdirectory called MEMOS, then MYSTUFF is the parent directory of, MEMOS. Each directory except the root directory has a parent directory.

parent process   A process that initiates one or more processes. Generally a process will not be completed until all the processes that it has initiated are also completed. *See also* **child process**.

parity The even or odd quality of the number of 1s or 0s in a set group of bits, often marked by an added parity bit and used to determine the integrity of data especially after transmission.

parity bit A bit added to a set group of bits to indicate parity so that the data can be checked for integrity.

park To lock the head of a hard disk drive above a part of the disk that contains no data. If you handle your disk drive too roughly, the head could fall, causing a head crash. If you park the disk before moving it, even if the head falls it won't cause a crash. Many new hard disks park themselves automatically whenever the power is turned off, and many disk utility packages have parking programs.

parse To break a string of characters into groups of smaller strings using a specific set of rules. For example, a program can count the number of words on a line by parsing the line using blank space as an indication of word boundaries.

partition *n.* A section of a hard disk that functions as an independent hard disk. An entire disk may consist of only one partition, or it may have several. Partitions must be created before the disk can be formatted and used by an operating system. Different types of disks and interfaces may require different formatting procedures.

v. To separate a hard disk into partitions.

Pascal A high-level language designed by Nicklaus Wirth in the early 1970s. Pascal is a highly structured language with a relatively simple syntax. Because Pascal insists on careful organization, it is popular for teaching programming and widely used in colleges and universities. Pascal is named after Blaise Pascal, a 17th-century French mathematician and religious philosopher who developed one of the first mechanical adding machines.

passive-matrix display A type of liquid-crystal display that controls an entire row of pixels in the liquid-crystal layer with a single transistor. Passive-matrix displays tend to be less bright and clear than active-matrix displays, but they also cost less. *See also* **flat-panel display**.

password A secret sequence of characters that is used as an access code for a file, program, computer, or network. All authorized users have a password; no one else can gain access to the file, program, computer, or network in question. To maintain security, some systems ask users to change their passwords on a regular basis.

paste   To insert text or graphics into a document from a buffer. *See also* **clipboard, copy, cut.**

patch   *n.* A piece of code added to software in order to fix a bug, especially as a temporary correction between two releases.

   v. To correct a bug in an item of software, especially as a temporary correction between two releases.

path   1. A sequence of commands or a link between points that is needed to reach a particular goal. Every programming routine, for example, has a path leading through a number of commands. A modem establishes a path for communication between a computer and a network or another computer. You can create a path in a graphics program and insert text along it so that the text appears as a curved line. The Apple Macintosh computer sets up a path to every file that you open and identifies each path internally with a distinct number. In DOS, a path is the list of directories in which the operating system will search for an executable file if you type in the file name as a command.   2. *See* **pathname.**

pathname   In a hierarchical file system, the name of the file you are accessing, together with the names of all the folders or directories that you have to go through to reach it from the drive and folder or directory you are in now. For example, if you are working in Windows in the C: drive (the primary hard disk drive) in a directory called \WORK, and you want to reach the file QUERIES.DOC, which is in a subdirectory LEFTOVER, then the pathname would be LEFTOVER\ QUERIES.DOC. If you had to get to QUERIES.DOC from the A: drive (a floppy disk drive), the pathname would be C:\WORK\LEFTOVER\QUERIES.DOC.

pattern recognition   The capability of a computer to identify patterns in order to pick out images in streams of visual data or sounds in streams of audio data.

Pause key   A key that interrupts a command, a program, or the on screen display of data when pressed. Keyboards for IBM PC and compatible computers have a Pause key that stops the display of data when you are scrolling through several screens. Many games have Pause keys so that you can interrupt the game and come back to it later.

PC   *Abbreviation of* **personal computer.**

PCB   *Abbreviation of* **printed circuit board.**

PC card   *See* **PCMCIA** (sense 2).

PC-DOS The version of DOS sold by IBM.

PCI *Abbreviation of* **Peripheral Component Interface.** A local computer bus designed by Intel that runs at 33MHz. The PCI bus is very common in computers that use Pentium, Alpha, and PowerPC microprocessors.

PCL *Abbreviation of* **Printer Control Language.** A set of commands developed by Hewlett-Packard used to control its printers and also used by all HP-compatible printers. Recent versions of PCL support a scalable font technology, Intellifont.

PCM *Abbreviation of* **pulse code modulation.** One manner by which an analog signal can be converted into a digital signal. PCM involves measuring the magnitude of the analog signal; the data is sent as digital information at rapid uniform intervals. PCM is used in modern modem protocols such as v.90.

PCMCIA *Abbreviation of* **Personal Computer Memory Card International Association.** **1.** An association founded in 1989 to create a standard for a credit card-sized card originally designed to function as a memory card for personal computers, especially portables. **2.** The card, also called a **PC card**, designed as a standard by this association. The Type I PCMCIA card is 3.3mm thick and functions as a memory card; other types of PCMCIA have taken on additional functions. The Type II card is 5mm thick and can be used for attaching a modem and fax, and the Type III card is 10.5mm thick and can be used for attaching hard disks and other peripherals that can accommodate more memory.

PDA *Abbreviation of* **personal digital assistant.** A lightweight, hand-held computer, often featuring an internal modem and cellular phone to be used as a link to a larger computer. Most PDAs are pen computers, which have an operating system that supports handwriting recognition. Some support voice recognition, allowing you to use your voice as input. *See also* **palmtop, pen computer.**

PDF *Abbreviation of* **Portable Document Format.** A format for graphical data that allows a document to retain its appearance for display or printing purposes between different operating system platforms.

PDL *Abbreviation of* **page description language.**

peer-to-peer network A network of personal computers, each of which acts as both client and server, so that each can exchange files and email directly with every other computer on the network. Each computer can tap into any of the others, although access can be restricted to those files a computer's user chooses to make public. Peer-to-peer networks are cheaper than client/server networks but less efficient when large amounts of data need to be exchanged. They work best with 20-25 users. *Also called* **file sharing network**.

pel   *A shortening of* **pixel**.

pen computer   A computer, especially a PDA, that lets you input and retrieve data by writing with a special pen. One kind of pen computer has a light-sensitive detector that allows you to use a light pen to select objects on the screen. Most pen computers, however, instead have a pressure-sensitive screen that allows you to use a stylus directly on the screen. Pen computers can recognize handwritten characters, and many contain slots in which you can insert devices such as modems.

Pentium   A microprocessor designed by Intel for personal computers and workstations and introduced in 1993. Pentium is so named because it represents the fifth generation of microprocessors from Intel, succeeding the popular 80486 series. Pentium performs calculations many times faster than the 486 microprocessor and is fast enough to support such CPU-intensive applications as speech recognition and high-bandwidth video. *See table at* **Intel microprocessors**.

Pentium II   A version of the Pentium Pro microprocessor, developed by Intel. Pentium II's processing speeds range from 233 to 450 megahertz. The PII (as it is known) was the first Intel microprocessor to incorporate MMX technology for improved multimedia performance.

Pentium III   A Pentium processor developed by Intel, released in 1999. The PIII operates at processing speeds of up to 1.13 gigahertz.

Pentium Pro   The successor to the Pentium microprocessor, developed by Intel and released in 1996. The Pentium Pro combines CISC and RISC technologies to increase processing speed and is optimized for 32-bit applications.

peripheral   A device, such as a printer, modem, keyboard, monitor, or hard disk, perceived as distinct from and external to a computer's CPU (central processing unit). Some people call monitors and keyboards peripherals, but since a computer might be unusable without these devices, others would not consider them truly peripheral.

Peripheral Component Interface   *See* **PCI**.

Perl A programming language, developed by Larry Wall, designed to process strings. Perl is widely used for web server applications. Perl stands for *Practical Extraction and Report Language.*

personal communicator A lightweight, hand-held pen computer that can access a PIM, fax, modem, voice mail, electronic mail, and telephone. Personal communicators are designed to allow people who work away from their desks to use their electronic equipment from a distance.

personal computer *Abbreviated* **PC** A computer built around a single microprocessor and designed to be independent of a mainframe or any other computer. Personal computers have their own operating systems, software, and peripherals so that they can be set up and run without any additional equipment. Personal computers can be linked to networks by modems or by cables. Personal computers tend to be less costly and less powerful than workstations, but at the high end of the market personal computers can and often do substitute for workstations. *Also called* **microcomputer.**

personal digital assistant *See* **PDA.**

personal information manager *See* **PIM.**

petabyte A unit of measurement of computer memory or data storage capacity equal to 1,125,899,906,842,624 (2^{50} bytes). One petabyte equals 1,024 terabytes. Informally, the term is sometimes used to refer to one quadrillion (1,000,000,000,000,000) bytes.

PGA *See* **pin grid array.**

PgDn *Abbreviation of* **Page Down key.**

PGP *Abbreviation of* **Pretty Good Privacy.** A powerful public key encryption algorithm created by Philip Zimmerman. This algorithm, which is in the public domain, is the most common method of encrypting messages transmitted over the Internet. *See also* **encryption, decryption, public key cryptography.**

PgUp *Abbreviation of* **Page Up key.**

phosphor The phosphorescent coating inside the screen of a cathode-ray tube.

Photo CD **1.** A CD on which the digitized image data of still photographs is stored. **2.** A CD on which digitized image data, illustrations, text, and audio data for interactive multimedia presentations can be stored. **3.** An imaging technology developed by Eastman Kodak to read and write image data to CDs.

phreak   One who engages in phreaking.

phreaking   The manipulation of telephone systems to allow one to make free calls or charge them to others' accounts. One early form of phreaking involved replicating the tones used by the switching systems, effectively allowing the user to make free long distance phone calls.

physical   Of, relating to, or being hardware. A physical hard disk, for example, is a piece of hardware that you can see and feel. It may be partitioned into a number of logical drives that function as if they were physically separate, so that you could have several logical drives but only one physical drive. *See also* **virtual**.

physical address   An address for data located in physical memory. Programs that use virtual memory must swap virtual addresses for physical addresses.

physical memory   The chips that are installed in a computer and used as random access memory (RAM). *See also* **virtual memory**.

PIC   A graphics file format developed by the Lotus Development Corporation and originally used with the spreadsheet program Lotus 1-2-3. The PIC format is still used with many popular graphics packages. *See table at* **graphics file format**.

pica   In typesetting, word processing, and desktop publishing, a unit of measurement equal to twelve points or approximately ⅙ of an inch.

pico-   *Abbreviated* **p**   A prefix indicating one trillionth (10^{-12}), as in *picosecond*.

picosecond   *Abbreviated* **psec**   A unit of time equal to one trillionth of a second (10^{-12}).

PICT   A graphics file format that supports both object-oriented and bit-mapped graphics. PICT was developed by Apple Computer and is used by almost all Macintosh graphics programs to store and exchange graphics documents. The original PICT format supported 8 colors along with black-and-white images. An updated version, PICT2, supports 256 colors. *See table at* **graphics file format**.

pie chart or **pie graph**   A graph in which each value is presented as a proportional slice or wedge of a whole, represented by the complete circle.

PIF   *See* **program information file**.

PIM   *Abbreviation of* **personal information manager**.   A database management system geared to personal information, such as notes, appointments, and addresses. PIMs often come with calculators, calendars, and schedulers.

pin **1.** One of the small metal prongs at the end of a connector that fit into the holes in a port. **2.** One of the wires attached to a magnet on the head of a dot-matrix printer. The greater the number of pins in a dot-matrix printer, the higher the resolution. **3.** One of the plastic sprockets on a dot-matrix printer. The pins fit into the holes along the edges of the paper and hold the paper in place. *See also* **tractor feed**. **4.** One of the prongs at the bottom of a chip. The pins connect the chip to the printed circuit board.

pincushion distortion The distortion on a monitor in which the horizontal and vertical lines curve inward toward the center of the screen. Most monitors have controls that allow you to correct distortion. *See also* **barrel distortion**.

pine A Unix program for reading and composing email, developed by the University of Washington. Pine stands for *pine is not elm* or *Program for Internet News and Email. See also* **elm**.

pin feed *See* **tractor feed**.

PING *Abbreviation of* **Packet Internet Groper**. A program that sends a message to another computer and waits for an acknowledgment in response. PING is normally used to check if another computer on the network is reachable.

pin grid array *Abbreviated* **PGA** The mounting of pins on a chip so that they protrude from the bottom, rather than from the sides. This method is used for chips with a large number of pins as opposed to dual or single inline processors, such as modern microprocessors.

pipe **1.** A temporary connection in memory that acts a conduit in passing data, in which the output of one process is the input to another process. **2.** The symbol | on a keyboard, usually the shift character of the backslash (\ ). **3.** A Unix and DOS command that instructs the operating system to send the output of one command to be the input to another command. For example, the command DIR lists the current directory's contents. The command MORE places breaks in long streams of data into so that the data displays screen by screen instead of scrolling by all at once. Thus, DIR | MORE takes the output of DIR, the directory's contents, and makes that the input for the MORE command, so that the contents of the directory will appear on the screen one screen at a time, prompting you to go on to the next screen when you want to. **4.** *See* **bandwidth.**

pipeline burst cache A type of memory caching that pre-fetches data in a burst mode into a small cache close to the microprocessor. Values are passed in and out of the microprocessor through this cache, setting up a pipeline feeding to and from the main cache and disk storage.

pipelining The ability in modern microprocessors to continue processing a sequence of instructions before the processing of the first instruction is complete. This is analogous to a factory assembling cars where many cars roll through the assembly line at various stages before the first car is completed. In a computer processor, this is accomplished by having one instruction being fetched from memory while the arithmetic part of the previous instruction is completed.

piracy *See* **software piracy.**

pitch In word processing, the number of printed characters per inch. In proportional pitch fonts, pitch is an average. Ten pitch, for example, would mean an average of ten characters per inch in proportional pitch, or precisely ten characters per inch in fixed pitch or fixed space.

pixel *Abbreviation of* **picture element.** The smallest unit of an image. A display screen is divided into millions of tiny dots of light called pixels, arranged in rows and columns. When you type a character or draw a line onscreen, the computer turns the pixels on in a specific pattern to render the image. If a pixel has only two color values (for example, black and white) it can be encoded by one bit of information. Colors or shades of gray can be displayed by increasing the number of bits used to represent each pixel. An 8-bit color monitor, for instance, uses 8 bits for each pixel, making it possible to display

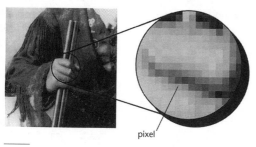

pixel

PIXEL

2^8 or 256 different colors or shades of gray. Technically, an image of 2 colors is called a bit map, and an image of more than 2 colors is called a pixel map. *See illustration. See also* **convergence, resolution**.

PKUNZIP   A method of file decompression developed by PKWARE, Inc, and distributed as shareware. PKUNZIP decompresses files that have been compressed using PKZIP or compatible compression programs.

PKZIP   A method of file compression developed by PKWARE, Inc. and distributed as shareware.

plaintext   **1.** The unencrypted form of a piece of text that has been encrypted, as for transmission. *See also* **ciphertext, decryption, encryption.**   **2.** ASCII text as opposed to a graphic image of text or a word processor file with embedded formatting characters.

plasma display   A kind of flat-panel display used in some laptop computers. Most plasma displays produce orange images on a black background. Research is being conducted on ways to make color plasma displays, which, if they prove practical, might be used in high-definition television screens.

platform   The part of a computer system that is perceived as most fundamental and with which any additional hardware and software must be compatible. Thus, one could refer to an Apple Macintosh or IBM PC platform, but one might also consider an operating system to be part of the platform.

platter   One of the round metal plates inside a hard disk. The platters are coated with a magnetic film containing scattered iron particles. Data is encoded by the alignment of the iron particles in a magnetic field. Each platter has two read/write heads, one on each side. *See illustration at* **hard disk**.

plot   To draw an image mapped onto a grid so that each point in the image can be located in relation to the x-axes, y-axes, and sometimes z-axes.

plotter   An output device that physically draws by moving a pen. The computer tells the plotter how the graphics map on to x-axes and y-axes. In many plotters, the paper moves along one axis while the pen moves along the other.

plug   A connector linking two devices.

plug and play *also* **plug 'n' play**   **1.** An architecture for personal computers characterized by the ability to identify an added component and configure itself with respect to this component. The Apple Macintosh system, with its closed architecture, is functionally plug and play. For example, on a Mac that you wanted to upgrade to multimedia, you could install a CD-ROM drive and plug in the speakers, and the computer would understand what they were and what to do with them. **2. Plug and Play** A specification for plug and play architecture designed by Microsoft and Intel as a subsystem of Windows 95.

plug-compatible Being a hardware device that can connect without modification to a computer or device made by a different company. For example, a plug-compatible modem can be plugged into a computer without the cables having to be rewired.

plug-in *See* **add-in**.

PMS *Abbreviation of* **Pantone Matching System**.

PNG *Abbreviation of* **Portable Network Graphics**. A bit-mapped graphics format that is similar to GIF. There are no patent or licensing issues restricting the use of PNG, which was developed so that users can avoid the legal issues involved with using GIF, which uses a patented compression algorithm.

point *v.* In a graphical user interface, to move a pointer to an item you plan to select.

n. **1.** In typography, approximately ¹/₇₂ of an inch, used to measure character height and leading between lines of text. **2.** In graphics, a pixel. **3.** In graphics, a unique location where two axes meet in a geometric figure. For example, you can identify the center of a circle as a point.

point and click In a graphical user interface (GUI), to choose an option by sliding a mouse that controls the cursor position (*pointing*) over a level surface and activating one of the mouse buttons (*clicking*) one or more times. It is the primary means of command execution when the GUI cursor is controlled by a mouse.

point and shoot *See* **point and click**.

pointer **1.** In a graphical user interface, a symbol appearing on a display screen that lets the user select a command by clicking with a mouse when the symbol is on the appropriate button or option. You move the pointer, which often appears in the shape of an arrow, with a mouse. **2.** In programming and database management systems, a variable that gives the memory address of a piece of data.

pointing device   An input device with which you can move a cursor or a pointer. Common pointing devices are mice, joysticks, light pens, and trackballs.

point of presence   *See* **POP** (sense 1).

point-to-point protocol   *See* **PPP**.

polling   The ongoing requests that a computer makes sequentially to each device with which it is connected as a way of determining if any device has data that it needs to transmit.

polyline   A drawing tool used to create polygons. You can create a polygon by drawing a line up to a point, then moving on in a different direction to the next point, until the figure is closed. The polygon can then be manipulated as a single entity.

POP   **1.** *Abbreviation of* **point of presence**.   In a wide area network (WAN), a point where you can obtain dial-up access with a local telephone call. Most Internet service providers (ISPs) provide POPs in many of the cities and towns that they serve.   **2.** *Abbreviation of* **Post Office Protocol**.   A protocol for Internet servers that stores and transmits email for clients who connect to the server for their email services.

pop-up menu   A menu that appears on the screen in response to a user action and is separate from the primary application menus. It generally remains onscreen until you select a command from the menu. *See also* **pull-down menu**.

pop-up utility   A memory-resident program that can be accessed from within any application by pressing a hot key. *See also* **desk accessory, terminate and stay resident**.

pop-up window   A window that appears on the screen when you select an option or press a function key. The window may supply information or allow you to choose options. Generally, the window will remain open until you explicitly close it. Sometimes other processing in that application is inhibited until the window is closed.

port   *n.* A place where data can pass into or out of a CPU (central processing unit), computer, or peripheral. In the case of computers and peripherals, a port is generally a socket into which a connector can be plugged. In the case of microprocessors, a port is a particular point in memory reserved for incoming and outgoing data. *See also* **parallel port, SCSI, serial port**.

v. To modify software so that it may be run on a different machine or platform.

portable 1. Designating software that is capable of running on two or more kinds of computers or with two or more kinds of operating systems; machine-independent. 2. Designating hardware that is capable of being carried around. The first computers termed portable weighed more than 25 pounds. Today most people would not consider anything heavier than a laptop truly portable.

Portable Document Format *See* **PDF.**

Portable Network Graphics *See* **PNG.**

portal A website considered as an entry point to other websites. A portal may provide access to a search engine, or the site might itself provide a search engine.

portrait Of or relating to a mode in which a page is oriented so that it is taller than it is wide. Most documents are printed in portrait mode. *See also* **landscape**.

POSIX *Abbreviation of* **Portable Operating System Interface.** A set of standards that defines the way in which software is to be written so that it can be run on compliant operating systems, including most versions of Unix and Windows NT.

post *v.* To send a message to a public forum on a network, such as to a newsgroup, website, or bulletin board.
    n. A message sent to a public forum on a network.

POST *Abbreviation of* **power-on self-test.** A set of operations stored in ROM (read-only memory) that tests each of a computer's components every time it is turned on. If the POST detects a problem, it will display an error message on the screen (if possible) and issue a beep or series of beeps as a warning in case the problem is in the monitor. If the POST does not detect any problems, the computer begins to boot, or load the operating system.

posterize In graphics and desktop publishing, to transform an image into a starker version by rounding all tonal values to a smaller number of possible values. An example is printing an image in black and white only, eliminating any shades of gray.

Post Office Protocol *See* **POP** (sense 2).

PostScript A high-level, object-oriented page description language developed by Adobe Systems, used to print high-resolution text and graphics. PostScript is used most often with laser printers, but it can be adapted to run on any kind of printer. PostScript uses outline fonts that are considerably smoother and better-looking than bit-mapped fonts. PostScript fonts are scalable; that is, they can be scaled to any desired size without distortions. PostScript fonts will also print at the full resolution offered by the printer. *See illustration at* **outline font**.

POTS *Abbreviation of* **Plain Old Telephone Service**. An informal acronym used to refer to a simple phone line connected to a telephone without any features or functions except for basic telephone service.

PowerBook Any of a group of Apple Macintosh laptop computers first released in 1992. All PowerBook computers have a built-in pointing device, and later versions come with an internal modem and an audio I/O device.

PowerBuilder A proprietary development environment for programming client/server database applications that supports many database environments including SQL Server, Oracle, and ODBC. Developers can create windows and controls using a graphical user interface from within the PowerBuilder environment.

power down To turn a computer or other device off.

Power-On Self Test *See* **POST**.

PowerPC A RISC-based microprocessor architecture jointly developed by IBM, Motorola, and Apple Computer. The initial PowerPC microprocessor, the Motorola MPC601, had a clock speed of 80 megahertz and could execute 3 instructions per clock cycle. Subsequent models include the Motorola PowerPC 603e and the Motorola PowerPC 604e. The current version is the Motorola PowerPC 7400, which operates at speeds of up to 450 megahertz.

power supply The electrical device that converts the alternating current (AC) of standard outlets to the lower-voltage direct current (DC) a computer requires. Most computer power supplies provide between 5 and 12 volts and anywhere from 90 to 250 watts. The higher the wattage, the more powerful the computer and the more peripherals it can support. Most modern computers that support peripherals require a power supply of at least 200 watts.

power up To turn a computer or other device on.

power user An experienced computer user who feels comfortable with the most complicated features of applications and learns new applications relatively quickly, but who is not necessarily a programmer.

ppm *Abbreviation of* **pages per minute**.

PPP   *Abbreviation of* **point-to-point protocol**.   A communications protocol developed as an improvement over SLIP. PPP can establish a direct serial connection between two computers over any full-duplex path. It then emulates other protocols, such as TCP/IP, allowing network connections over the serial line. With built-in error detection, security, as well as line-monitoring functions, it is quite a popular protocol for connecting to the Internet via modem.

PRAM   [PEE-ram]   *Abbreviation of* **parameter RAM**.

precision   The exactness with which a number is represented in memory. Precision depends on the number of bits allotted to a number; the more bits are allotted, the more digits can be used to represent a fraction. Some systems for representing floating-point numbers distinguish between double precision and single precision. Double precision allots twice as many bits to a number as single precision.

preemptive multitasking   A kind of multitasking in which the CPU (central processing unit) controls the sequence in which processes execute and the amount of time that is allotted to each process. It will interrupt one process and allow another process to run so that a single process does not monopolize the CPU. Unix and most Windows operating systems from Windows 95 onward use preemptive multitasking.

presentation graphics   A kind of graphics geared to business presentations of statistical information and featuring a wide variety of graphs and charts including pie charts, flow charts, and bar graphs. Presentation graphics lets you insert titles, labels, text, and clip art to make a graph or chart clearer and more interesting.

presentation layer   The software layer that accepts and displays data input by the user and displays data output to the user.

Presentation Manager   A graphical user interface (GUI) that provides a windowing environment for the IBM OS/2 operating system. Presentation Manager has many of the same features as the GUI on Apple Macintosh computers, such as pull-down menus, multiple on-screen windows, and desk accessories.

Pretty Good Privacy   *See* **PGP**.

preview   **1.** In word processing, a feature that allows the user to format a document for the printer and then view it on the display screen instead of printing it. The user can check to see if the appearance of the printed document will be satisfactory or not and can reset margins, spacing, and so on before printing. *Also called* **page preview**. *See also* **greeking, thumbnail**. **2.** The ability to examine how a page will appear before committing to an activity. Graphics packages may let you preview before exporting a certain format. Many packages allow you to preview clip art before choosing which image to insert.

primary cache   *See* **Level 1 cache**.

primary storage   The computer's RAM (random-access memory). Primary storage is directly accessible to the computer's CPU (central processing unit), unlike mass storage devices such as disk drives and tapes, which are sometimes referred to as secondary storage.

print   To send a document to the printer in order to obtain a hard copy; to route output to a printer rather than to a disk file.

printed circuit board   *Abbreviated* **PCB**   A flat plastic or fiberglass board on which electrically conductive circuits have been etched or laminated. Chips and other electronic components are mounted on the circuits. Computers consist of one or more printed circuit boards, usually called cards or adapters. The board that contains the CPU (central processing unit) is typically called the motherboard. *See illustration.*

PRINTED CIRCUIT BOARD (left) AND DETAIL (right)

printer   A device for printing text and graphics, especially onto paper. Table 20 compares features of various kinds of printers. *See also* **dot-matrix printer, impact printer, ink-jet printer, laser printer, line printer, liquid-crystal shutter printer, nonimpact printer, thermal printer, thermal wax printer**.

TABLE 20 Common Printer Types

Type	Letter Quality	Relative Speed	Other Characteristics
Bubble-jet printer	Near	Moderate	• Ink has a tendency to run immediately after printing • Often used for small, portable printers.
Dot-matrix printer	Near	Slow to moderate (slower speed for letter-quality printing)	• Can print on multilayer forms • Limited font availability • Uses a tractor-feed mechanism for paper handling
Impact printer	Yes	Slow	• Also called daisywheel printer • Used for multilayer forms
Line printer	No	Very fast	• Used in scientific research and business offices for high-speed printing • Extremely noisy
Laser printer; Liquid-crystal shutter printer; Light-emitting diode printer	Yes	Fast	• Unlimited font availability
Ink-jet printer	Yes	Moderate (often has faster draft-quality speed)	• Fonts readily available • Some models are portable • Some models can print in several colors • Ink can smear or spread on the page after printing • Inexpensive alternative to a laser printer
Thermal printer	No	Slow to fast	• Often comes built into many fax machines and adding machines; also sold separately as a label printer • Paper is slippery and tends to discolor over time
Thermal wax printer	No	Slow	• Usually can print in several colors with fairly high quality

Printer Control Language   *See* **PCL**.

printer driver   A program that enables a computer to work and communicate with a particular brand and model of printer. *See also* **Chooser, device driver**.

printer font   A font that is only available for use by a printer and cannot be displayed onscreen. If text is formatted with a printer font, it is displayed onscreen using a default screen font. You must wait until you print to see what the printer fonts used in a document look like. Printer fonts can be built into the printer (resident fonts), downloaded from disk into the printer's memory, or stored in a font cartridge. Users of Apple Macintosh computers or Microsoft Windows who may wish to avoid the discrepancy between screen and printer fonts can buy Adobe Type Manager (ATM) or Apple's TrueType outline fonts, which look the same on-screen as when printed.

printout   Printed output of text or data; hard copy.

Print Screen key   *Abbreviated* **Prt Sc**   A key on many IBM PC and compatible computer keyboards that when pressed sends whatever text and graphics are currently on the display screen to the printer (under DOS) or to the clipboard (under Microsoft Windows).

print server   *See* **server**.

print spooler   *See* **spooler**.

process   *n.*   **1.** A program.   **2.** A part of a program that does a single task.

v. To perform an operation, such as sorting or calculating, on data.

process color   Cyan, magenta, yellow, or black. *See* **CYMK**.

processor   **1.** *See* **microprocessor**.   **2.** *See* **CPU**.

program   *v.* To write a set of instructions that a computer can execute.
n. A set of instructions that a computer can execute. A program is a sequence of directions, called statements, that specify exactly what the computer needs to do to accomplish a predetermined task. A program is written in a programming language, a specially constructed vocabulary and set of rules for instructing a computer. Generally, one programs in a high-level language, such as Pascal, C, C++, or BASIC. Programs can also be written in assembly language, a low-level language one step removed from the machine language understood by the computer.

Programming instructions are often referred to as code. The program as written by the programmer is called the source code. A program that has been translated into machine language and is ready to run is known as an *executable program* or *executable code*. Software that you purchase consists of one or more executable programs.

program file   A file that contains an application or program. A data file contains work created with an application or program.

program information file   *Abbreviated* **PIF**.   A file that contains the instructions that allow a non-Windows application to run in Microsoft Windows.

programmable read-only memory   *See* **PROM**.

programmer   One who writes computer programs.

programming language   An artificial language consisting of a vocabulary along with grammatical rules used to write a set of instructions that can be translated into machine language and then executed by a computer. Machine language is the language the computer actually understands. Each different type of CPU (central processing unit) has its own unique machine language. English and other natural languages are not programming languages because they cannot be easily translated into machine language.

   The term programming language usually refers to high-level languages, such as FORTRAN, C, C++, Java, COBOL, Pascal, or BASIC. Lying below high-level languages are assembly languages, which are similar to machine languages. Programmers can also program in assembly languages.

   Lying above high-level languages are fourth-generation languages, usually called 4GLs. 4GLs are the closest to natural languages.

   Regardless of the language in which it's written, the program must be translated into machine language. This is done by either compiling the program or interpreting the program.

PROLOG   A high-level language widely used for programming in the field of artificial intelligence, especially expert systems. It was developed in the early 1970s by Alain Colmerauer and Philippe Roussel. PROLOG works with the logical relationships between pieces of data rather than with their mathematical relationships. A program is constructed as a set of facts and a set of rules for deriving new facts. The name PROLOG comes from *programming in logic*.

PROM   *Abbreviation of* **programmable read-only memory**.   A type of ROM (read-only memory) chip onto which data can be written, or programmed, only once. PROMs retain the contents of their memory even when the computer is turned off. PROMs are programmed at the factory for use with a particular computer. Unlike ROMs, PROMs can also be manufactured as blank memory, and data can be programmed onto the chip by the user with a special device called a PROM programmer or PROM burner. Programming a PROM chip is often referred to as burning the PROM. An EPROM (erasable programmable read-only memory) is a type of PROM that can be erased and reprogrammed. *See also* **ROM**.

prompt   A symbol, or sometimes a phrase, that appears on a display screen to indicate that the computer is ready to receive input. Depending on which program is running, the symbol could be a colon (:), a backslash (\), a greater than sign (>), or one of various others. Some programs will wait indefinitely for input; others will resume execution after a time-out, a set interval that passes without user input.

propagated error   An error that is used as input to an operation, causing another error.

property   A characteristic of a device or of an object such as an application or a file.

proportional font   A font in which the characters have varying pitches, or widths. *See also* **fixed space**, **monospace font**.

proportional pitch   The allocation of space of varying widths to different characters in a font. Proportional pitch contrasts with fixed pitch or fixed space, in which each character is given a space of the same width. Thus, in a proportional pitch font, narrow letters such as *i* and *l* are given a smaller width than wide letters such as *m* and *w*. *Also called* **proportional space**, **proportional spacing**.

proprietary   Privately owned, especially by an individual or corporation under a trademark or patent. A proprietary product, program, or technology cannot be duplicated or used unless an explicit license is purchased from its owner. In order to legally use proprietary software, for example, one must either purchase it or obtain permission from the owner.

protected mode   An operating mode available on the Intel 80286 and later microprocessors. It supports more advanced features than real mode, the default operating mode of Intel microprocessors (including the earlier 8088 and 8086). Protected mode supports multitasking by allocating each program a certain area of memory that other programs cannot access. Each program is thus protected from interference from other programs running simultaneously. Such interference can cause a computer to crash in real mode. Protected mode also provides for extended memory.

The DOS operating system cannot take advantage of protected mode. The OS/2 operating system runs in protected mode, as does Unix, and current versions of Microsoft Windows.

protocol   A standard procedure for regulating data transmission between computers or between devices such as modems. *See also* **communications protocol, FTP.**

proxy   A program running on an internal network that intercepts information requests. The proxy is configured by the administrator to allow certain kinds of requests and deny others. If the proxy denies the request, it sends a response back to the requester. If the proxy fulfills the request, it transmits the request onward to an internal server, so that the external source will be unable to ascertain the exact location of the information. Proxies may be used to control both incoming and outgoing requests. As part of a firewall, a proxy helps secure internal networks.

proxy server   A server of an ISP (Internet service provider) that stores frequently accessed webpages. When a subscriber of the ISP requests a webpage stored in the proxy server, the server shows the stored webpage instead of requesting it from the Internet. This can allow the customer to access pages more quickly, and it manages the resources of the ISP more efficiently. The downside is that the page may have been updated since the proxy server last stored it. *See also* **proxy.**

Prt Sc   *Abbreviation of* **Print Screen key.**

psec   *Abbreviation of* **picosecond.**

pseudocode   Code that is written in a form that allows the programmer to focus on the algorithms instead of the syntax of the programming language. Generally, a natural language such as English is used to outline or draft the steps of the program, then the programmer translates it into a programming language so that it can be executed.

public domain software   Software that is not copyrighted and is available to users without charge or restriction. Public domain software is not the same as shareware or freeware. Shareware is copyrighted and users are asked to pay a fee to the author. Freeware is also copyrighted but is given away for free.

public key cryptography   A technique for the encryption and decryption of data that uses two different keys, one public and one private, for encryption and decryption. Public key cryptography is useful in situations in which a sender and a recipient wish to communicate securely and in which speed is not important. In public key cryptography there is a public list of encryption keys each corresponding to one individual recipient. In order for a person to send an encrypted message, the sender must look up the intended recipient's public key and encrypt the message using that. Each recipient privately holds the key necessary for decryption; it is impossible, in practical terms, for anyone to guess the private decryption key from the public encryption key.

Public key cryptography is different from traditional encryption, in which the encryption and decryption keys are fundamentally identical. Traditional encryption is less secure, since one has to communicate the key in some manner, but it is a faster system for decoding than public cryptography. *See also* **ciphertext, encryption, plaintext.**

publish and subscribe The capability for linking portions of documents and establishing how updates to the data in one document affect the data in other documents. If a portion of a document is published, then a change made to this portion is automatically updated to subscriber versions contained in other documents. Publish and subscribe became available in Apple Computer's System 7 operating system, which was a major upgrade of the Macintosh System.

puck An input device that resembles a mouse but has a clear plastic section that is marked with cross hairs. It is used on a digitizer to trace accurately a hard copy of a graphical image into a form that can be used by the computer. Pucks are often used in architectural and engineering applications.

pull-down menu A pop-up window that appears directly beneath the item selected on a menu bar. *Also called* **drop-down menu.** *See illustration at* **menu.**

pull medium A service that distributes information only when a user specifically makes a request. The Internet and its services, such as FTP, are pull media.

pulse code modulation *See* **PCM.**

push medium A service that distributes information by sending data to the user at a time determined by the server. The user may have signed up for a subscription service, in which case the server sends out information, such as stock quotes or news items, at intervals. Or, the user may be the recipient of unrequested email sent out by a spamming program.

pushbutton   *See* **button** (sense 1).

push-pull   Of or relating to an arrangement of two identical electronic devices that that are set in opposite phase in order to minimize distortion.

[Q]

QBE   *Abbreviation of* **query by example**.

QIC   [kwik]   *Abbreviation of* **quarter-inch cartridge**.   A tape cartridge in which the magnetic tape is ¼ inch wide, used especially for back-ups. Such cartridges may be the same size as standard cassette tapes or they may be miniature. The manufacturers of these tapes have established a set of standards for identifying and distinguishing their different sizes. *See table at* **access time**.

quantum bit   The smallest unit of information in a computer designed to manipulate or store information through effects predicted by quantum physics. Unlike bits in classical systems, a quantum bit has more than two possible states: a state labeled 0, a state labeled 1, and a combination of the two states that obeys the superposition principle.

quarter-inch cartridge   *See* QIC.

qubit   A quantum bit.

qubyte   A sequence of eight quantum bits operated on as a unit by a computer.

query   A request to a database for information. For example, if you have a database with the wholesale prices of widgets from every company in the United States and the United Kingdom for every month from 1999 to 2009, you might send a query asking for a list of companies selling widgets in a certain price range in January 2000.

query by example   *Abbreviated* **QBE**   A form of sending queries to a database in which the database management system gives a template with all the fields for the database. You then enter any restrictions under the field to which they apply. For example, if your database has names, addresses, telephone numbers, and birthdays of your friends, you could type *March* in the *birthday* field to elicit a list of the names, addresses, telephone numbers, and birthdays of your friends with birthdays in March.

query language   The language used by a database management system for queries. Query languages are usually small and highly structured.

queue   *n.*   **1.** In programming, a place in which data items can be stored and from which they can be removed only in the same order in which they were placed there. *See also* **stack.**   **2.** A buffer that stores commands waiting for the computer or device to attend to them. For example, if you tell the computer to print several documents, it will begin printing one document and put the commands to print each of the others in the queue until it can get to them.

v. To place commands in a buffer until the computer or device can attend to them. For example, if you tell the computer to print several documents, the operating system will queue the commands to print each document until it can carry them out.

QuickDraw   An object-oriented system developed by Apple Computer for displaying graphics and text that is used by all Macintosh computers and programs and by some printers. QuickDraw enables applications for Macintosh computers to create dialog boxes, icons, menus, and the other features that distinguish the Macintosh graphical user interface. Different versions of QuickDraw have different color capabilities.

QuickTime   Originally an extension of Apple Computer's System 7 operating system that incorporates digital video and other time-based data, QuickTime has evolved into a multimedia standard that can be incorporated in both Netscape Navigator and Microsoft Internet Explorer. QuickTime allows either local file storage or networked multimedia applications.

quit   To turn off a program with the appropriate command, usually QUIT or EXIT, so as to save all your data and configuration choices. While you work, many programs store your data in temporary buffers that may get lost if you turn off the computer without quitting. When you quit, the computer asks you to save anything that hasn't yet been saved on your hard disk, floppy disk, or other storage device. It then erases any extra copies from the buffer so as not to waste memory with unnecessary copies.

QWERTY keyboard   [KWUR-tee]   A keyboard having the traditional arrangement of keys on a standard English keyboard or typewriter.

The name comes from the letters of the first six keys on the left side at the top row of the keyboard. Several alternative keyboards have been designed to facilitate faster typing, of which the best known is the Dvorak keyboard. *See illustration.*

QWERTY KEYBOARD

[R]

radio button   In a graphical user interface, a button representing one of a group of mutually exclusive options. For example, a menu may have radio buttons for various fonts. Since only one font can be selected at a time, clicking on a particular radio button selects that font and rejects all the others.

radix   The base number of a number system. For example, the radix is 10 in the decimal system and 2 in the binary system.

radix point   A character that separates the integer in a mixed number from the fraction. In the number 3.14, for example, the decimal point is the radix point.

ragged   Not aligned evenly with a margin. *Ragged right* refers to text that is not aligned, or justified, along the right margin. *See also* **flush, justification**.

RAID   *Abbreviation of* **redundant array of inexpensive disks**.   A group of disk drives over which data is distributed. The disk drives are used together to facilitate faster storage and retrieval and greater data security than would be possible with a single disk drive. RAID is somewhat of a misnomer, since it is not usually inexpensive at all.

RAM   *Abbreviation of* **random-access memory**.   The main memory of a computer. Because RAM allows random access, the central processing unit can access the data it needs in RAM without having to go through other data first, making RAM faster than memory that offers sequential access. When a computer is turned on, the information from the startup disk is immediately loaded into RAM. Next, the operating system is loaded into RAM. Any program instructions or data to be worked with must first be moved to RAM, and any new or changed data will be stored in RAM until it can be written to a hard disk or other storage device. The microprocessor can also write data to RAM. Most RAM consists of semiconductors that provide volatile memory, which is destroyed every time the computer is turned off or experiences a power outage. *See also* **ROM.**

RAM cache   *See* **cache** (sense 2).

RAM disk   A part of RAM configured so as to be treated as a peripheral disk by the operating system. RAM works much faster than a disk, so using a RAM disk can speed a computer up considerably. However, a RAM disk uses the same RAM that serves as the computer's main memory, so before setting up a RAM disk you need to be sure that you will have enough RAM left to run the software. Because RAM is volatile memory, anything left on a RAM disk when you turn your computer off will be lost unless you have copied it to a hard disk or some other storage device. *Also called* **virtual disk.**

RAM-resident   *See* **memory-resident.**

random access   Immediate access to data items from their addresses. When a data record that is stored in RAM is retrieved, for example, an electrical pulse goes directly to the address of the data requested. If the record is on a hard disk, the head will be positioned directly above the first sector with data from the record. The computer won't have to sift through extra data on the way to the record it is looking for as it would with a tape. *Also called* **direct access.** *See also* **sequential access.**

random-access memory   *See* **RAM.**

range   In a spreadsheet, a set of one or more contiguous cells that form a rectangle and have been selected so that an operation can be performed on all of them at once.

You usually identify a range by the address of the cells in the upper left and lower right corners. For example, B2..P7 would define a rectangle border by the cells from B2 to B7, from B7 to P7, from P2 to P7, and from B2 to P2. *Also called* **cell block.** *See illustration.*

raster   A scanning pattern of parallel lines that form the display of an image projected on a cathode-ray tube of a display screen or television set.

	A	B	C	D
1		Canada (dollar)	France (franc)	Japan (yen)
2	1993	1.2896	5.6642	111.10
3	1994	1.3657	5.5454	102.16
4	1995	1.3718	4.9875	94.02
5	1996	1.3632	5.1148	108.77
6	1997	1.3844	5.8335	120.99
7	1998	1.4830	5.8964	130.75
8	1999	1.4848	6.2585	113.71
9	2000	1.4672	6.8454	106.93

RANGE   Three valid ranges

raster font   *See* **bit-mapped font**.

raster graphics   The use of bit maps by software or hardware to create, display, or store graphics.

raster image processor   *Abbreviated* **RIP**   A device that converts vector graphics into a bit-mapped image, usually so that the image can be printed. This term includes both the hardware and the software that make up this device.

raster scanning   A process for creating and refreshing an image on a display screen. In raster scanning, the cathode-ray tube sends electrons across the top of the screen from the left edge to the right edge. The cathode-ray tube then begins again from the left edge, but this time it directs the electron path to begin each line slightly below the line just covered. When the electron beams reach the bottom right corner, the process begins again.

raw data   Information that has not been formatted or processed.

RDBMS   *Abbreviation of* **relational database management system**.

read   To get data from a hard disk or other storage device. When a computer reads a hard disk, it copies the data it needs into RAM. When it reads RAM, it accesses the data from RAM and proceeds to process it.

readme file   A text file in many programs that tells the user of any modifications in or requirements for the program. It is often the first file a user will be given the option to use after a program is installed.

A readme file may, for example, explain how to install the program and warn about bugs recently discovered in the program and provide tips on how to deal with them.

read-only   Designating information that is permanently stored and can be read but not changed or deleted. It is impossible to alter the content of a read-only file, and the instructions and information contained in ROM (read-only memory) are also unalterable. *See also* **RAM, ROM.**

read-only memory   *See* **ROM.**

read/write   Of or relating to a storage device that is capable of having data written to or from it.

read/write head   *See* **head.**

real address   *See* **absolute address.**

RealAudio   A client/server system developed by RealNetworks that plays audio over the Internet. The RealAudio server compresses audio files and sends the data to the RealAudio client, which decompresses these files and plays them on the client computer. *See also* **adapter, expansion board.**

real mode   The default operating mode for IBM PC and compatible computers that uses conventional memory only, allows only one program to run at a time, and allots that program 640 kilobytes of RAM. *See also* **conventional memory, protected mode.**

real time   **1.** The processing of data by a computer as rapidly as the data is input or within some small upper limit of response time, typically milliseconds or microseconds. For example, an automatic pilot must respond to data on changing flight conditions or the position of other aircraft immediately. Accordingly, automatic aircraft guidance systems must use real time.   **2.** Animated computer graphics or multimedia applications in which real-life situations are simulated at the speed at which they would normally occur. For example, flight simulation programs used to train pilots use real time.

real-time   Of, using, or operating in real time, as a conversation conducted by IRC (Internet Relay Chat).

real-time clock   A battery-powered clock that is part of a computer's circuitry and that keeps the time regardless of whether the computer is off or on. *See also* **real-time clock.**

reboot   To restart a computer. *See also* **cold boot, warm boot.**

recalculate   To determine the value of cells in a spreadsheet again to reflect new data or a change in a formula. Some spreadsheet programs recalculate automatically whenever new data is entered or a formula is changed, while other programs have a special recalculation command that the user must enter, as by a function key.

record   1. In database management systems, a single set of related data organized into fields. For example, if you have a database to help you keep track of personal correspondence, you might keep a record for each letter you receive. Within the record, you might have separate fields telling you when you received the letter, when it was written, what it was about, who sent it, the address of the person who wrote it, and when you replied. *See also* **field, report.**   2. In certain programming languages, a collection of data set up as a unit.

record locking   A database feature that prevents a data record from being edited. This feature is useful when more than one person has access to a database, because if a record locks while one person is editing it, a second person is prevented from editing that record at the same time.

recover   1. For a program to automatically return a computer system to an operative state after an error. This kind of recovery does not require human intervention.   2. To restore a computer system to an operative state. If data is damaged or lost, you can run a program to salvage data that remains in storage.

recycle bin   A system folder in Microsoft Windows where deleted files are stored. You can access the recycle bin to restore or expunge those files. This folder is represented on the desktop by an icon of a recycle bin.

Red Book   A standard for audio CDs, developed by Phillips and Sony and approved by the ISO. It is one of several CD standards now in use.

recoverable error   An error that does not cause a crash or the loss of data; an error that the user, the computer, or the software can deal with so as to continue working without serious or lasting consequences.

red-green-blue monitor   *See* **RGB monitor.**

redirect   To direct a program or file to send output to or receive input from a device that is not the default. For example, the default input device is usually the keyboard or the mouse, but you could redirect the program to take input from a stylus. The default output device is the display screen, but when you print, you redirect the program to send output to your printer. Many programs allow the second person to accept or reject changes with a click.

redline   In word processing, to mark pages in a text so that they can easily be reviewed by another person. For example, if you are writing an article with a colleague, you may want to redline your proposed changes in order to show them to your colleague later. The redlined text may appear in boldface or in a color that you have selected.

reduced instruction set computer   *See* RISC.

redundant array of inexpensive disks   *See* RAID.

reformat   **1.** To erase existing data on a storage device so that it can be reused.   **2.** In applications such as word processing programs, to alter a document's stylistic features, such as font, point size, and margins.

refresh   **1.** To renew the image on a display screen by renewing the flow of electrons from the cathode ray tube. This frequency is measured in hertz.   **2.** To renew the data in dynamic RAM by sending a new electric pulse to recharge the chips.

refresh rate   The frequency with which the image on a display screen must be renewed by refreshing. The standard refresh rate on most monitors is 75 hertz.

register   A temporary storage area in a microprocessor. A register holds either bits of data that are currently being processed or addresses for data that are currently being processed. If you need to add two numbers, for example, each number (or its address) will be placed in a register, and the sum will be placed in a third register. The more registers a microprocessor has, and the more bits those registers can hold, the faster the microprocessor.

registry   A database maintained by all versions of Microsoft Windows and Windows NT that contains configuration information. It can be used to hold information for DDE and OLE communications or information about all the hardware and software in the system.

relational database   A database system in which any database file can be a component of more than one of the database's tables. When searching, data from a field in one table is matched with data from an equivalent field in a second table, resulting in a third table that combines the data from both tables. Thus, a relational database allows you to combine data, correlating information in different tables and devise a new table with the data. For example, you might draw up a table with a row for places you would like to visit and columns showing the best time of year to go, friends you hope to see, tourist attractions, and approximate transportation costs. Then you might draw up another table with a row for each of your friends and columns showing their addresses and phone numbers, how many nights they could put you up for, and what kind of gifts they like. If you were planning a vacation for January, you could get a table showing you where to go, transportation costs, friends you could stay with, their phone numbers, and what presents to bring.

relational database management system   *Abbreviated* **RDMBS**
A program that allows you to make and manipulate relational databases.

relational operator   An operator, such as =, >, or <, that is used to compare two or more values. Table 21 lists relational operator symbols and their meanings.

TABLE 21 Relational Operators

Symbol	Meaning
=	Equal to
! or <>	Not equal to
>	Greater than
>=	Greater than or equal to
<	Less than
<=	Less than or equal to

relative   Defined with respect to the current location of something. For example, a relative path is the sequence of directories between the current directory and the target directory. Mechanical mice use a relative coordinate system; the computer does not know where they are, only that they have moved a certain distance in a certain direction. *See also* **absolute**.

relative cell reference   In spreadsheets, the identification of one or more cells by referring to the location relative to an initial base point. For example, B4 may intially refer to the cell that is the intersection of the second column and fourth row (that is, relative to cell A1), but the cell it refers to could change if you modify the spreadsheet or if you copy that reference to another cell. If the cell reference B4 were placed in or copied to cell D5, for example, the reference would point to cell F9, which is two columns over and four rows down from D5. *See also* **absolute cell reference**.

release number   The number that identifies a new release of a program. Numbers under 1 indicate a beta, or pre-release version. 1.0 indicates the first release. Integers indicate a new version, whereas numbers between integers indicate minor modifications such as bug fixes and other performance upgrades. Version 2.0 usually represents a major change from Version 1.0; Version 2.5, a minor change from 2.0. Software designers and marketers, however, are not always consistent in the use of this system.

remote   Controlled, operated, or used from a distance, as by modem or over cables.

remote access   The use of a modem to access a network or host computer, in contrast with being directly connected to a local access network (LAN).

remote procedure call   *Abbreviated* **RPC**   A protocol by which a program on a networked computer is capable of executing a program on another computer in the network.

remote terminal   A terminal that is at a different location than its host computer and is not directly linked by cables or similar hardware. A remote terminal connects to a host computer by means of a modem.

removable hard disk   A portable plastic or metal cartridge for data storage. Removable cartridges are almost as easy to disconnect, transport, and connect elsewhere as floppy disks, but they can store much more data. *Also called* **removable cartridge**.

render   To add features such as color and shading to an image so that it appears more three-dimensional.

repaginate   To cause a document to paginate again. Most programs repaginate automatically, so that if you add or delete material from a document, the locations where pages break shift accordingly.

repetitive strain injury   *Abbreviated* **RSI**   Damage to tendons, nerves, and other soft tissues that is caused by the repeated performance of a limited number of physical movements. RSI is characterized by numbness, pain, and a wasting and weakening of muscles. *Also called* **repetitive stress injury**.

replace   *n. See* **search and replace**.

v. To do a search and replace so as to change a given string of characters.

replication   The process of creating copies of a networked database or part of a database and the synchronization of the copies so that any edits that are made on one copy are made in all of the other copies.

report   Information that has been output from a database in response to a query and organized and presented according to particular specifications. For example, if you have a database that gives the dates and costs of home repair projects and specifies the type of repair, you could request a report showing dates and costs of all repairs in the calendar year 2001, arranged alphabetically by the type of repair.

report generator   A program that creates reports from a database in response to a query. Most database management systems come with a report generator. The report generator generally lets you specify the form of the report, which may be a table, a graph, or a chart, for example.

report writer   *See* **report generator**.

reserved word   A word or string of characters that has been assigned a particular meaning in a program, system, or programming language and that therefore cannot be used in other circumstances, as in naming a file in a word processing program. For example, *then* is a reserved word in BASIC; you may call a variable *neht* but you cannot call it *then.*

reset button   A button, key, or sequence of keystrokes pressed to restart the computer.

resident font   A font stored in a printer's ROM (read-only memory). All laser printers come with one or more resident fonts, but additional fonts can usually be added to a printer's repertoire by downloading soft fonts. *Also called* **built-in font, internal font**.   *See also* **soft font**.

resident program   *See* **terminate-and-stay resident program**.

resolution   The clarity or fineness of detail that can be distinguished in an image, especially one produced by a monitor or printer.

For printers, resolution is generally measured in dots per inch, or dpi. The higher the dpi, the sharper the resolution. A low-quality dot-matrix printer may print at 125 dpi, an ink-jet printer at 600 dpi, and a laser printer at 1,200 dpi. Professional typesetters print at 1,200 dpi or better.

For monitors, resolution is measured as the number of pixels horizontally displayed, and the number of lines vertically displayed on the screen. The denser the pixels, the clearer the image will be. A 640 × 480 pixel screen, typical for a VGA monitor in graphics mode, displays 640 distinct dots on each of 480 lines, or about 3 million pixels. A Super VGA monitor has a resolution of 1,024 × 768, or almost 8 million pixels, more than 2½ times the resolution of the VGA monitor.

The terms high resolution and low resolution are often used to describe printers and monitors. The meanings of these classifications shift as the technology improves.

restore   **1.** To retrieve a file from a backup. This may involve finding the file on a storage device, such as a Zip disk, a CD-ROM, or tape, uncompressing it, and copying it back to its original place on the disk. Software used to perform a backup can usually automate this process.   **2.** In graphical user interfaces, to bring back a window to its previous size after it has been minimized or maximized.

retrieve   To access information or a file, as from a database or storage device. When you sit down at your computer to revise a document, you begin by retrieving the file containing your document.

return   **1.** In word processing, a command that moves the cursor to the next line on the display screen. In most programs, soft returns are entered automatically whenever you reach the end of the line. If you want an additional line break, however, you must enter a hard return.   **2.** A command that enters or confirms another command. For example, when you select an option from a menu, you first move your cursor to that option and then either click or press the Return key to enter your selection.

Return key   **1.** The key used to enter or confirm a command. The program receives and responds to your command only after you press the Return key.   **2.** In word processing, the key used to enter a hard return. *Also called* **Enter key**.

reverse video   The reversal of background and foreground colors on a display screen to highlight certain characters. For example, if your screen normally displays white characters on a blue background, highlighted characters may appear in blue on a white background. *Also called* **inverse video**.

RGB monitor   *Abbreviation of* **red-green-blue monitor**.   A monitor with a cathode-ray tube that houses three electron guns directing separate streams of electrons at the screen to represent the colors red, green, and blue. An RGB monitor creates other colors by combining these three.

ribbon cable   A flat, broad cable, containing from 8 to 100 parallel conducting wires. A ribbon cable is often used to make direct connections between peripheral components and the motherboard. For example, a ribbon cable with 40 parallel wires can be used to connect an IDE drive to the motherboard.

rich text format   *Abbreviated* **RTF**.   A standard developed by Microsoft Corporation for specifying the format of text without using hidden formatting codes. This format allows documents to be run on different platforms. RTF supports some basic formatting, such as bolding and italicizing. For example, you could save a Microsoft Word document in the RTF format before sending a copy to someone who uses a word processing program that is not compatible with Microsoft Word. Not all of the formatting features might appear, but they would be able to read the basic text.

right justify   To justify a text on the right margin, so that the right edge of the text is even. *See also* **justification**.

ring   One of the three principal topologies for a local area network, in which all computers and devices, known as nodes, are arranged in a circle and connected by cables. Data is passed in one direction along the ring from one computer or device to the next. Each computer or device renews the data with a new electric pulse and sends it on its way. When the data reaches its destination, the computer or device to which it is addressed copies it before sending it to the next node in the network. When it returns to the sender, the sender takes it out of circulation. *See also* **bus, star, token-ring network**. *See illustration at* **network**.

RIP   *Abbreviation of* **raster image processor**.

RISC   *Abbreviation of* **reduced instruction set computer**.   A design that restricts the number of instructions that a microprocessor can handle. The more instructions a microprocessor can handle, the slower the execution of each instruction. RISC architecture speeds up processing by eliminating the instructions that are needed least often. When they are needed, they must be composed from the smaller group of instructions selected for inclusion. Intel's Pentium chips are CISC while Motorola's PowerPC chip is RISC. *See also* **CISC**.

RLL   *Abbreviation of* **run-length limited**.

robot   **1.** A mechanical device that is programmed to perform complex tasks, such as machines in factories that are designed to do the repetitive mechanical work of humans. Some robots respond to input from their environment and adjust their response automatically without intervention from humans.   **2.** *See* **bot**.

robotics   The branch of engineering that applies artificial intelligence and engineering to the creation and programming of robots able to detect and react to sensory input and designed to perform useful tasks. Robots are now being used to perform some manufacturing operations and to carry out certain tasks, such as cleaning toxic waste sites, that would pose serious danger to humans.

robust   Relating to or being a software product that performs consistently well in a range of conditions or when receiving a wide variety of input data. A robust program will run well under unusual or extraordinary circumstances.

ROM   *Abbreviation of* **read-only memory**.   Nonvolatile memory consisting of chips that store data that cannot be changed, expanded, or erased and that was installed when the chips were manufactured. ROM stores the BIOS and sometimes parts of the operating system. *See also* **EPROM, PROM, RAM**. *See table at* **access time**.

roman   A font style marked by upright letters with serifs and in which the vertical lines are thicker than the horizontal lines. *See also* **italic**. *See illustration at* **font family**.

root directory   The uppermost directory in a hierarchy of directories or folders; the directory from which all other directories or folders branch out. For example, when you format a floppy disk in Unix, Unix sets up a root directory marked by a back slash. You can create folders or other directories and subdirectories within this directory, or you can place your files directly into the root directory. *See also* **directory**.

router   [ROO-ter or ROU-ter]   **1.** A device in a network that handles message transfer between computers. A router receives information and forwards it based on what the router determines to be the most efficient route at the time of transfer. *See also* **bridge**. **2.** *See* **gateway** (sense 2).

routine A set of programming instructions designed to perform a specific, limited task within a larger program. A routine usually has an identifier that serves as a command to execute the routine. Each module in a program may consist of several routines. *See also* **function, subroutine**.

RPC *Abbreviation of* **remote procedure call**.

RSA encryption A public key encryption algorithm invented by Ronald Rivest, Adi Shamir, and Leonard Adelman. RSA is the basis of many popular encryption systems, including DES.

RSI *Abbreviation of* **repetitive strain injury**.

RTF *Abbreviation of* **rich text format**.

rule **1.** In word processing, graphics, and desktop publishing programs, a straight vertical or horizontal line used to set a graphics image or a small section of text, such as a column or a footnote, apart from the rest of the page. **2.** In expert systems, a conditional statement that tells the program how to respond to particular input.

ruler In word processing, desktop publishing, and graphics programs, a short window covering the width of the display screen and containing a line with inches, picas, or points marked off and indicators for margins and tab settings. In many programs, these indicators can be moved to adjust the margins and tab settings.

run **1.** To process or execute a program or instruction. **2.** To be processed or executed.

run-length limited *Abbreviated* **RLL** A method of encoding data on a hard disk that greatly increases the storage capacity over that of the modified frequency modulation method.

running head *Another term for* **header** (sense 1).

runtime The time during which a program is running.

runtime error An error that occurs while a program is running.

runtime version A limited version of a program, usually an operating environment or interpreter, sold with another application for the sole use of that application.

[S]

sampling   A technique for digitizing analog input. Sampling involves recording audio and visual information by taking numerous readings at regular intervals. Digitizing analog sound recordings involves capturing a series of individual readings of sound waves. When these individual captures are played, they are perceived by the human ear as a continuous stream of sound. The greater the frequency of such captures per unit of time, the more realistic the digital recording will be; however, the greater the frequency, the more storage space is necessary to hold the data.

sans serif   Of, relating to, or being a font that does not have serifs. Helvetica and Geneva are sans serif fonts, for example. *See illustration at* **serif.**

saturation   **1.** The state of a ferromagnetic substance in which an increase in applied magnetic field strength does not produce an increase in magnetization.   **2.** The vividness of a color, measured as a degree of difference from a gray of the same lightness or brightness.

save   To copy a file or files from a buffer to a disk or other long-term storage device. While you work, everything you do stays in a buffer, but since the buffer is volatile memory, it can be erased by a power failure. The more often you save, the less work you can lose in case of a crash. Saving to more than one storage device increases the chances that data will not be lost.

scalable   **1.** Designating a computer file, as an audio or a video file, for example, that can be played at varying rates and levels of quality in accordance with the resources of the computer being used.   **2.** Designating an architecture in which a microprocessor can be replaced with a more powerful one without necessitating the rewriting of any software.

scalable font   A font whose size can be changed freely without changing the proportions of the characters. This means that you do not need a new font for every size you want to use; you can enlarge or reduce the same font and it will look just as good. PostScript and TrueType are scalable fonts for printing. The screen fonts for graphical user interfaces are also scalable fonts.

scaling   **1.** The process of adjusting the size of an image or font without changing its proportions.   **2.** The process of adjusting the scale of an image, such as a graph or design, so as to change the perspective from which the image is viewed. Many presentation graphics programs, for example, allow scaling of the y-axis on bar graphs to highlight certain features.

scan   **1.** To move a finely focused beam of light or electrons in a systematic pattern over a surface in order to reproduce and subsequently transmit an image.   **2.** To search stored data automatically for specific data.

Scandisk   A utility on MS-DOS and Microsoft Windows that checks disks for errors and defects. Often, Scandisk is capable of correcting such errors, as well.

scanner   *See* **optical scanner**.

scheduler   **1.** In an operating system, a program that allocates the use of such resources as the CPU (central processing unit) or a printer so that several tasks can be handled at the same time without interfering with each other.   **2.** A program that helps people using a network schedule meetings. The scheduler compares the relevant calendars, sends out invitations, and distributes follow-up reminders. Some schedulers can also reserve conference rooms, slide projectors, and similar items.

scientific notation   A way of representing a number, especially a very large or a very small number, by showing it as the product of a power of 10 and a number between 1 and 10. For example, the number 23,456,000,000,000,000 would be written in scientific notation as 2.3456×10^{16} or as 2.3456E16, with "E" standing for "10 to the exponential power of." Similarly, .0000007 would be written as 7×10^{-7} or as 7E–7. Scientific notation is widely used in science and engineering because it allows precise calculations with very large or very small numbers. Table 22 lists some examples of numbers in scientific notation. *See also* **floating-point notation**.

TABLE 22 Examples of Scientific Notation

Scientific Notation	Decimal Expansion
1.2345E4	12,345.0
1.0E–5	0.00001
–6.789E3	–6,789.0
–9.0E–2	–0.09

scrapbook   A desk accessory that allows you to save frequently used pictures or passages of text. The scrapbook can store multiple images. You can cut, copy, or paste images from the scrapbook into documents created with most application programs.

scratch pad   A section of memory, especially a high-speed memory circuit in a microprocessor, used for temporary storage of preliminary data during processing. Data held in the scratch pad is erased when the computer is turned off.

screen   *See* **display screen**.

screen capture   The act or process of sending a copy of whatever is on the display screen to the printer or to the clipboard.

screen dump   The act or process of sending a copy of whatever is on the display screen to the printer or file.

screen flicker   The appearance of a flicker or other distortion on the display screen. A low refresh rate is the most frequent cause of screen flicker. Monitors use phosphors of various durations to create the display, and the fading of these phosphors may also give the appearance of screen flicker.

screen font   A bit-mapped font used to show text on the display screen. Screen fonts are designed to look as similar as possible to the printer fonts used by the same program, but printers, especially laser printers, can often achieve higher resolutions than monitors.

screen saver   A utility program designed to protect monitors from ghosting. Screen savers work by blanking the screen or replacing its contents with a constantly moving graphic image; this prevents an image from being etched into the screen. Screen savers are frequently set up to run automatically after the computer has been idle for a period of time and to restore the screen contents when the user resumes work. Screen savers have recently found a new use: putting Energy Star–compliant monitors into low-power mode during periods of inactivity.

screen shot   *See* **screen capture**.

script   A short program that does not need to be assembled or compiled. Scripts may be run directly from the operating system, but are often launched by more complex programs.

scripting language   A relatively simple high-level programming language, such as HyperTalk, that is used to write scripts. *See also* **macro**.

scroll To move a file within a window so as to change what can be seen in the window. For example, you may originally see only the top half of your page, but if you scroll down, you will see the middle half, losing a quarter at the top and at the bottom. You can scroll vertically or horizontally by using the arrow keys and the Page Up and Page Down keys or by using a scroll bar.

scroll bar In graphical user interfaces, a narrow bar that appears on the side of or beneath a window to let you scroll by clicking or dragging with the mouse. A scroll bar will generally have arrows at each end, and by clicking on an arrow you can scroll a document or menu in the direction in which the arrow points. Scroll bars usually also have a box indicating the relative position of the document within the window. You move a document by dragging the box along the scroll bar in the desired direction. *See illustrations at* **desktop** *and* **frame**.

scroll box A box within a scroll bar that indicates the relative position of the document within the window. You move a document by dragging the box along the scroll bar in the desired direction. *See illustration at* **desktop**.

Scroll Lock key A key that is pressed to change the effect of the cursor control keys as determined by the application. In some applications, for example, when the Scroll Lock key is depressed the cursor control keys scroll the document rather than moving the cursor.

SCSI [SKUZ-ee] *Abbreviation of* **small computer systems interface.** A standard parallel interface for rapid data transmission. As many as 7 devices can be connected to one SCSI port. Because only one transmission can be made at a time, each device is assigned an address reflecting the priority to be given to transmissions to and from that device relative to transmissions to and from the other devices connected to the same port. The SCSI then dispatches data in priority order. Even though some data must wait to be dispatched, it is still transmitted faster over a SCSI than over most other interfaces because a SCSI can handle up to 40 megabits per second. Hard disks are the peripherals most often connected over a SCSI. Apple Macintosh computers, some IBM PC and compatible computers, and many Unix systems use SCSI interfaces.

SCSI-2 The current version of SCSI that can transmit between 10 megabytes and 40 megabytes of data per second. An earlier version, SCSI-1, was considerably slower.

SDI   *Abbreviation of* **single document interface.**   A user interface in the Microsoft Windows operating environment in which a single running application allows only one document per active window. An example of an SDI application is the Notepad in Windows 3.1. To concurrently enter input into several documents in an SDI application, the application must be loaded and be run independently for each document. *See also* **MDI.**

SDK   *Abbreviation of* **Software Development Kit.**   A set of software tools that allow programmers to modify or use an existing application from within other applications.

SDRAM   *Abbreviation of* **Synchronous Dynamic Random-Access Memory** *or* **Synchronous DRAM**   A kind of DRAM that synchronizes with the internal clock of the CPU (central processing unit), with a maximum operational speed of 100 megahertz. A technology called SDRAM II can operate at higher speeds. As faster and faster CPUs come on the market, new kinds of DRAMs are being developed to meet their clock speeds. By using SDRAM, the CPU is seldom idle while waiting on memory.

search   To find and review every occurrence of a string of characters in a document. For example, if you were writing a review of a new book and you wanted to make sure you had underlined the book's title at each occurrence, a search for the title would allow you to underline those occurrences that you had missed the first time.

search and replace   A procedure for changing a string of characters to a different string of characters throughout a document. For example, you might want to replace *don't* with *do not* in a letter. In some programs, the search and replace feature comes with an option to review and confirm the change each time. While this obviously takes much longer, it can prevent you from accidentally making a change you don't want to make. For example, if you used the phrase *do's and don'ts* in your letter, you might not want it to become *do's and do nots.*

search engine   A program that allows you to perform searches for data on the Internet.

secondary cache   *See* **Level 2 cache.**

secondary storage   *See* **mass storage.**

sector   An area on a disk that contains the smallest addressable unit of information. When a disk is formatted, the operating system divides it into sectors and tracks. Tracks are concentric circles around

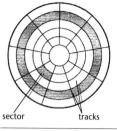 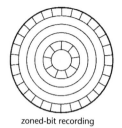

sector   tracks   zoned-bit recording

SECTOR   Sectors and tracks

the disk; sectors are segments within each circle. Generally, each track contains the same number of sectors. The operating system and disk drive know where information is stored on the disk by noting its track and sector number, or address.

Some hard disk drives use zoned-bit recording. Here tracks on the outside have more sectors than tracks on the inside. *See also* **bad sector**. *See illustration.*

Secure Sockets Layer   *See* SSL.

security   The prevention of unauthorized use of a program or device. On networks or any other system where more than one user can access programs and data, security usually involves the use of passwords to identify authorized users, and encryption, which renders data unintelligible to unauthorized users. More recently, companies with access to the Internet have been installing firewalls to prevent unauthorized users from accessing their local area networks. *See also* **encryption, password**.

seek time   The amount of time required for a disk drive's read/write head to move to a specific location on a disk. Seek time is expressed in milliseconds, or thousandths of a second. It differs from access time, the amount of time that elapses before the read/write head locates a piece of data and is ready to transfer it from the disk. *See also* **access time, disk drive, head**.

select   **1.** To choose a portion of a document, spreadsheet, or database by highlighting it, as by changing the background color, so that an operation can be performed specifically on that portion. *See also* **block**.   **2.** In a graphical user interface, to choose a command or action by moving the mouse until the pointer touches a specific object on the screen, and then clicking on that object.

semantics   The meaning of a programming instruction as opposed to the syntax, or the rules governing its spelling and structure. The semantic rules of a programming language are violated when a command is syntactically correct but makes no sense in the context of its program.

semiconductor   **1.** A crystalline substance, such as silicon or germanium, having electrical conductivity that is greater than an insulator (such as rubber) but less than a good conductor (copper, for example). Computer chips and a variety of other electronic devices are made of semiconductor material. By adding impurities called dopants to semiconductor materials, manufacturers can precisely control the semiconductor's electrical resistance.   **2.** An integrated circuit or another device made up of semiconductor material.

sequential access   A method of storing and retrieving information in sequential order. A sequential access device must search from the beginning of a sequence of locations each time it seeks data. Sequential access contrasts with random access, which allows a device to access data directly, without passing through all locations preceding the one where the data is stored. *See also* **random access**.

serial   **1.** Of or relating to the transmission of the bits of a byte over one wire, one bit at a time. Serial communication contrasts with parallel communication, in which data is transmitted and received in many bits at once. *See also* **parallel, serial port**.   **2.** Of or relating to the execution of computer instructions in sequence. Most computers are serial by nature, although most supercomputers are parallel processors.

Serial Line Internet Protocol   *See* **SLIP**.

serial mouse   A mouse that is attached to the computer through a serial port. A bus mouse, on the other hand, is connected to the computer through an expansion board. A serial port is adequate for the limited amount of data that is transmitted by a mouse, and a serial mouse is easy to install. *See also* **mouse**.

serial port   A port at the back of a computer that is used for serial communication. Devices such as modems and serial mice are connected to a computer's serial port. A serial port transmits data on series— one bit of data at a time. It is often referred to as an RS-232 port. RS-232 is the Electronics Industries Association's designation for a standard for how the various connections in a serial port are to be used. The serial port contains one line for transmitting data, one line to receive data, and several other lines that signal when transmission or reception will occur and generally maintain a smooth flow of data between the computer and whatever device is attached. Serial port technology is becoming superseded by the USB port, which allows for faster connection speeds and the ability to add peripherals without shutting off the computer. *Also called* **serial interface**.

serif   A fine line finishing off the main strokes of a letter. Typefaces without these fine lines are called sans serif. Serif fonts are often preferred for printed documents, whereas sans serif is often preferred for documents published on the Web. *See illustration*.

Mm   Mm

Mm   *Mm*

SERIF   Serif (left) and sans serif fonts in roman (top) and italic

server   In a client/server network, a computer that stores files and provides them to individual workstations, or clients. Additionally, the server often controls access to peripherals such as printers and executes complex programs or tasks that the client requests. *Also called* **file server**.

service provider   *See* **ISP**.

SGML   *Abbreviation of* **Standard Generalized Markup Language**.   A text formatting language that is widely used for large database and multiple media projects. The fields in an SGML document are indicated by embedded tags. The tags and the relationships among the fields they represent are specified in the DTD (Document Type Definition). The tags do not specify how the fields are to be displayed, allowing different applications to display them differently. SGML is particularly well suited for works that involve heavy cross-referencing, indexing, or hypertext linking.

shadowing   A technique that speeds up a computer by taking certain programs stored in the slower ROM (read-only memory) and copying them into the faster RAM (random-access memory). Although shadowing improves computer performance, it can cause a shortage of RAM, especially if you are running programs designed to use extended memory.

shareware Copyrighted programs that are made available on a trial basis. Users who like the software and would like to keep using it are asked to pay a small fee to the author and are often registered so that they can receive program updates, bug fixes, and assistance. Shareware differs from public domain software, which is not copyrighted. See also **freeware, public domain software**.

sheet-fed scanner An optical scanner into which documents can be fed. In a sheet-fed scanner, the document is rolled past the scan head. A flatbed scanner, on the other hand, moves the scan head past a stationary page, much in the same way as a photocopier does. A sheet-fed scanner is suited for scanning unbound documents or single pages, while a flatbed scanner can handle bound books. *See also* **hand-held scanner**.

sheet feeder A mechanism that feeds paper one sheet at a time. Sheet feeders are standard with laser printers and most kinds of fax machines. *Also called* **cut-sheet feeder**.

shell A program that facilitates communication between the user and the operating system, often presenting a menu-driven user interface that makes it easier to select files and choose and process commands.

shift clicking The act of holding down the Shift key and clicking the mouse button at the same time. Shift clicking can have different effects depending on what application you are using, but on Apple Macintosh computers and in Microsoft Windows, it allows you to select more than one item from a screen.

Shift key A key on a computer keyboard that, when pressed and held down, changes letters from lowercase to uppercase. In many applications, the Shift key changes the meaning of a function key when the two keys are pushed at the same time. The Shift key can also change the function of mouse button.

shortcut In Microsoft Windows, a file that points to another file. Instead of having to go through menus or directories to open a file that you use frequently, you can create a shortcut for it. By doing so, an icon representing that file appears on your desktop. Double clicking on the icon allows you to open the file. This allows you a quick way to access programs whose icons can't be moved to the desktop.

shortcut key   *See* **hot key.**

shrink-wrap   Relating to a legal agreement, such as a software license, to which you indicate acceptance by opening the shrink-wrap that encloses the product subject to the agreement.

shrink-wrapped software   *See* **packaged software.**

S-HTTP   An extension of HTTP, originally developed by Enterprise Integration Technologies and the National Center for Supercomputer Applications, for transmitting data, such as business transactions, securely over the World Wide Web. Unlike the Secure Sockets Layer standard, S-HTTP cannot be used to support encrypted data that is transmitted over the Internet by means of FTP or other non-HTTP protocols.

shut down   To exit applications and the operating system properly in preparation for turning off the computer. If you merely switch off the computer while applications are running, data could be lost or damaged. You can either close each application manually or select your operating system's command to do so.

SIG   *Abbreviation of* **special interest group.**   A group of computer users who share an interest in a specific subject. The members of a SIG can share information and have discussions electronically, through a mailing list, website, Usenet newsgroup, or other online forum.

Silicon Valley   A region of California southeast of San Francisco known for its high-technology design and manufacturing industries. Once encompassing the communities immediately southeast of San Francisco, collectively known as the South Bay, it is generally used now to describe the entire region. Hewlett-Packard moved to the area in the 1930s, but Silicon Valley was mostly farmland until the 1970s, when technology companies, many of which were associated with the space program and military projects, began to move there. Apple Computer drew attention to the region in the mid-1970s, and its consumer products opened the market for a wave of new companies, drawing on the talent pools of the University of California-Berkeley, Stanford University, and the California Institute of Technology. In the 1990s, the Valley became home for a wave of Internet companies.

SIMM   *Abbreviation of* **single in-line memory module.**   A small printed circuit board that contains up to nine memory chips. SIMMs plug into sockets inside the computer. Installing them increases the RAM (random-access memory) of your computer. Common SIMM capacities range from 4MB to 32MB. *See illustration at* **chip**.

Simple Mail Transport Protocol *See* **SMTP**.

sine wave A waveform with deviation that can be expressed as the graph of the equation $y = \sin x$. *See also* **wavetable synthesis**.

single document interface *See* **SDI**.

single in-line memory module *See* **SIMM**.

single in-line package *See* **SIP**.

single-density disk An floppy disk with far less storage capacity than a double-density or high-density disk. Single-density disks are now obsolete.

single-sided disk A floppy disk that can store data on one side only. Double-sided disks have about twice as much storage capacity, and single-sided disks are now obsolete.

SIP *Abbreviation of* **single in-line package**. An electrical component housing whose connecting pins stick out from one side, as contrasted with the pins on a DIP switch. *See illustration at* **chip**.

site *See* **website**.

size To shrink or enlarge an object. In word processing, text can be sized to fit a new page size; in graphical user interfaces, sizing a window means enlarging or reducing it on the screen. Sizing a graphical image is accomplished with object-oriented graphics, a method of storing and representing images with mathematical descriptions. When an object is sized, its mathematical description is recalculated, yielding a distortion-free enlargement or reduction. *See also* **object-oriented graphics, window**.

slate PC A notebook computer or PDA that has a surface, or slate, onto which you can input data and commands by writing with a stylus or an electronic pen. The slate PC can translate printed words, numbers, and punctuation into ASCII characters.

SLIP *Abbreviation of* **Serial Line Internet Protocol**. A communications protocol allowing TCP/IP to run over a serial connection. It has been commonly used for connecting to the Internet via modem. SLIP is slow and lacks security and error-correction features, and so is being replaced by PPP.

slot *See* **expansion slot**.

small computer systems interface *See* **SCSI**.

Smalltalk   An object-oriented development environment provided by the Software Concepts Group. Smalltalk was one of the first object-oriented programming languages.

smart   Designating a program that performs correctly in a wide variety of complicated circumstances without having to be explicitly instructed by the user. A program that is able to anticipate the information that will next be requested from a disk is said to be smart software.

smart card   A plastic card containing a computer chip and enabling the holder to purchase goods and services, enter restricted areas, access medical, financial, or other records, or perform other operations requiring data stored on the chip.

smart terminal   A terminal in a multi-user system that has a processor and therefore has some processing capabilities independent of the host computer. The phrase *like a smart terminal* is sometimes used to describe the behavior of workstations or personal computers with respect to programs that run almost entirely from a remote server's storage.

smiley   An emoticon, especially a smiling facial glyph [:-) or :)] used to express delight or to indicate humor or irony.

S/MIME   *Abbreviation of* **Secure Multipurpose Internet Mail Extensions**   An extension of the MIME protocol for the transmission of encrypted email over the Internet.

smoothing   A technique used by laser printers for eliminating jaggies, the jagged distortions that appear on curves. Smoothing usually involves reducing the size or alignment of the dots that make up a curved line. *See illustration at* **antialiasing**.

SMTP   *Abbreviation of* **Simple Mail Transfer Protocol**.   A protocol used on TCP/IP networks to govern the transfer of electronic mail, usually over the Internet.

smurfing   The malicious disabling of a network by flooding it with replies to PING requests. The attackers send out PING requests using the forged return address of the company being attacked. The responses bombard the company's network, causing their system to crash. Smurfing is one kind of a denial-of-service attack.

snail mail   Mail delivered by a postal system, as distinct from email.

snapshot   A text or graphics file containing a copy of the information a screen at a particular moment. Such a file can be printed out or emailed to show an image of what was on the screen at the time the snapshot was taken. This can be useful for troubleshooting problems by having a record of error messages that appear on the screen, and for guiding readers of a manual through the various steps of using an application by showing them screen-by-screen steps for accomplishing a task.

sniffer   *See* **packet sniffer.**

soft   **1.** Designating something intangible, such as a program or concept, as opposed to something that exists physically, such as a keyboard or disk drive.   **2.** Designating something that is changeable or impermanent, such as a soft copy. *See also* **hard.**

soft copy   A temporary representation of a program or document on a computer's display screen.

soft font   A font that must be downloaded from a disk to a printer. Soft fonts contrast with hard fonts (fonts that are permanently stored in a printer's memory) and fonts contained in a font cartridge that is plugged directly into the printer. *Also called* **downloadable font.** *See also* **font, font cartridge.**

soft hyphen   In word processing and desktop publishing programs with hyphenation, a hyphen that is automatically inserted to break a word at the end of a line. Soft hyphens are inserted and deleted by the program as a document is revised. Hard hyphens, on the other hand, are added and deleted by the user.

soft return   In word processing and desktop publishing programs, a line break that occurs automatically when the cursor reaches the right margin. If the document is changed, the soft returns are moved by the program to the appropriate places at the end of each line. A hard return is supplied by the user, and it remains at the same place unless the user deletes it.

software   The programs, programming languages, and data that control the functioning of the hardware and direct its operations. Software and hardware are integrally connected, and the distinction between them can be subtle. When you buy a word processing program, you are buying software, but the disk on which the program is recorded is hardware.

Software is usually divided into two categories. Systems software controls the workings of the computer. It includes operating systems, utilities, compilers, assemblers, and file management tools.

Applications handle the multitude of tasks that users want their computers to perform. Examples are word processing programs, database management systems, spreadsheets, and games. Applications software is unable to run without the operating system and utilities.

Two additional categories that contain elements of systems and applications software are network software, which enables computers to communicate, and programming languages, which give programmers the tools to write programs.

Software Development Kit *See* **SDK.**

software piracy The copying and distribution of software to unauthorized users. Some software has copy protection, which acts as a deterrent but is not foolproof against those with enough skill to circumvent it. Some software companies have responded to piracy with incentives for purchasing, such as documentation, upgrades, and support; and lawsuits against those who deal in large-scale piracy. Still other software developers make shareware. *See also* **copy protection, dongle.**

SoHo or **SOHO** *Abbreviation of* **Small Office/Home Office.** An important and rapidly growing market for computer and computer-related products. SOHO equipment is more sophisticated than what the average consumer would need, while being less expensive (and less functional) than the equipment used in larger offices.

sort An operation that takes a set of data and arranges it in alphabetical or numerical order. Sorting is a common procedure in word processing, database management, and spreadsheet programs.

sound card A printed circuit board that plugs into a computer, enabling it to digitally reproduce a wide range of sounds. On some motherboards, the sound card is integrated into the system. *Also called* **sound board.**

source The place, such as a file, a disk, or a device, from which data is moved. *See also* **destination.**

source code Programming instructions in their original high-level language, such as C or C++, as written by a programmer. Before a program can be read and executed by a computer, it must be converted from source code to object code or machine language by a compiler or an interpreter. *See also* **high-level language, machine code, programming language.**

space bar   A bar at the bottom of the keyboard that when pressed down introduces a blank space to the right of the preceding character.

spamming   Sending a mass mailing to newsgroups, email users, or list servers, usually without regarding whether the message is appropriate for the recipients. Spamming is very bad netiquette. Many newsgroups will blacklist spammers, causing their messages to be rejected at the server.

special character   A character that is not a letter, number, or space. Punctuation marks and symbols may be considered special characters, depending on the context, and control characters are always considered special characters.

special interest group   *See* SIG.

speech recognition   The ability of a computer to accept human speech as an input device. Speech recognition allows you to speak words that the computer either understands as commands or stores as data, making it possible for people who cannot use a mouse or keyboard to input information into their computers. Such programs require relatively powerful computers to work efficiently because of the demands on the CPU (central processing unit) and memory. *Also called* **voice recognition**.

speech synthesis   The ability of a computer to produce speech in such a way that sounds like human speech.

spell checker   A program that searches a document for misspelled words by comparing each word in the document to a dictionary file of correctly spelled words. The spell checker will stop at an incorrectly spelled word and offer a list of correctly spelled substitute words.

Other useful spell checker features in many word processing programs include the capacity to add new words to the dictionary file, the ability to stop at a word that occurs twice in a row, and the ability to count the number of words in a document.

spider   A program used by search engines to retrieve webpages. *Also called* **webcrawler**.

split screen   A display screen that is divided in two, allowing you to view two documents at the same time or to view one document in two different ways.

spoof   1. To emulate the identity of another device. For example, to include in an encrypted message a forged identifying label. This action spoofs the source of the transmission and allows only users who have the correct identifying label to decrypt the transmission. **2.** To assume the identity of another user, as in sending an email under another person's username, for example.

spool *Abbreviation of* **simultaneous peripheral operations online**. To put commands or requests temporarily into a buffer, so that they are carried out when they are able to be processed.

spooler A program that paces print jobs by temporarily storing them in a buffer and sending them to the printer when the printer is able to process them. This frees up the CPU (central processing unit), allowing the user to work on something else while a document is printing. *Also called* **print spooler**.

spot color A printing process in which each color used on the page is printed separately with its own ink, in layers. This is the process that ink-jet printers use. This process contrasts with CMYK printing processes, in which all colors are created with cyan, magenta, yellow, and black.

spreadsheet **1.** A table of values arranged in rows and columns in an onscreen display. The intersections of columns and rows are called cells. The rows are numbered and the columns are alphabetized, so each cell can be identified by its row number and column letter. B9, for instance, is the cell in column B and row 9.

Spreadsheet applications are accounting and bookkeeping programs that let you create and manipulate spreadsheets electronically. You define what data is in each cell and how different cells depend on each other. The relationships between cells are formulas, and the names of the cells are labels.

Formulas make spreadsheets powerful by linking data in different cells together. After you complete a calculation, you can enter new values, recalculate, and see how a change in one value affects the results. For example, you may use a spreadsheet to keep track of your annual budget. If your rent goes up, you adjust the value in the cell indicating rent, and the application recalculates your budget.

Two of the most well-known spreadsheet applications are Lotus 1-2-3 and Excel. *Also called* **worksheet**. **2.** A document created in a spreadsheet application.

spreadsheet notebook *See* **three-dimensional spreadsheet**.

SQL [SEE-kwel] *Abbreviation of* **Structured Query Language**. A standard interface language for the issuing of queries to a relational database. SQL commands can be issued interactively or can be embedded within a program.

SRAM [ESS-ram] *Abbreviation of* **static random-access memory**. *See* **static RAM**.

SSL *Abbreviation of* **Secure Sockets Layer**. An encryption standard developed by Netscape for transmitting data, especially business transactions, securely over the Internet. Another encryption standard, S-HTTP, applies specifically to the World Wide Web, but SSL operates on the network level, allowing for the encryption of data transmitted by other protocols, including FTP.

stack A section of memory used for temporary storage of information in which the item most recently stored is the first to be retrieved, and the first item stored is the last to be retrieved.

standalone A term describing a self-contained, independently operating computer or device.

standard An agreed-upon procedure or structure for a specific type of communication. There are standard physical structures that enable a device such as a printer to plug into a variety of different computers, and there are standard communications methods, called protocols, that make the data in one computer usable by other computers and devices.

Some standards are set by an official organization, such as ANSI (American National Standards Institute), which establishes standards for programming languages. Other standards evolve naturally as hardware and software developers attempt to create products that will be compatible with the more popular computers and devices. Some commonly used standards include the ASCII standard for characters and TCP/IP, a communications protocol.

Standard Generalized Markup Language *See* **SGML**.

star One of the three principal topologies for a local area network, in which all computers and devices, known as nodes, are connected to one central computer, known as the hub. All communication between nodes is routed by the hub. *See also* **bus, ring**. *See illustration at* **network**.

start bit In asynchronous communication, the bit that signals the beginning of a byte of data. *See also* **stop bit**.

startup disk A disk that contains the operating system files that a computer needs to start working. The startup disk is usually a hard disk; if a computer does not have a hard startup disk, a floppy startup disk must be inserted into one of the disk drives every time the computer is turned on. *Also called* **boot disk, system disk.**

statement   An elementary instruction in a high-level language. Programs are made up of statements and expressions, operations, and values stated in symbolic form.

static   Unchanging or fixed. *See also* **dynamic.**

static RAM   *Abbreviated* **SRAM**   A type of random-access memory that does not need to be refreshed by the CPU (central processing unit) as often as dynamic RAM. Substantially faster than dynamic RAM, static RAM chips are also more expensive and are used for cache memory, a reserved area of memory that stores frequently used data or instructions for fast access. *See table at* **access time.**

static random-access memory   *See* **static RAM.**

stop bit   In asynchronous communication, the bit that signals the end of a byte of data. *See also* **start bit.**

storage   The places that hold computer information for subsequent use or retrieval. There are two types of storage: primary storage consists of a computer's RAM (random-access memory); secondary storage, or mass storage, refers to the places, such as hard disks or floppy disks, where large amounts of information can be permanently stored.

storage device   Any device used to record and store computer data. Among storage devices are hard disks, floppy disks, CD-ROMS, and tape.

store   To copy data onto a mass storage device, such as a floppy disk, or into memory from the CPU (central processing unit).

streaming audio   The sending and playing of audio in real time over the Internet, instead of first sending a file and playing after it has been downloaded.

streaming video   The sending and displaying of video in real time over the Internet, instead of first sending a file and displaying after it has been downloaded.

string   A set of consecutive characters treated by a computer as a single unit. Computers can perform operations on text by treating words as strings. *Also called* **character string.**

striping   On an array of disk drives, a technique for improving disk drive speed. Each file written into a striped array is spread, or striped, over several drives. Striping is accomplished by writing chunks, usually bits, of a single piece of data on multiple disk drives. This allows the user to access all the chunks in parallel, thus speeding disk performance. *See also* **array**, **RAID**.

structured query language   *See* **SQL**.

style sheet   In word processing or desktop publishing, a file of instructions for the format of a document. The style sheet gives such specifications as margins, page size, fonts, and line spacing. The style sheet can be easily adjusted to change the format.

stylus   A pen-shaped instrument used with computers that accept input by pressing or drawing on pressure-sensitive screens. This technology is used with many kinds of personal digital assistants (PDAs).

subdirectory   A subdivision within a larger computer directory that stores related files. All subdirectories are branches of the root directory. The directory immediately above the one you are working in is called the parent directory.

submenu   A menu that appears and presents further options or commands after a selection from a previous menu has been made.

subnet or **subnetwork**   A network that is part of a larger network. Subnetworks are usually connected to larger networks using routers and switching hubs.

subnotebook   A portable computer that is lighter and smaller than a notebook computer.

subroutine   A sequence of programming statements that can be repeatedly executed from different parts of a program to form a specific task within a program.

subscript   A letter or number that is printed slightly below the level of other characters on the same line.

subsystem   A system whose jurisdiction is lesser than the primary system of which it is a part. A subsystem is usually capable of operating independently of its larger system, which may be a program or an operating system, for example.

suite   **1.** A group of business software products packaged and sold together. A standard suite will include a word processing program, a spreadsheet application, and a database program; it may also include other applications, such as graphics or mail programs. Each different component of a suite should have certain things in common with the others, including a consistent look-and-feel, a common installation, and shared macros.   **2.** A group of procedures that work cooperatively. For example, the suite of protocols for Internet services includes FTP, HTTP, SMTP, and Telnet.

supercomputer   A computer that is among the fastest and most powerful available at a given time. Supercomputers are designed to execute computation-intensive programs as quickly as possible. They generally handle fewer programs at a time than ordinary mainframes; but the programs they handle are far more complex, and they execute them much faster. Supercomputers are used in scientific research, especially in performing the enormous number of calculations required in modeling complex phenomena such as weather patterns or nuclear explosions. Supercomputers generally use parallel processing to achieve their computation speed and require specialized software.

SuperDisk   A disk storage system developed by Imation Corporation, having a removable drive that uses a 3.5 inch disk with a capacity of 120 megabytes. The system is backwards compatible, allowing the drive to read regular 1.44MB diskettes as well.

SuperDrive   A 3.5-inch floppy disk drive that can read all Apple Macintosh formats (400KB, 800KB, and 1.4MB) and can read and format 720KB and 1.4MB DOS disks. The SuperDrive is now standard on Macintosh computers, and it allows you to move files between Apple Macintosh and IBM PC compatible systems.

superposition principle   A principle holding that two or more solutions to a linear equation or set of linear equations can be added together so that their sum is also a solution.

superscalar architecture   A microprocessor architecture, used by almost all modern microprocessors, that allows for the execution of more than one instruction each second.

superscript   A letter or number that is printed slightly above the level of other characters on the same line.

superuser   A Unix account having no restrictions on privileges. Usually only network administrators have superuser accounts, because they allow the user to read or modify all files on the system. *Also called* avatar.

Super VGA   *See* SVGA.

support   *v.* To have the ability to work in a certain way, to interact with a certain device or program, or to perform a certain task. For example, Adobe Photoshop, a desktop publishing program, supports TIFF files.

n. Assistance with the installation or use of a computer product. Most vendors offer telephone support for installation problems. Some hardware vendors offer onsite support.

surf   To browse through information presented on the Internet by casually following links you might think lead to something interesting from site to site, in contrast to the activity of focused searching for specific information.

surge protector   A device that prevents electrical power surges from damaging a computer. Another device, called the uninterruptible power supply (UPS), prevents the loss of data from brownouts. *Also called* **surge suppressor**.

SVGA   *Abbreviation of* **Super Video Graphics Array**.   A display standard for IBM PC and compatible computers that offers better resolution than VGA (Video Graphics Array). SVGA video adapters and monitors are able to display up to 1,280 by 1,024 pixels and over 16 million different colors. *Also called* **extended VGA**.

S-Video   Of or relating to the technology involved in sending video signals over cable by splitting them into two signals, one for chrominance (color) and one for luminance (brightness), resulting in a sharper onscreen picture.

swap   In a system using virtual memory, to copy a segment or page between RAM and the hard disk. The system usually sets aside a certain portion of the disk to hold such copies. The segment or page is copied to disk when it is not needed and copied back into RAM when it is needed again.

swap file   A file used by an operating system to swap memory locations.

switch   *See* **option** (sense 1).

Sybase   A database server developed by Sybase, Inc. that utilizes SQL. Sybase is a popular database management system in Unix and Windows NT environments.

synchronous   A type of communication in which the flow of data is synchronized by an electronic clock. Synchronous communication takes place within the components of a computer and between computers in certain networks. Asynchronous communication is not governed by a clock signal; data is transmitted intermittently with a start bit and a stop bit signaling the beginning and end of each byte of data. Asynchronous communication can be carried out over telephone lines and is commonly used for communication between a computer and another device. *See also* **asynchronous.**

Synchronous Dynamic Random-Access Memory or **Synchronous DRAM** *See* **SDRAM.**

syntax The spelling and grammatical rules governing a computer language. Programming language syntax is very precise, and a command that violates a grammatical rule will generate a syntax error. *See also* **semantics.**

sysadmin A system administrator.

sysop A system operator.

system A combination of components working together. A computer system is made up of all of the hardware and software that allow a computer to accept input, to process and store it, and to produce output. Within a computer, the operating system consists of the programs that allow the different components such as the keyboard, memory, CPU (central processing unit), and monitor to function together. The operating system also provides a software base from which applications can run. *See table at* **operating system.**

System On Apple Macintosh computers, one of the two programs that make up the operating system. The other operating system program, called Finder, is a file and program manager.

System 9 is an updated version of Apple's Macintosh operating system, which includes true virtual memory, multitasking, and several other features. *See table at* operating system.

system administrator A person who manages and maintains computer systems and software, as for a business, institution, or organization.

system board *See* **motherboard.**

system call A request for the execution of an operating system's routine by an application or program.

system clock An electronic timer circuit that sends out a pulse at regular intervals that are measured in megahertz (one megahertz equals a million cycles per second). All of the processes executed by the computer are synchronized according to these pulses.

system disk *See* **startup disk.**

System folder In Apple Macintosh computers, the folder that contains files for the System, Finder, device drivers, fonts, and other resources needed by the operating system.

system operator A person who manages, and sometimes owns, a bulletin board system.

systems analysis The study of a problem or task, followed by the design and implementation of computer hardware and software to solve that problem or task.

systems analyst One who performs systems analyses, designing and implementing computer systems for specific settings and requirements.

systems software Software that is concerned with the actual operation of the computer as opposed to the work that is done with it. Systems software primarily includes the operating system and related utility programs, as well as configuration files, compilers, linkers, and other files and programs that cannot be considered applications software.

[T]

T *Abbreviation of* **tera-**.

T1 A digital carrier used to transmit data at a rate of 1.544 megabits per second.

T3 A digital carrier used to transmit data at a rate of 44.736 megabits per second.

TA *See* **terminal adapter**.

Tab key A key that moves the cursor a preset distance, as to the next cell in a spreadsheet or to another part of a dialog box.

table An arrangement of data, such as text or fields in a database, in rows and columns.

tablet *See* **digitizer** (sense 2).

tab stop In word processing, a position along a line of text where the cursor will stop when the Tab key is pressed. Tab stops are useful for indenting the first line of a paragraph, but their most important function is to make it easier to type text in columns without filling lines with spaces. Most word processors set default tab stops every half inch, but these can be deleted or changed. Usually they can also be set to align text flush left or right with the stop, centered on it, or with decimal points aligned on it.

tag 1. A character or string that is attached to a database field or other item of data and encodes information about that item, often used in performing a sort.   **2.** In HTML, text enclosed in a pair of angle brackets ($<$ $>$) that indicate to the browser how the text should be displayed. For example, <ITL> is a tag to indicate that the text that follows should be italicized.

Tagged Image File Format   *Abbreviated* **TIFF**   A format for storing and transferring graphics images, especially gray scale images, as in bit maps. The TIFF format can be read by both Apple Macintosh and IBM PC and compatible computers, and is commonly used in desktop publishing. *See table at* **graphics file format.**

tape   A thin strip of plastic coated with iron oxide or some other material on which data can be recorded magnetically. Magnetic tape has been used for recording sound since the 1950s and was a natural choice as a storage medium for the earliest electronic computers. But in order to retrieve data from any point on a reel of tape, it is necessary to move the entire tape until that point is reached, a process which causes continual wear and tear and takes a long time, even with high-speed drives. With the development of the much faster random access capabilities of the hard disk, tape was no longer competitive as a primary storage medium. Because of its relatively low cost and high reliability, however, it remains the preferred medium for long-term storage and backup for computers of all sizes. *See also* **QIC,** **tape drive.**

tape drive   A device that holds magnetic tape, mounted on reels or in cartridges, and includes a transport mechanism that moves the tape across read/write heads that read data from it and write new data to it. Tape drives are widely used as backup storage devices; they have capacities ranging up to several gigabytes and use tape of different sizes. Mainframe and minicomputers often use ½-inch 9-track tape. More common types used with personal computers are 8 mm videocassette cartridge drives, 4 mm digital audio tape (DAT) drives, and especially the less expensive QIC (quarter-inch cartridge) drives, many of which can use standard audio cassette tapes. Tape backup drives were long regarded as unnecessary because the contents of a small hard disk could usually be restored without too much trouble in case of a failure. The increased use of large capacity hard disks and multitasking software, however, has made tape drives a valuable part of a reliable personal computer system.

target   The destination to which the output of a command or an operation is directed. *See also* **source**.

target language   The language into which a document written in another language, called the source language, is to be translated. The term is used to refer to a natural language as well as to the object code or machine language produced by a compiler or an assembler.

task   An operation, job, or process carried out by a computer or program.

taskbar   A row of buttons or graphical controls on a computer screen that represent open programs. The user can switch back and forth between programs by clicking on the appropriate button. *See illustration at* **desktop**.

task switching   A technique that allows a user to load two or more programs simultaneously and switch from one to another without having to close and open them in turn. For example, you can type a letter with a word processor, switch quickly to a database or spreadsheet to check information, and return to the letter without losing your place or saving and exiting the program. This technique differs from multitasking in that the program that is not active does not continue to run in the background; it is suspended until you return to it, and all of the microprocessor's attention goes to the active program. Task switching is typically performed by a shell program, such as the Apple Macintosh MultiFinder, the DOS Shell, or XTree. *Also called* **context switching**.

TB   *Abbreviation of* **terabyte**.

TCP   *Abbreviation of* **Transmission Control Protocol**.   A protocol that specifies the way two hosts are connected and the way packets are exchanged between them in sequential order. This protocol is generally used in conjunction with the Internet Protocol. *See also* **IP**, **TCP/IP**.

TCP/IP   *Abbreviation of* **Transfer Control Protocol/Internet Protocol**. Two interrelated protocols for network communications routing and data transfer developed for the precursor to the Internet, the ARPAnet. It is the accepted standard for Unix-based operating systems and for the Internet. TCP is used to break data into packets, and IP routes the packets. In theory, either of these protocols could be used with a different counterpart, but in practice they are used together and are instrumental to the growth of the Internet.

tear-off menu   A pop-up menu that can be moved around the screen. A tear-off menu does not disappear once you have made a selection from it; it stays on the screen for you to use as often as you want.

technical support The service provided by a hardware or software manufacturer to customers who have problems with the product or questions that are not answered by the supporting documentation. The level and quality of technical support is an important factor to consider when deciding on the purchase of a computer system. All large, reputable companies offer telephone support to customers.

telecommunications The transmission and reception of information, especially computer data, over telephone lines.

telecommuting The practice of working at home by using a modem and a computer terminal connected with a business office.

teletypewriter *Abbreviated* **TTY** An electromechanical typewriter that either transmits or receives messages coded in electrical signals carried by telegraph or telephone wires.

Telnet *n.* A protocol for terminal emulation that provides the capability for remote log in.
v. To remotely access another computer using the Telnet protocol.

template **1.** A pattern or model that is used as a starting point for an operation, with the user adding to it or modifying it as needed. Templates are often used in word processing programs as the basis for résumés, letterheads, business cards, and so on; in spreadsheet programs to do calculations for standardized procedures such as loan amortizations and investment returns; and in databases to eliminate the work of designing and building common structures such as address directories. **2.** A sheet of paper or plastic that fits over all or part of a keyboard and contains labels describing the functions of each key within a particular application program or for a particular terminal emulation.

tera- *Abbreviated* **T** **1.** A prefix indicating one trillion (10^{12}), as in *terahertz.* **2.** A prefix indicating 1,099,511,627,776 (2^{40}), as in *terabyte.* This is the sense in which *tera-* is generally used in terms of data storage capacity, which, due to the binary nature of bits, is based on powers of two.

terabyte *Abbreviated* **TB** A unit of measurement of computer memory or data storage capacity equal to 1,099,511,627,776 (2^{40}) bytes.

One terabyte equals 1,024 gigabytes. Informally, the term is sometimes used to refer to one trillion (1,000,000,000,000) bytes.

terminal   A device with a keyboard and a video display, through which data or information can enter or leave a computer system. The most basic configuration lacks any local data processing or storage capabilities and depends on the mainframe or minicomputer it is connected to for these services. Although there are many different types and models of terminals, any given central computer is compatible with only one or a few of them. It is equally possible to access these machines with a microcomputer by means of an emulation program; the computer then acts as a smart terminal. Most communications software programs provide emulation options of this sort for a number of widely used terminal types. *Also called* **video terminal**. *See also* **diskless workstation**.

terminal adapter   An adapter that enables a PC to connect to an ISDN communications line. The signals passed to and from a terminal adapter are purely digital, unlike a modem, which converts the computer's output to analog. Many terminal adapters provide a separate analog jack so you can use the same line to send analog (voice) data. This means you can talk on the phone while your computer accesses the Internet over the same line.

terminate and stay resident program   *Abbreviated* **TSR (program)** A program that remains in RAM (random-access memory) even after the program has been exited. TSRs are sometimes called pop-up utilities because, once loaded, they can be called up from within another application by pressing a single hot key. TSRs include calculators, appointment reminders, telephone dialers, notepads, screen-color programs, and spell checkers. Many of these tools are quite sophisticated and add a great deal to the convenience of operating a personal computer, but the user should be aware that they take up space in RAM that is then unavailable to the main applications that they are meant to support. However, many TSRs now swap much of their code out of RAM when they are not in use, leaving just enough code to recognize hot keys and swap the bulk of the code back in. The growing use of multitasking makes TSRs unnecessary, as any accessory program can simply be run as a standard background process that can be switched to the foreground when needed. *See also* **memory-resident**.

TeX   A page description language developed by Donald Knuth, a prominent computer scientist and programmer. TeX is used for formatting a page's typographical layout. *See also* **LaTeX**.

text   **1.** Data consisting of only standard ASCII characters, without formatting or any other codes.   **2.** In word processing, data in the form of words and sentences, as distinct from material such as graphics, tabular material, charts, and graphs.

text editor   *See* **editor**.

text file   A file that contains only characters in the standard ASCII character set and not extended ASCII characters, control characters, or formatting codes. *See table at* **file**.

text flow   *See* **text wrap**.

text mode   A mode of operation of video adapters in which the display is limited to the characters and symbols of the extended ASCII character set. These characters are the smallest units available to the display, which is divided into a number of horizontal lines and vertical columns of characters, such as 50 x 80 for VGA. Because the total number of units and choices is smaller, displays in text mode are faster than those in graphics mode, but text mode permits no more graphics than straight lines and simple box drawings. Some word processing and spreadsheet programs enable you to switch from character mode, used for editing the text, to graphics mode for viewing graphs, pictures, or text as it will appear when printed. *See also* **WYSIWYG**.

text wrap   A feature supported by some word processors that allows you to contour type around a graphic. Such type is harder to read than noncontoured type, so this feature should be used carefully. *Also called* **text flow**, **wrap-around type**.

TFT display   *See* **thin film transistor display**.

thermal printer   A nonimpact printer that works by pushing heated pins against treated paper. Thermal printers are used in most calculators and fax machines. *See table at* **printer**.

thermal wax printer   A nonimpact printer that works by applying heated pins to a ribbon covered with colored wax. The wax melts onto the paper to print an image. Although most thermal wax printers were designed to print in color, there are also black-and-white thermal wax printers. *See table at* **printer**.

thin client   **1.** A client/server architecture in which most, if not all, of the processing is run on the server.   **2.** A computer that serves as a client in a client/server architecture.

thin film transistor display   *Abbreviated* **TFT display**   A display using a refinement of LCD technology in which each liquid-crystal cell, or pixel, is controlled by three separate transistors, one each for red, blue, and green. *See also* **active-matrix, flat-panel display.**

thread   **1.** A portion of a program running somewhat separately from the rest. For example, in a communications program, one thread might handle communications with the modem while another thread handles interaction with the user.   **2.** A series of messages on a certain topic that have been posted on a Usenet newsgroup or bulletin board system.

three-dimensional spreadsheet   A program that allows two or more spreadsheets to be linked together and incorporated into another spreadsheet. All of the spreadsheets can then be viewed at the same time. For example, monthly or yearly reports from a number of accounts can be analyzed on separate individual spreadsheets, and then combined into a composite sheet that uses formulas to total the data from the individual sheets. The total is automatically recalculated when changes are made in any one of the single spreadsheets. *Also called* **spreadsheet notebook, 3-D notebook, workbook.**

three-tier architecture   A client/server architecture that separates the application into three distinct parts: a presentation layer, a functional layer, and a data storage layer. The presentation layer is part of the system responsible for taking user input and displaying output. The functional layer is the core of the system where most of its functionality resides. The data storage layer is the part of the system that is responsible for storing and retrieving data from the database. Each one of these layers could be an independent application running on a separate computer or platform. For example, the presentation layer may run on a Windows-based workstation, the functional layer may execute on a Unix workstation, and the database layer could be a database server running on another computer.

throughput   **1.** The rate, measured in characters or bytes per second, at which data can be processed and transferred from one place to another within a system.   **2.** The ability to transfer data across all parts of a computer system.   **3.** In telecommunications, the rate, measured in characters or bytes per second, at which data is sent and received over a given channel.

thumbnail In desktop publishing, a small image showing the preliminary layout of a page. It is convenient to view a number of thumbnails on the screen at once so that pages can be checked against each other for balance and consistency.

TIFF *Abbreviation of* **Tagged Image File Format.**

tiled windows Windows that are arranged so that they are all completely visible. Tiled windows do not overlap.

timed backup *See* **autosave.**

time-out The automatic cancellation of a process if the expected input is not received after a specified time.

time-sharing In multi-user systems, the process by which CPU (central processing unit) time is assigned to each user in sequence, so that no user has to wait for another to finish and log out before beginning to work. Most modern operating systems use time-sharing, and it usually works smoothly enough that individual users are unaware of each other's simultaneous use of the system. At times of peak load on large systems, however, the CPU resources can be spread so thin as to cause a noticeable slowdown.

tin A program for reading Usenet newsgroups on the Unix platform.

title bar In a graphical user interface, a line at the top of a window that shows the name of the program or file in that window.

toggle **1.** To switch from one to the other of two possible states. For example, some word processors and editors use the Insert key to toggle between insert mode and overwrite mode. **2.** To change the state of a bit from 1 to 0 or 0 to 1.

toggle switch A switch key, or key combination that moves a function from one to the other of two possible states. For example, the Num Lock key switches the numeric keypad between its numeric and cursor control modes. *See illustration at* **DIP switch.**

token A file that contains permission to transmit over a local area network. *See* **token-ring network.**

token-ring network A type of local area network in which permission to transmit over the network is contained in a special file called a token. The ring topology of the network allows the token to be circulated continuously from one station to the next. When a station wishes to transmit, it seizes the token, marks it as busy, inserts its message together with the intended address, and sends the package back into the loop. All other stations on the network must pass the busy token along to its destination and are prohibited from transmitting any new data themselves. After the message is delivered, the token returns to the originating station, where it is once again marked free and returned to circulation. *See also* **bus, star.**

toner   A fine, electrically charged, powdered pigment that is fused to paper to form an image in laser printers and photocopying machines.

tool   **1.** A program used primarily to create, manipulate, modify, or analyze other programs, such as a compiler, editor, or cross-referencing program.   **2.** In a draw or paint program, a design element, such as a pattern, brush width, line width, color, or shape, that a user can select from a toolbar.

toolbar   In programs using a graphical user interface, a row of icons across the top of a window that serve as buttons to activate commands or functions.

toolbox   A set of compiled routines that can be used by programmers as ready-made modules or building blocks with which to write new software.

top-level domain   The broadest category in the hierarchy of Internet addresses. In the United States, top-level domains include .com, .edu., .mil., .gov, .org, and well as .us. Each country has their own top-level domain, such as .de for Germany or .mx for Mexico.

topology   The geometric arrangement in which the nodes of a local area network are connected to each other, usually a bus, ring, or star configuration. *See illustration at* **network.**

touch pad   A pointing device consisting of a soft pad sensitized to finger movement or pressure and used especially on laptop computers as an alternative to a mouse.

touch screen   A display consisting of a monitor behind a pressure-sensitive transparent panel. Touching the panel with a fingertip activates the functions represented by elements of the display. Touch screen displays are widely used for such purposes as informational displays in museums and hotels and for automated ticket purchases in airports. *Also called* **touch-sensitive display.**

tower configuration A cabinet for a personal computer system that is designed to stand upright, usually on the floor, with components, such as the power supply and mass storage devices, stacked on top of each other. *Also called* **minitower configuration.** *See also* **desktop configuration.**

TPI *Abbreviation of* **tracks per inch.** A measure of the storage density of magnetic media, such as floppy disks. TPI represents the number of tracks that can be recorded per radial inch on the surface of the disk. Densities for common types of DOS-formatted disks are 48 TPI for double-density 5.25-inch disks, 96 TPI for high-density 5.25-inch disks, and 135 TPI for high-density 3.5-inch disks. As the width of disk tracks varies with density, the read/write heads in disk drives must be the correct size for the disk to be used.

track One of the concentric magnetic rings that form the separate data storage areas on a floppy or hard disk. Tracks are created in the process of formatting a disk. Double-density disks formatted in DOS generally contain 40 tracks, and high-density disks contain 80. *See also* **cylinder, sector.**

trackball An input device similar to an upside-down mouse. You move the on-screen pointer by rotating the ball with your fingers or palm. A trackball usually has one or more buttons that are just like mouse buttons. A trackball is stationary, however, and does not require a flat surface to operate. Consequently, trackballs are often used with laptop or notebook computers. *See illustration.*

tracks per inch *See* **TPI.**

tractor feed A mechanism for advancing continuous-form paper through a printer by means of two pin-studded rotating belts. The pins catch matching perforations along the edges of the paper.

TRACKBALL

Tractor feed printers do not have to be fed paper as often as sheet-fed ones, but the mechanism can easily go out of alignment and require repositioning of the paper. Tractor feed is commonly found in dot-matrix printers, many of which also provide the option of using a friction feed mechanism for single sheets. *Also called* **pinfeed**.

transaction A group of related operations marked to form one unit. Either all of the operations must complete successfully, or else all must be discarded. An example of a transaction is a transfer of funds between banking accounts. Both the withdrawal from an account and the deposit to another account must be completed for the transaction to be successful.

transaction processing A type of processing, generally used with database applications, that controls how data is entered into a database or updated in a storage location. Transaction processing is used to ensure database integrity even in the event of catastrophic failure such as a drive crash or power failure.

transceiver A transmitter and receiver housed together in a single unit and having some circuits in common. In a local area network (LAN), a transceiver connects computers to the network.

transfer rate The rate at which data moves between two points. In modems, for example, transfer rates are measured in terms of bits per second.

transistor A tiny electronic device containing a semiconductor and having at least three electrical contacts, used in an integrated circuit as a switch to create a bit. If electrical current passes through, the switch is on and the bit is a 1. If no current passes through, the switch is off and the bit is a 0.

translation software Software that is designed to translate texts from one natural language into another natural language. Most translation software uses an internal dictionary to find vocabulary equivalents and subroutines that analyze a sentence to locate such things as the subject and verb and to identify grammatical features such as verb tenses. Translation software usually yields an approximate translation that must be reviewed and edited by a human translator.

Transmission Control Protocol/Internet Protocol *See* **TCP/IP**.

tree structure A logical structure for classifying and organizing data in which every item can be traced to a single origin through a unique path. Such a structure is usually represented graphically in the manner of a family tree, with the starting point, called the root, at the top. The root is usually divided into subdivisions, which are connected to it by branches and may themselves be further divided. Any point where two or more branches meet is called a node. A node is referred to as the *child* or *daughter* of the node directly above it, which in turn is called its *parent*.

Tree structures are used in computing as a way of organizing directories and the files they contain. The root directory is logically the first on a disk, with all other directories classified as subdirectories of it. Every directory except the root has a single parent directory, whose name can often be abbreviated to the sequence of two dots (..) in commands and file names. *See also* **file name, folder, pathname**.

trn A program for reading Usenet newsgroups on the Unix platform. trn allows you to read posts in the order that they appear in a thread, so you can follow the logical sequence of posts and replies to posts.

Trojan horse A computer program that appears to be benign, such as a directory lister, an archiver, or a game, but is actually designed to break security or damage a system. A Trojan horse differs from a virus in that the damaging code is unable to replicate itself and spread to other programs.

TrueType A high-level outline font technology developed by Apple Computer and available with Apple's System 7 and later releases, Microsoft Windows 3.1 and later releases, and certain laser printers. TrueType provides scalable fonts to both the display screen and the printer with no need for additional cartridges, printer fonts, or printer microprocessors, and uses hints to make the fonts look better on the screen. TrueType fonts will also print at the full resolution offered by the printer, and can print to any kind of printer. Since TrueType is an open industry standard, TrueType font packages are being developed and distributed by several different companies. *See illustration at* **outline font**.

truncate To cut off the end of a number or string when it is too large to fit into the space allotted to it. In DOS, for example, file names are limited to eight characters; if more are entered, DOS will only recognize the first eight. Truncation is most commonly applied to numbers in floating-point notation, which can often extend to many decimal places. If the number of digits exceeds what fits in memory, the number may be rounded off and its excess digits dropped. This method always rounds numbers downward, but the digits that are lost are normally too insignificant to matter for most calculations.

TSR program *Abbreviation of* **terminate and stay resident program.**

TTY *Abbreviation of* **teletypewriter.**

turnkey system A complete computer system designed for a specific application, assembled and delivered to the end user ready to run. The system includes all necessary hardware, software, peripherals, and documentation. For example, a specialized CAD system for commercial patternmaking or architectural drafting might include a file server, fast workstations with large hard disks and extra memory for graphics use, plotters, digitizers, and customized software. Turnkey systems are often designed for professional, medical, order processing, and CAD/CAM applications.

tutorial A program that instructs the user of a system or software package by simulating the capabilities of the system or software. Most large commercial applications provide tutorials that usually consist of a series of short, graduated lessons demonstrating how to use the features of the program.

tweak To adjust or fine-tune something, such as a computer program, in order to improve it.

tween To show the successive steps that occur as one object is transformed into another in the process of morphing shapes in graphics programs.

twisted-pair cable A cable made of two strands of wire that are twisted around each other. One wire carries the signal, and the other wire is grounded.

type 1. To display text by or as if by pressing keys on the keyboard. 2. A DOS command to display the contents of a text file on the display screen.

typeface The design of a set of printed letters. The typeface specifies the exact shape of each letter and character. Some common typefaces are Courier, Helvetica, Times Roman, and Times New Roman. Typefaces that have the same shapes but differ in obliqueness (e.g., italic) and weight (bold, demi-bold, lightface, etc.) are grouped into font families. The two broad categories of typefaces are serif and sans serif. The growth of desktop publishing and the development of outline font technology have made a large variety of standard and decorative typefaces available for personal computers, so that the appearance of business and personal documents produced by laser printers can now approximate that of professionally printed ones. *See illustrations at* **font family, serif.**

typesetter *See* **imagesetter.**

[U]

ultra-large scale integration *Abbreviated* **ULSI** The technology for placing over 1,000,000 electronic components on a single integrated circuit. *See table at* **integrated circuit.**

uncompress To restore a compressed file to its original state. *Also called* **unpack.**

undelete To restore text to a document, or a file to a directory, after it has been deleted.

underflow error A data-processing error arising when a computed quantity is a smaller number than the device is capable of displaying. Underflow errors most often occur when dividing very small numbers by very large ones.

underscore A line placed under text to indicate emphasis. The text in this sentence has an underscore. In programming, a single underscore character is often used to represent multiple words without using a space, as in new_variable.

undo To reverse the action of a command and return to a previous state.

undocumented Relating to a feature of a program that is not mentioned in the program's official documentation. In Microsoft Windows, for example, double clicking on the title bar of a window is a method of maximizing or minimizing the window, yet this fact is undocumented in that it does not appear in the manual. Features are occasionally undocumented through oversight; more often they are functions that were included by programmers for their own convenience but deemed unnecessary, trivial, or troublesome for customers. The largest source of undocumented features is in operating system software, for which large volumes have been compiled by experimenters who have discovered function calls and other information not published in the official manuals.

Unicode A standard for encoding characters. Each character is represented by sixteen bits. ASCII, being an 8-bit encoding scheme, can only represent 256 characters. With 65,536 combinations, Unicode can encode the letters of all written languages, as well as, for example, thousands of Chinese and Japanese characters.

Uniform Resource Locator *See* URL.

uninstall To remove the software associated with a program completely from a computer.

uninterruptible power supply *See* UPS.

Universal Serial Bus *See* USB.

Unix or **UNIX** [YOO-nicks] A proprietary, interactive time-sharing system originally invented in 1969 at AT&T Bell Labs. When it was reimplemented in the high-level programming language C some five years later, it became the first operating system that could be moved from one computer to another easily, because source code written in C can be recompiled by another computer easily. Today Unix is the most widely used multi-user general-purpose operating system in the world. There are several varieties (often called *flavors*) of Unix, among them versions developed at the University of California at Berkeley from 1979 on and AT&T's own later version, System V. More recent modifications have been made by Sun Computer and by the Open Systems Foundation (OSF). Standardization is increasing across versions.

Unix has long been favored in technical, scientific, and educational circles for its flexibility, power, security, and large networking capabilities. In recent years a number of more convenient graphical user interfaces have been developed which add greatly to its ease of use. *See table at* **operating system**.

unpack *See* **uncompress**.

unzip To uncompress a file using a data compression utility such as PKUNZIP or WinZip. *See also* **zip**.

upgrade To replace a software program with a more recently released version or a hardware device with one that provides better performance.

upload To transfer data or programs over a digital communications link from a smaller or peripheral system to a larger or central host. For example, many computer users like to upload news articles to specific newsgroups on the Internet. *See also* **download**.

uppercase Of, relating to, or being a capital letter. *See also* **case-sensitive**.

upper memory area *See* **high memory area**.

UPS *Abbreviation of* **uninterruptible power supply**. A power supply containing a battery source that will supply power to the computer in case electrical power fails. A UPS may last from fifteen minutes to several hours after a power failure.

upward compatible Of or relating to a software program designed to run on the present model of a computer as well as on future, more powerful models. For example, all software that runs on IBM PC-compatibles based on the Intel 80486 microprocessor will also run on later models based on the Pentium series. Software developers strive for upward compatibility because it enables users to upgrade their computer systems without the expense of replacing software and data. New systems can become so technologically advanced, however, that upward compatibility must often be sacrificed. *Also called* **forward compatible**. *See also* **backward compatible, compatible**.

URL *Abbreviation of* **Uniform Resource Locator** *or* **Universal Resource Locator**. The specific name or identifier of a file on the Internet. Used especially on the World Wide Web, a URL is structured like this: http//www.whitehouse.gov

USB *Abbreviation of* **Universal Serial Bus**. An external bus that allows you to connect up 127 peripheral devices to your computer, an amount far greater than what regular ports will connect. USBs have a bandwidth of up to 12 megabits per second, but they can also support slower devices at 1.5 megabits per second.

USENET A worldwide public network on the Internet that can be accessed with a news reader. The material on USENET consists of a large number of newsgroups on various topics. You can follow a thread by reading a sequence of messages posted on a single topic, or respond to a message through a newsgroup or one-on-one through email.

user *See* **end user**.

user-friendly Designed to be easy for those without much experience to learn and use. User-friendly systems include such features as menu-driven or graphical user interfaces, online help, and a logical function organization that conforms to established standards.

user group   A group of people who share a common interest in a particular topic that relates to computers or computer programming. Many have technical newsgroups on Usenet where pertinent information is regularly discussed. Some have developed into large organizations which hold conventions or seminars.

User ID   *See* **username.**

user interface   The way in which a user enters commands in a given program. There are three main types of interface. In the command-driven interface, the user types commands from the keyboard. In a menu-driven interface, either the keyboard or a mouse is used to select an option from a menu displayed on the screen. In a graphical user interface, the user selects and activates functions by manipulating icons and pop-up windows on the screen. While the menu-driven and graphical user interfaces are generally easier to learn and use, many expert users still prefer the command line interface because of its speed and efficiency.

user memory   The portion of a computer's memory that is available to the user for programs. When the system starts, before any programs are loaded, a number of areas in memory are set aside for use by the operating system, BIOS, drivers, video adapters, and the like. Once these areas are allocated, the rest of memory can be used by applications, TSRs, and utilities. Memory management programs can search the reserved areas of a specific machine, locate regions that are not being used, and make them available as additional user memory.

username   An identification string, distinct from the password, that is required for logging on to a multi-user system, bulletin board system, local area network (LAN), or online service. *Also called* **login name, User ID.**

utility   A program that performs a specific task related to the management of computer functions, resources, or files. Utility programs range from the simple to the sophisticated, and many programmers specialize in producing and distributing them as shareware. There are utilities that perform file and directory management, data compression, disk defragmentation and repair, system diagnostics, graphics viewing, and system security, for example. Many utilities are written as memory-resident programs meant to serve as adjuncts to operating systems. Many operating systems incorporate such popular utility functions as undeleting, password protection, memory management, virus protection, and file compression. *See also* **pop-up utility, terminate and stay resident.**

UUCP *Abbreviation of* **Unix to Unix copy.** A set of utility programs for Unix systems that allow for the communication of data over serial connections.

uudecode [yoo-yoo-dee-KODE] *n.* A set of programs for decoding uuencoded binary data out of ASCII.

v. To decode ASCII text into binary data using this set of programs. *See also* **decryption, encryption, uuencode.**

uuencode [yoo-yoo-en-KODE] *n.* A set of programs for converting binary data as ASCII text. These programs were originally used to encrypt communications for transmission using UUCP, and have also been used with SMTP and for sending messages to USENET groups. Problems may occur when uuencoded data passes through non–ASCII-based systems, however, such as computers that use the EBCDIC character set.

v. To encode binary data as ASCII text using this set of programs. *See also* **decryption, encryption, uudecode.**

[V]

vaccine Software designed to detect and stop the progress of a computer virus. Computer vaccines usually include an antivirus function that searches files, especially executable files, for patterns of code that belong to known viruses and then removes them. The program also watches for and prevents unexpected or anomalous changes in the file allocation table and the area on the disk that stores boot information. Some vaccines can detect even unknown viruses by monitoring all executable program files and sending an alarm if an unauthorized attempt is made to change their program code.

Value Added Reseller *See* **VAR.**

vaporware New products that have been announced or marketed but have not yet been produced.

VAR *Abbreviation of* **Value Added Reseller.** An organization that combines computers and peripheral hardware, adds software, and then resells the system as a single product.

variable In programming, a location in memory that is referenced by name and used to store values that may change during the execution of the program. *See also* **constant**.

variable length In database systems, designating a field whose length depends on the information it contains. Strings of text, such as names and addresses, are usually stored as variable length fields. *See also* **field length**.

variable-length record A record that contains one or more variable length fields.

VBScript A scripting language developed by Microsoft resembling Visual Basic. VBScript can be interpreted by some browsers and is often used in writing Web applications. *See also* **high-level language, script, Visual Basic**.

VDT *Abbreviation of* **video display terminal**. *See* **monitor**.

VDT radiation The electromagnetic radiation emitted by video display terminals. Studies have shown that exposure to these emissions may have harmful effects on users' health, but other studies have reached contradictory conclusions. Debate continues over how much protection users should have from them and what levels they should be limited to. In the absence of conclusive evidence, many monitor manufacturers comply with the strictest emissions standards currently in existence. Whatever standard your monitor meets, consumer groups usually advise to work at least two or three feet from the display screen. Furthermore, since emissions are stronger from the back and sides of a monitor, care should be taken not to place a monitor too close to a worker.

vector An array of only one dimension.

vector font *See* **outline font**.

vector-graphics *See* **object-oriented graphics**.

Veronica *Abbreviation of* **Very Easy Rodent-Oriented Netwide Index to Computerized Archives**. A utility used on the Internet to search for keywords in Gopher file names.

vertical justification In word processing and desktop publishing, the automatic alignment of columns so that they end evenly at the bottom margin. Vertical justification is accomplished by feathering, the adding of space between lines of text.

very large-scale integration *Abbreviated* **VLSI** The fitting of at least 100,000, and often over a million, transistors and other electronic components onto a single integrated circuit or chip. *See table at* **integrated circuit**.

VESA [VEE-suh] *Abbreviation of* **Video Electronics Standards Association**. A group consisting of personal computer manufacturers concerned with the establishment and improvement of industry standards for graphics and multimedia. Standards that VESA has introduced include VGA, SVGA, and the VESA local bus.

VGA *Abbreviation of* **Video Graphics Array**. The graphics display system introduced by IBM in 1987 that was an industry standard for IBM PC and compatible computers. VGA works with an analog monitor and offers a palette of 16 to 256 continuously variable colors. When displaying text, VGA has a resolution of 720 pixels across by 400 down. When displaying graphics and using 16 colors, VGA has a resolution of 640 pixels across by 480 down. VGA is downward compatible with all earlier IBM graphics display systems. Higher resolution interfaces have replaced VGA for desktop usage. However, VGA is still used as a minimum graphics standard for the configuration of new systems and in instances where integration problems prevent display at higher resolutions. VGA may also be used for nonstandard displays such as flat panel liquid-crystal displays or projectors. VGA is sometimes used on servers where direct interaction with the video display is limited. *See table at* **video standard**.

vi A full-screen text editor supported by Unix. Although many people consider emacs easier to use, vi still maintains a popular following. The name *vi* comes from the word *visual.*

video accelerator *See* **graphics accelerator**.

video adapter An expansion board designed to provide or enhance the display of graphics and text on a monitor. A video adapter, however, is only as good as the monitor permits; a monochrome monitor, for example, will never display colors, no matter what video adapter you use, and a digital monitor will never offer the same resolution as an analog monitor. Most video adapters offer at least two video modes, one for text and one for graphics. Within each mode, some monitors offer two or more different resolutions. With higher resolution, the image is clearer but fewer colors can be displayed. Many video adapters come with extra modes for backward compatibility, but if you need to run programs designed for particular video standards, you should make sure that your adapter can run under those standards. Some video adapters also come with their own memory so that they do not have to compete with applications for RAM. *Also called* **graphics adapter, video board, video card, video display adapter.**

video display terminal *Abbreviated* VDT **1.** *See* monitor. **2.** *See* cathode-ray tube.

Video Graphics Array *See* VGA.

video memory RAM (random-access memory) located on a video adapter, used in the creation of images.

video mode The form in which a video adapter displays information on the monitor. Video adapters generally offer at least two modes, one for text and one for graphics. In text mode, the adapter can display any letter, number, or symbol in the ASCII character set. In graphics mode, it displays bit-mapped graphics using pixels. Some video adapters offer two or more graphics and text modes that differ in resolution and the number of colors that can be displayed simultaneously.

video RAM *See* VRAM.

video standard One of a set of standards establishing the resolution and number of colors that can be displayed simultaneously for any given system of graphics display in a particular mode. Most video standards require backward compatibility and call for separate video modes for graphics and text. Most video standards for IBM PC and compatible computers are now being set by the Video Electronics Standards Association (VESA), although some are proprietary. Proprietary standards usually suit specific applications rather than general use. Bear in mind that video standards require tripartite cooperation: the video adapter, monitor, and applications must all support the same standard. Table 23 compares the features of various common video standards.

video terminal *See* terminal.

view *n.* In database management systems, a response to a query that appears to the user as a table on the screen. A view is useful because it allows you to combine specified parts of distinct tables temporarily, without altering those tables. Some systems allow you to store and manipulate views as if they were real tables.

v. **1.** To request and peruse such a view. **2.** To peruse a file without making changes in it. Some word processing programs have a different command for viewing documents than for accessing them.

TABLE 23 Widely Used Video Standards

Video Standard	Resolution*	Mode	Simultaneous Colors (Maximum)	Characteristics
VGA (Video Graphics Array)	720 × 400 360 × 400 640 × 480 320 × 200	Text Text Graphics Graphics	16 16 16 256	• Uses analog signals • Used in most IBM PS/2 models • Also available for conventional IBM computers • Maximum palette size of 262,144 colors
IBM 8514/A	1,024 × 768	Graphics	256	• Provides 64 shades of gray on monochrome display screen • Designed for Micro Channel Architecture–based IBM PS/2 • Uses interlacing
TIGA (Texas Instruments Graphics Architecture)	1,024 × 768	Graphics	256	• Supports same resolution as 8514/A but is noninterlaced • Based on the TI 34010 and TI 34020 graphics coprocessors
XGA (Extended Graphics Array)	640 × 480 1,024 × 768 1,056 × 400	Graphics Graphics Text	65,536 256 16	• Emulates VGA and has additional modes • Used in IBM PS/2 Model 90 and up
SVGA (Super VGA)	800 × 600 1,024 × 768 1,280 × 1,024 1,600 × 1,200	Graphics Graphics Graphics Graphics	16,777,216 16,777,216 16,777,216 16,777,216	• Emulates VGA and has one or more high-resolution modes • Although 16 million colors supported, not all SVGA products have this capability; more colors require more memory • Listed SVGA resolutions also support 16; 256; 32,768; and 65,536 simultaneous colors

*The resolutions are given in the form: horizontal × vertical.

virtual   **1.** Capable of functioning or being used as, but not constituting, the physical object or entity represented. For example, virtual memory is memory that a microprocessor can use, but it doesn't correspond to actual chips in RAM. Virtual reality mimics reality so as to let a user respond to it and thus practice techniques that would be appropriate to the actual situation being simulated. For example, pilots train on the ground with interactive computer systems that imitate flight conditions.   **2.** Of, relating to, or existing in virtual reality.

virtual address   An address in virtual memory. The operating system must map the virtual address onto an address in a physical storage device, such as a hard disk drive, in order to access the necessary data and transfer it to RAM.

virtual disk   *See* **RAM disk**.

virtual machine   **1.** A virtual computer simulated by an actual computer that runs two or more operating systems, or two or more copies of the same operating system, at the same time and thus functions as if it were two computers.   **2.** A software program that simulates a hardware device not physically present.

virtual memory   A way of organizing computer memory so that there appears to be more memory space available than there is in physical RAM chips. The operating system breaks programs into pieces, called segments or pages, and loads into RAM only those that are actually being used. When a piece is called for, the operating system makes room for it by copying some other piece that has not been used in a while to a special place on the hard disk. This allows the user to run very large programs, or to multitask several smaller ones, without buying a lot of RAM.

Since the operating system copies program pieces into arbitrary places in memory and may even move them about to make room for others, the addresses that the program references do not correspond to actual bytes in physical RAM. These virtual addresses are converted into physical addresses by the operating system, usually with the help of special tables in the CPU (central processing unit).

Since only a small portion of most programs is active at any one time, the active portions can usually all fit in physical RAM, resulting in very little slowdown in system performance. But if too many programs are active at once, or if a program is poorly written, the system may spend all its time swapping and get very little work done.

virtual reality   An interactive computer system that simulates reality by using such I/O devices as gloves that transmit information about the position of the user's hands and fingers, goggles that use a small display screen for each eye to provide a stereoscopic view of the virtual world, and headphones. Both the simulations and the responses to user input take place in real time so as to allow the user to practice techniques that would be appropriate to the actual situation being simulated. For example, pilots train on the ground with virtual reality systems that imitate flight conditions and respond to their input as an actual airplane might.

Virtual Reality Modeling Language *See* **VRML.**

virus A program or series of commands that can duplicate themselves in a manner that is harmful to normal computer use. The amount of damage can vary; viruses may erase all your data or do nothing but reproduce themselves. Most viruses work by attaching themselves to another program. They may replicate themselves over long periods of time before any damage occurs, so that they may be in a system for months before they are detected. There are many virus protection programs now available to identify and remove the most common viruses. Bear in mind, however, that you put your system at risk whenever you copy files or programs from sources you do not know.

Visual Basic A compiler and development environment developed by Microsoft Corporation that is widely used for creating Windows and DOS applications. In Visual Basic, programmers create applications by dragging and dropping buttons and other components and writing small subroutines to control these components.

VLSI *Abbreviation of* **very large-scale integration.**

voice mail An interactive computer system for answering and routing telephone calls, recording, saving, and relaying messages, and sometimes paging the user. The section of the hard disk reserved for an individual's messages is called a *voice mailbox. See also* **email.**

voice recognition *See* **speech recognition.**

volatile memory Memory that loses its data when the power is turned off or disconnected. RAM, for example, consists of volatile memory, whereas a hard disk stores nonvolatile memory.

volume 1. A predetermined amount of memory on a tape or disk. The volume usually comprises all the memory on the storage device, but sometimes a single disk is divided into two or more volumes, and sometimes one volume is distributed over two or more disks. 2. A disk or tape used to store data.

volume label The name assigned to a specific disk or tape in order to distinguish the disk or tape in question from other storage devices. Usually, the user chooses a volume label when formatting the disk or tape. *Also called* **volume name.**

VRAM [VEE-ram] *Abbreviation of* **Video Random Access Memory.** A form of dynamic RAM for visual data that is located on the video adaptor and features separate communication paths for the processor and the circuitry for the video display. It is useful for video applications that require high-speed processing, and the two ports to the memory allow it to operate faster than conventional dynamic RAM.

VRML   [VUR-mull or vee-ar-em-ELL]   *Abbreviation of* **Virtual Reality Modeling Language**.   A programming language used for implementing multimedia virtual reality programs.

[W]

wafer-scale integration   The fabrication of an entire computer (including ROM and RAM, for example) as a single integrated circuit having such a large number of components that a single semiconductor wafer is completely filled.

WAIS   [ways or wayce]   *Abbreviation of* **Wide Area Information Server**.   An early protocol for searching and retrieving text on the Internet. As the capabilities of search engines developed, WAIS became generally obsolete.

wait state   A period of time when the CPU (central processing unit) or other processor waits idly for data from RAM or an I/O device such as the keyboard. A wait state occurs, for example, when the CPU processes data faster than RAM can supply it. A CPU that works with memory at maximum efficiency so as to have no wait states is called a *zero wait state* machine or microprocessor.

wallpaper   A picture or design in the background of a graphical user interface on a display screen.

WAN   [wan]   *Abbreviation of* **wide area network**.

warez   A slang term for proprietary software that is illegally distributed over the Internet or other network. In order to pirate the software, generally someone has overridden copy protection features or found away around registration protocols. Transmitting and using such pirated software is in violation of copyright laws.

warm boot   The process of restarting a computer without turning the power off. When you do a warm boot, your computer erases everything from RAM, including all your data, whether or not you have saved it. Then the computer reloads the operating system into RAM. On IBM PC and compatible computers, pressing Ctrl-Alt-Del causes a warm boot. On Apple Macintosh computers, you can start a warm boot by selecting RESTART from the SPECIAL menu.

WAV   A format developed by Microsoft Corporation and IBM for files containing digitized audio material. The extension .WAV is used with sound files using this format.

wavetable synthesis   A technique for mimicking the sound of a musical instrument used by systems that utilize MIDI (Musical Instrument Digital Interface). Wavetable synthesis operates by retrieving from a memory bank a recorded digital sample of the sound of a musical instrument, such as a piano, trumpet, flute, guitar, or drum. The digitized sounds are stored in ROM or RAM. Wavetable synthesis can work with 16-bit audio data, and is held to produce truer musical sounds than FM synthesis. *See also* **FM synthesis, sine wave.**

Web or **web**   *See* **World Wide Web.** Generally, *Web* is capitalized when used as a noun, as in *browsing the Web.* When used as an adjective, it is becoming increasingly common to use a lowercase letter, as in *web browser, webmaster,* and *webpage.*

web browser   A program, such as Netscape Navigator and Microsoft Internet Explorer, that allows the user to access hypertext links to different sites on the World Wide Web.

webcrawler   *See* **spider.**

webmaster   A person responsible for designing, developing, marketing, or maintaining websites.

webpage or **Web page**   A file on the World Wide Web that is accessible using a Web browser.

web server   A computer on which server software has been installed and that is connected to the Internet, allowing the computer to accept requests for information using the HTTP protocol. Each web server has its own IP address. Usually each IP address corresponds to a domain name. When you access a web server, the server transmits to you the particular webpage that you request.

website or **Web site**   A set of interconnected webpages, usually including a homepage, generally located on the same server, and prepared and maintained as a collection of information by a person, group, or organization. The transition from *World Wide Web site* to *Web site* to *website* seems to have progressed as rapidly as the technology itself. The development of *website* as a single uncapitalized word mirrors the development of other technological expressions which have tended to evolve into unhyphenated forms as they become more familiar. Thus *email* has recently been gaining ground over the forms *E-mail* and *e-mail,* especially in texts that are more technologically oriented. Similarly, there has been an increasing preference for closed forms like *homepage, online,* and *printout.*

weight   The degree of thickness of the strokes used to form the characters of a font. For example, boldface characters have thicker strokes than lightface characters.

what you see is what you get   *See* WYSIWYG.

whitespace   **1.** The space on a piece of paper where no characters or graphics appear when a document, record, or file is printed.   **2.** Any of the characters that cause blank space to appear on the screen or in print. Tabs and spaces, for example, are whitespaces.

Wide Area Information Server   *See* WAIS.

wide area network   *Abbreviated* **WAN**   A network that uses such devices as telephone lines, satellite dishes, or radio waves to span a larger geographic area than can be covered by a local area network (LAN). BITNET, Internet, and USENET are wide area networks.

widow   In word processing, a last line of a paragraph that appears as the first line of a page. *See also* **orphan**.

wild card   A symbol that stands for one or more characters, used in many operating systems as a means of selecting more than one file or directory with a single specification. In Unix, a question mark (?) can stand for any single character and an asterisk (*) can stand for any number of characters. For example, FIL?.DOC would refer to FILE.DOC, FILL.DOC, FILM.DOC, and so on. *.DOC would refer to all file names ending in the extension .DOC. Most word processors also use wild cards in search and search and replace procedures.

Winchester drive   A hard disk. This term was originated by IBM in the early days of computer technology development, taken from the Winchester tradename for a .30-30 rifle. Early hard disks had a storage capacity of 30 MB and an access time of 30 milliseconds, which was likened to the Winchester, which shoots a .30-caliber bullet with a powder grain size designation of 30.

Win32   A proprietary 32-bit API supported by Windows NT. Win32 is not tied to any particular hardware architecture or line of microprocessors. It includes a number of advanced features, such as multiple threads, the Unicode international character set, and remote control of other computers over a network. A subset of the features of Win32, known as Win32c, is supported by Windows 95. A somewhat different subset, called Win32s, is supported by an add-on to Microsoft Windows.

window   A rectangular portion of a display screen set aside for a specific purpose. Many operating systems and applications that have graphical user interfaces allow the user to divide the display screen into several windows and work with a different file or part of a file within each one. In multitasking environments, which can run several programs at once, each window can display output from a different program. To enter input into a particular file or program, the user clicks on the file or program's window to bring it into the foreground.

Each window often has its own menu or other controls, as for size, shape, and positioning. A window can be reduced to an icon representing the program running in the window in order to save space on the display screen. The icon can then be expanded back to a window. *See also* **overlaid window, pop, tiled windows, zoom.**

windowing   Designating an environment that allows you to create windows. Operating systems for Apple Macintosh computers and Microsoft Windows, for example, offer a windowing environment.

Windows   Any of a series of graphical user interfaces or GUI-based operating developed by Microsoft Corporation, in use in 90 percent of all computers sold today. Originally designed to run as a GUI over DOS, the newest edition, Windows ME (Millennium Edition) has no DOS support. Application programs must be written to run specifically under Windows. This results in a consistent look-and-feel for all programs, based on pull-down menus, icons, and (of course) windows. All programs are able to use the tools and common file formats provided by Windows, which allows data and graphics to be easily transferred from one program to another. Windows supports multitasking, the running of more than one program at the same time. Windows also takes full advantage of the protected mode offered by the Intel Pentium microprocessors, using extended memory to run more powerful applications.

The family of Windows operating systems developed by Microsoft includes Microsoft Windows, Windows NT, Windows 95, Windows 98, Windows 2000, and Windows ME. Both Windows NT and Windows 95 and later versions, unlike Microsoft Windows, do not rely upon the presence of MS-DOS and are true operating systems. They also support the 32-bit API Win32, and take full advantage of the 32-bit processing offered by the Intel and AMD families of microprocessors.

Microsoft Windows has enabled IBM PC and compatible computers to tap into some of the most successful features of Apple

Macintosh computers, including a graphical user interface and a consistency in the look and operation of different programs. While Macintoshes still dominate publishing, graphics, and Web design, the Windows family has come to dominate business and technical applications. Another competitor, Linux, is used in network operations and as an alternative desktop operating system.

Prior to Windows 95 and Windows NT, versions of Windows were known by release numbers, such as Windows 2.0 or Windows 3.2. They were operating environments that used MS-DOS as the operating system. Although the term Windows can be understood to refer specifically to those pre-95 versions, Windows is now generally used to refer to the current Windows operating systems.

Windows 95 An operating system developed by Microsoft Corporation. Windows 95 does not require the presence of MS-DOS in order to function, and is therefore a true operating system. This is in contrast to Microsoft Windows, which is more correctly termed an operating environment. Windows 95 supports most of the 32-bit API Win32, and uses the 32-bit processing of the Intel 386 and its successors. Windows 95 also features plug and play architecture.

Windows 98 A successor to the Windows 95 operating system developed by Microsoft Corporation, introduced in 1998.

Windows 2000 An operating system developed by Microsoft Corporation, introduced in 2000. There are versions for servers and for desktops. Windows 2000 is targeted toward computers used in a business environment. Windows 2000 is built with a network-centric model in contrast to Windows NT, which was built as a standalone operating system with networking features as an add-on. Windows 2000 includes enhanced security and more support for laptops, and it supports more hardware features than Windows NT.

Windows CE A version of the Windows operating system developed by Microsoft Corporation that is designed to run on hand-held computers such as PDAs.

Windows keyboard A keyboard that has additional keys that activate functions specific to Windows operating systems.

Windows ME An operating system developed by Microsoft Corporation, introduced in 2000. Windows ME is targeted to the home computer market. Windows ME provides increased multimedia resources, increased networking capabilities, and more support for home applications and nontechnical users than Windows 98.

Windows NT   An operating system developed by Microsoft Corporation, introduced in 1993. Windows NT does not rely on an underlying operating system, as Windows does on DOS, and is able to run DOS, OS/2, and Windows applications. It is largely hardware-independent, and can run on Intel Pentium machines, among others. Windows NT is available in two versions: one acts as a server in networks and another for client or stand-alone workstations. Windows NT uses the security features of Intel 386 processors and higher to incorporate logon security, making it more suitable for network computers than Windows 95 or Windows 98.

WinZip   A program that runs under Microsoft Windows developed by Niko Mak Computing that compresses many files into a single archive. *See* **data compression**.

Wizard   An automated instructional guide that is a feature of some Microsoft and other applications. Wizards can provide application shortcuts for accomplishing specific tasks. For example, a Wizard in MS Access can help a user set up a sophisticated query by following simple steps.

word   **1.** In word processing, a group of characters with spaces or punctuation on both sides.   **2.** A unit of memory, measured in bits. The length of a word for a given computer is equal to the largest amount of data that can be handled by its CPU (central processing unit) in one operation. The most common word lengths for personal computers are 8, 16, and 32 bits. A more powerful computer may use words that are up to 64 bits long.

word processing   *Abbreviated* **WP**   The act or practice of using a computer to create, edit, and print out documents such as letters, papers, and manuscripts. With a word processor the tasks of deleting, inserting, and moving sections of text can be made through a few keystrokes instead of through laborious retyping, as with a typewriter.

A simple word processing program such as an editor has several basic features, such as inserting and deleting text, defining page size and margins, word wrap, cut and paste, search and replace, copy, and print. More sophisticated applications can check spelling and grammar, find synonyms, number pages, create page headings and footnotes, generate form letters, and merge text or graphics in other files. *See also* **WYSIWYG**.

word processor   *Abbreviated* **WP**   A program or computer designed for word processing.

word wrap   In word processing, a feature that automatically moves a word to the beginning of a new line if it goes beyond the margin of the document. The feature rearranges lines to avoid breaking a word, unless the program supports hyphenation. Word wrap makes pressing the Return key at the end of each line unnecessary, contrasting in this respect with the functions of a mechanical typewriter. When the margins or other layout parameters of the document are changed, word wrap automatically rearranges the text to fit the new specifications.

workbook   *See* **three-dimensional spreadsheet.**

workgroup   A group of individuals working together on a single project. The computers of workgroup members are linked together in a local area network (LAN), allowing the members to share common data files and communicate via email.

working directory   The directory in which the user is currently working, or where an application and its files reside. A pathname that does not begin with the root directory is assumed by the operating system to begin with the working directory.

worksheet   *See* **spreadsheet.**

workstation   **1.** A powerful computer used for scientific and engineering applications, desktop publishing, CAD, and software development. Workstations are often linked together in a local area network (LAN), but they can also stand alone.   **2.** A computer connected to a local area network.

World Wide Web   *Abbreviated* **WWW**   Commonly referred to as the Web. All of the files residing on all Internet information servers that use hypertext as their primary navigation tool. The Web utilizes HTTP for data transfer, and documents may feature not just text but also multimedia elements, such as graphics, audio, and video. It was developed at the European Laboratory for Particle Physics (CERN), in Geneva, Switzerland, and can be accessed through browsers such as Netscape Navigator and Microsoft Internet Explorer.

worm   A malicious program that replicates itself until it fills all of the storage space on a drive or network.

WORM   *Abbreviation of* **write once read many.**   An optical disk that can be written to once but read many times. Once the data has been written to the disk, it cannot be changed. Because of their large storage capacity (up to one terabyte) and unchangeability, WORMs are suited for storing data archives.

WP   **1.** *Abbreviation of* **word processing.**   **2.** *Abbreviation of* **word processor.**

wraparound type   *See* **text wrap.**

write   To copy information from memory to a secondary storage device, usually a disk. *See also* **read.**

write-once   Of or relating to a medium that allows you to write data to it only once. Data once written to a write-once medium cannot be modified or deleted.

write once read many   *See* **WORM.**

write-protect   To modify a file or disk so that its data cannot be edited or erased. A file or disk modified in this way is read-only; data cannot be written to the disk or appended to the file. Many operating systems enable you to write-protect an individual file using software commands. A 3.5-inch floppy disk has a small switch in one corner of its plastic shell that may be slid open to write-protect the disk.

WWW   *See* **World Wide Web.**

WYSIWYG   [WIZ-ee-wig]   *Abbreviation of* **what you see is what you get.**   Relating to or being a word processing or desktop publishing system in which the screen displays text and graphics exactly as it will be printed. One advantage of a WYSIWYG system is that the layout of a document is much easier to set up.

In actual practice, the correspondence between what appears on the screen and what is printed out can be very close but not exact, because a standard laser printer has a resolution several times greater than that of the best display screens. Thus, what you see is usually only a good approximation of what you get.

[X]

x-axis   The horizontal axis in a two-dimensional graph or coordinate system.

XENIX   [ZEE-nicks]   An operating system that conforms to Unix, developed by Microsoft for IBM PC-compatible computers. XENIX is now no longer sold, and has been largely supplanted by Unix.

XGA   *Abbreviation of* **Extended Graphics Array.**   A video standard developed by IBM that is fully compatible with but supports higher resolutions and more colors than VGA. *See table at* **video standard.**

x-height The height of the lowercase *x* in a font. The x-height measures the height of the body of a lowercase letter, excluding ascenders (strokes that rise above the top of the *x*, as in the letter *b*) and descenders (strokes that fall beneath the bottom of the *x*, as in the letter *g*). Since some fonts have long ascenders or descenders, the x-height often gives a better idea of the actual size of a font than the given point size.

XML *Abbreviation of* **Extensible Markup Language** A metalanguage written in SGML with which you can design a markup language, used to allow for the easy interchange of documents on the World Wide Web.

Xmodem A protocol for transferring files from one personal computer to another and detecting errors in their transmission. Widely available as public domain software, Xmodem is commonly used to download files from bulletin board systems. Xmodem operates by transmitting data in blocks of 128 bytes, each block followed by a checksum, a technique for detecting errors in the transmission of data. If the checksum calculated from the data received in a particular block does not match the checksum originally transmitted with the block, the same block is then retransmitted. If the checksums match, then the next block of data is transmitted. *See also* **Ymodem, Zmodem**. *See table at* **communications protocol**.

XMS *Abbreviation of* **Extended Memory Specification**. A procedure developed by Lotus, Intel, Microsoft, and AST Research for using extended memory and certain portions of conventional memory not available to DOS. An extended memory device such as Microsoft's HIMEM.SYS or Quarterdeck Office System's QEMM386.SYS must be installed in order for an application to take advantage of the additional memory.

XOR [EKS-or or kzor] A Boolean operator that returns the value TRUE if one of its operands is true and the other false. Table 24 shows the results of the XOR operator. *Also called* **exclusive OR**. *See also* **AND, NOR, NOT, OR**.

X Window System A windowing system for bit map display devices that is used on Unix systems and was originally developed at MIT. The X Window System allows a user to log on to several computers simultaneously, as well as run applications and view output on a single display screen.

TABLE 24 Results of XOR Operator

a	b	a XOR b
FALSE	FALSE	FALSE
FALSE	TRUE	TRUE
TRUE	FALSE	TRUE
TRUE	TRUE	FALSE

[Y]

y-axis   The vertical axis in a two-dimensional graph or coordinate system.

Yahoo!   A proprietary Internet search engine and portal.

Y2K   *See Year* **2000**.

Year 2000 problem   *Abbreviated* **Y2K**   The set of problems that were encountered by computers at or around the turn of the year 2000. Earlier applications tried to conserve memory and disk space by limiting the representation of the year field to the last two digits. For example, 1997 is represented as 97 while the year 2000 is represented as 00, and 2010 as 10. Problems would arise because these applications read 10, for example, as referring to 1910, not 2010. *Also called* **millennium bug**.

Ymodem   An enhanced version of the Xmodem communications protocol that increases the transfer block size from 128 to 1,024 bytes. Ymodem also allows batch file transfers, whereby you can specify a list of files and send them at once. Xmodem transmits only one file at a time. *See also* **Zmodem**. *See table at* **file transfer protocol**.

[Z]

z-axis   The third axis in a three-dimensional graph or coordinate system, used to represent depth.

zero insertion force socket   *See* **ZIF socket**.

zero wait state   Relating to or being a microprocessor that has no wait states. A microprocessor inserts wait states when reading or writing to memory that is slower than the microprocessor in order to allow the memory to catch up. The microprocessor runs at maximum speed when zero wait states are inserted. *See also* **clock speed.**

ZIF socket *Abbreviation of* **zero insertion force socket.** A chip socket designed to accept the legs of a chip with no resistance. A chip is made secure in a ZIF socket by moving a small lever that clamps the socket shut.

zinc-air battery A lightweight battery that can store large amounts of energy. Zinc-air batteries have what is known as a flat discharge voltage characteristic. They deliver a constant amount of power dependably over most of their lifetimes, rather than draining slowly.

zine or **'zine** **1.** An inexpensively produced, self-published, underground publication. **2.** An e-zine.

zip To compress a file using a compression utility such as PKZIP or WinZip. *See also* **unzip.**

Zip A removable hard disk technology developed by Iomega Corporation that can store up to 100 megabytes of data. Because of its capacity and relatively low cost, Zip drives are beginning to replace floppy drives in many systems.

Zmodem An enhanced version of the Xmodem communications protocol that allows faster and larger data transfer rates with fewer errors. Zmodem includes a feature called checkpoint restart that resumes data transfer where it left off, rather than from the beginning, if transmission is interrupted. *See also* **Ymodem.** *See table at* **file transfer protocol.**

zoned-bit recording A technique for formatting a disk so that tracks on the outside have more sectors than tracks on the inside of the disk. Some hard disk drives use zoned-bit recording. *See illustration at* **sector.**

zoom In a graphical user interface, to make a window larger by selecting the zoom box in one corner of the window. Clicking the zoom box for the first time enlarges the window to fill the entire display screen. Clicking it again restores the window to its original size.